Gulliver as Slave Trader

Gulliver as Slave Trader

Racism Reviled by Jonathan Swift

ELAINE L. ROBINSON

McFarland & Company, Inc., Publishers
Jefferson, North Carolina, and London

LIBRARY OF CONGRESS CATALOGING-IN-PUBLICATION DATA

Robinson, Elaine, L., 1935–
    Gulliver as slave trader : racism reviled by Jonathan Swift / Elaine L. Robinson.
        p.   cm.
    Includes bibliographical references and index.

    ISBN-13: 978-0-7864-2586-0
    ISBN-10: 0-7864-2586-5 (softcover : 50# alkaline paper) ∞

    1. Swift, Jonathan, 1667–1745. Gulliver's travels. 2. Swift, Jonathan, 1667–1745 — Political and social views. 3. Slave trade in literature. 4. Racism in literature. 5. Swift, Jonathan, 1667–1745 — Criticism and interpretation. 6. Satire, English — History and criticism. I. Title.
PR3724.G8R59 2006
823'.5 dc22
                                    2006020492

British Library cataloguing data are available

©2006 Elaine L. Robinson. All rights reserved

No part of this book may be reproduced or transmitted in any form or by any means, electronic or mechanical, including photocopying or recording, or by any information storage and retrieval system, without permission in writing from the publisher.

On the cover ©2005 Clipart.com, ©2005 Pictures Now

Manufactured in the United States of America

McFarland & Company, Inc., Publishers
  Box 611, Jefferson, North Carolina 28640
    www.mcfarlandpub.com

To my Mother
Made to suffer because of your race,
You rose above it, full of grace.
You taught me freedom to embrace,
And inspired my journey to a higher place.

Acknowledgments

To Jim and Lou. I am eternally grateful for our Christian Social Action days of laboring in the vineyard with Martin Luther King, Jr., and Malcolm X, which centered me, and made this book possible.

Table of Contents

Acknowledgments — vii
Introduction — 1

1. The African Slave Trade — 25
2. Malignant Aggression — 67
3. "Flagitious and Facinorous Acts" — 92
4. Repository of Abominations — 126
5. Black Superiority — 154

Chapter Notes — 227
Bibliography — 235
Index — 239

Introduction

> He has gone
> Where fierce indignation
> Can lacerate his heart no more
> Go, Stranger,
> And if you can,
> Imitate this man,
> Who strove with all his might to vindicate freedom.[1]
> *Swift's self-written epitaph*

My study of *Gulliver's Travels* began in the seventies, in an English master of arts program at UCLA. At the end of a class in eighteenth-century English literature, which included *Gulliver's Travels*, a noted scholar of the literature said, "Some day someone is going to tell us the meaning of *Gulliver's Travels*." I thrilled to the challenge, but I made no conscious intention to take it on. In the eighties, in the PhD program in English at the University of Pennsylvania, one of my professors said, "Nobody knows the meaning of *Gulliver's Travels*," and quoting another scholar, added, "There are no Biblical allusions in *Gulliver's Travels*." Well, I knew that was wrong. Soon after, I had the honor and privilege of being a Reader at the prestigious Huntington Library, to which distinguished scholars from all over the world flocked to conduct research. One day one of these distinguished scholars, not without condescension and a touch of contempt, accosted me with, "Do you *really* think you can find something new to say about *Gulliver's Travels*?" In deference to his reputation, I just answered, "Oh, probably not!" Then, in the nineties, $30 or $60 million was squandered on the four-hour NBC TV production of *Gulliver's Travels*, which was an outrageous distortion and an alarming insult to Jonathan Swift. After all, *Gulliver's Travels is* considered one of the undisputed, all-time great masterpieces of the world literature; and Swift *is* one of the greatest satirists and masters of irony of all time. To categorize *Gulliver's Travels* as children's literature, or science fiction, or fantasy, as is usually done, is appalling.

Although scholars for almost 300 years have written about *Gulliver's Travels* in an unsuccessful attempt to determine its meaning, the purpose of my book is to demonstrate that Swift himself, in *Gulliver's Travels*, tells us his meaning. It just requires following the abundance of clues he provides. Most of these clues are allusions which provide evidence of his meaning. For example, through one such allusion, he reveals and defends his covert motive and method while defining the genre of *Gulliver's Travels* and its irony. The allusion is to "The Defense of Poetry" from *Genealogies of the Pagan Gods*, by Giovanni Boccaccio (1304–1374), one of the founders of the Italian Renaissance, who says:

> ... surely it is not one of the poet's functions to rip up and lay bare the meaning which lies hidden in his inventions.... I grant that poets are at times obscure, but invariably explicable if approached by a sane mind.... Surely no one can believe that poets invidiously veil the truth with fiction, either to deprive the reader of the hidden sense, or to appear the more clever; but to make truths which would otherwise cheapen by exposure the object of strong intellectual effort and various interpretation, that in ultimate discovery they shall be more precious. In a far higher degree is this the method of the Holy Spirit.[2]

And it is Swift's method in *Gulliver's Travels*. His allusion to Boccaccio is also for the purpose of revealing its genre according to Boccaccio's definition of fiction:

> Fiction is a form of discourse, which, under the guise of invention, illustrates or proves an idea; and, as its superficial aspect is removed, the meaning of the author is clear. If, then, sense is revealed from under the veil of fiction, the composition of fiction is not idle nonsense. Of fiction I distinguish four kinds: The first superficially lacks all appearance of truth; for example, when brutes or inanimate things converse. Aesop ... was the past master in this form.[3]

Boccaccio's first kind of fiction is depicted in *Gulliver's Travels* when the horses (Houyhnhnms) converse. He goes on to define the second kind of fiction:

> The second kind at times mingles fiction with truth.... This form has been employed from the beginning by the most ancient poets, whose object it has been to clothe in fiction divine and human matters alike.[4]

Both the fact that the *Travels* is a protest of white supremacy and the African slave trade, in defense of "real" Christianity, and the fact that the fundamental nature of the *Travels* is conversionary prove it clothes in fiction divine and human matters alike, and thus exemplifies Boccaccio's second kind of fiction. He goes next to the third kind of fiction:

The third kind of fiction is more like history than fiction, and famous poets have employed it in a variety of ways. For however much the heroic poets seem to be writing history — as Virgil in his description of Aeneas tossed by the storm — yet their hidden meaning is far other than appears on the surface.... If the events they describe have not actually taken place, yet since they are common, they could have occurred, or might at some time. My opponents need not be so squeamish — Christ, who is God, used this sort of fiction again and again in his parables.[5]

Swift uses this sort of fiction again and again in the *Travels*, in that however much he has Gulliver ostensibly writing "a faithful history of my travels" (234) — as in his description of Gulliver "tossed by storms" — yet Swift's "hidden meaning is far other than appears on the surface," for the events in the African slave trade, to which he alludes, *have* actually taken place and were *common* in his day, so that "as its superficial aspect is removed," *Gulliver's Travels* "is more like history than fiction."

Boccaccio mentions a fourth kind of fiction, which he says "contains no truth at all, either superficial or hidden, since it consists only of old wives' tales."[6] Perhaps the gossip about a clandestine love affair between the giant Gulliver and the six inch wife of the treasurer of Lilliput is an example of the fourth kind of fiction.

There are other allusions to Boccaccio which are clues to Swift's meaning. In "A Tritical Essay Upon the Faculties of the Mind," as well as in Gulliver's last leave-taking of the reader, Swift echoes Boccaccio's attack on critics, using some of Boccaccio's very epithets. In addition, the hidden meaning in Swift's depiction of "illustrious persons" (159) in Glubbdubdrib can be found in Boccaccio's *De Casibus Virorum Illustrium* (The Fates of Illustrious Men), which will be demonstrated. Moreover, Boccaccio's conclusion in his attack on critics is Swift's goal in *Gulliver's Travels*: "to make us all become apes of Christ." Boccaccio says to critics who "jeer" at what "they do not understand," calling poets "apes of nature":

It would be better for such critics if they would use their best efforts to make us all become apes of Christ.[7]

Another clue, coincidental rather than allusive, which nonetheless sheds light on *Gulliver's Travels*, is the observation of a twentieth-century Classics scholar:

The early Greeks did not depend upon logic and reason. The fifth century advanced upon rationalism but never became an age of enlightenment. Mythopoesis rather than reason was the chariot for the Greek mind. The literature reveals a genius that can encompass impossible contradictions, illogicalities and absurdities, can make them ring true in synthesis, reflecting reality in a way that a rational discourse does not know[8] [Charles Rowan Beye, *Ancient Greek Literature and Society*].

Beye could have used Swift's comparison to illustrate his point, when Swift has Gulliver say:

> I knew and could distinguish those two heroes at first sight, not only from the crowd, but from each other. Homer was the taller and comelier person of the two, walked very erect for one of his age, and his eyes were the most quick and piercing I ever beheld. Aristotle stooped much, and made use of a staff. His visage was meager, his hair lank and thin, and his voice hollow [159].

Unlike the fifth-century Greeks, the eighteenth-century English *did* depend upon logic (which St. Francis called Satan) and reason, and *did* advance upon rationalism, and, consequently, considered their period the "Age of Enlightenment," as it is called. But Swift set about to dig up the foundations of logic and rationalism and enlightenment, falsely so called, and projected "real" Christianity as the true enlightenment. Certainly "real" Christianity would have prevented white supremacy, the African slave trade, the animalization and extermination of black people, and the degeneration of white people to the level of monsters. His fierce indignation at the practice of substituting nominal Christianity for "real" Christianity can be felt in the irony he uses in pretending to defend nominal Christianity while really attacking it:

> I hope no reader imagines me so weak to stand up in the defence of real Christianity ... to have an influence upon men's belief and actions: to offer at the restoring of that would indeed be a wild project; it would be to dig up foundations; to destroy at one blow all the wit and half the learning of the kingdom; to break the entire frame and constitutions of things; to ruin trade, extinguish arts and sciences with the professors of them; in short, to turn our courts, exchanges, and shops into deserts.... Therefore I think this caution was in itself altogether unnecessary ... since every candid reader will easily understand my discourse to be intended only in defense of nominal Christianity; the other having been for some time wholly laid aside by general consent, as utterly inconsistent with our present schemes of wealth and power.[9]

That is why "real" Christianity is conspicuously absent from the pages of *Gulliver's Travels*. It is "utterly inconsistent with white people's schemes of wealth and power," such as the African slave trade, which is acceptable in nominal Christianity. So the purpose of the satire and irony in the *Travels* is to convert white people to "real" Christianity by exposing their urgent need of it, especially by allusions to their atrocities against black people.

To those who think it would be "for the benefit of church and state, that Christianity be abolished," Swift advises, "it may be more convenient to defer the execution to a time of peace...."[10] He goes on to add:

> If ... we are to trust to an alliance with the Turk, we shall find ourselves much deceived: for ... his people would be more scandalized at our infidelity, than our Christian neighbours. For the Turks are not only strict observers of

religious worship, but, what is worse, believe a God; which is more than is required of us, even while we preserve the name of Christians.

To conclude: whatever some may think of the great advantages to trade by this favourite scheme [of abolishing Christianity], I do very much apprehend, that in six months time after the act is passed for the extirpation of the Gospel, the Bank and East-India stock may fall at least one "per cent." And since that is fifty times more, than ever the wisdom of our age thought fit to venture, for the preservation of Christianity, there is no reason we should be at so great a loss, merely for the sake of destroying it.[11]

As to his mention of "East-India stock," the Dutch East India Company controlled most of the African slave trade at the time. Swift's "Argument To Prove That The Abolishing of Christianity In England May, As Things Now Stand, Be Attended With Some Inconveniences, And Perhaps Not Produce Those Many Good Effects Proposed Thereby" is a scathing attack on nominal Christianity, as is its prominence in *Gulliver's Travels*.

But both attacks are conversionary, in keeping with the purpose of satire in Swift's day, for "to the great satirists of the period satire was an affirmative thing, with constructive intentions. It seemed to offer the best corrective to the vices and follies of man and society as no other literary mode could; and if Swift's ironic wit derives mainly from the bent of his mind and temperament, he was fortunately born in an age that cherished and nourished this quality. The satirist, Henry Fielding once wrote, is to be regarded as our physician, not our enemy."[12] In *Gulliver's Travels*, according to Landa, "the best corrective to the vices and follies of man and society," prescribed by physician Swift, is conversion to "real" Christianity, which is alluded to throughout as the very basis of the satire and irony.

I therefore find the criticism of noted Swift scholar Louis Landa to be very much mistaken in the following exegesis concerning the religiousness of *Gulliver's Travels*:

> Even though the view of man as formulated in *Gulliver's Travels* may have received both coloring and substance from the currents of traditional Christian thought, we are obviously not to conceive of the work as a religious tract or as concerned with doctrine. *Gulliver's Travels* is secular, an exploration of man's social and moral nature in non-theological terms, done in the allegorical mode and embedded in fantasy. Nevertheless we may reasonably suppose that Swift's thinking as a divine had a yeasty influence, however difficult it is to define that influence precisely or indicate its full extent. It seems to go beyond the obvious use of the traditional symbols of sin — that is, those figures and images of the flesh which he utilizes in describing the Yahoos. The noisome putridity of these creatures, their envelopment in stench and dungy vileness, is, of course, emblematic of their moral natures.[13]

First of all, we *are* "obviously" to conceive of *Gulliver's Travels* as a religious tract, so to speak, and it is very much concerned with doctrine, chiefly with the doctrine of St. Bernard of Clairvaux. *Gulliver's Travels* is *not* "secular." It is *not* "an exploration of man's social and moral nature in non-theological terms." Rather, it exposes white people's social and moral nature precisely in *theological* terms. Moreover, it is *not* done in the allegorical mode and it is *not* embedded in fantasy. It is done in the parabolical mode, and it is symbolistic rather than fantastic. Further, Swift's thinking as a divine had far more than "a yeasty influence." Also contrary to Landa, the "Yahoos" are *not* "the traditional symbols of sin," except to a racist. Landa's description echoes Gulliver's animalization of black people, Gulliver's white supremacist perception of black people. This is not, of course, to say that Landa is a racist, but that he obviously does not realize that the yahoos he describes are black people, and that Swift is protesting the African slave trade. What Landa considers "emblematic of the Yahoos' moral natures" is in reality emblematic of the moral natures of white people. It is as stated by one of Bernard's followers:

> ... the soul itself is a mirror, whose spiritual condition dictates the rectitude with which it records the figures of nature, and only the soul/mirror which is able to subject itself to the will of Christ will be free of distortion. If distortions and lack of correspondence in the "speculum" of nature occur, it is not that there are distortions in creation, but rather in the attitude of the observer.[14]

In Gulliver's description of black people, Swift exposes racist perceptions as distortions indicative of an evil soul. According to Bernard, "Visible things are investigated by sense perception, which reveals corporeal objects not as they are in themselves but as they appear to our sensitivity."[15] This is why Bernard says, "We can know our neighbors only by love,"[16] which is another way of saying "...only the soul/mirror which is able to subject itself to the will of Christ will be free of distortion."[17] This is just one of many examples of Swift's exposing white people's social and moral natures in *theological* terms, and evidence that *Gulliver's Travels* is *not* "secular." It attacks the foundations of western civilization that caused the secularization of western civilizations. *Gulliver's Travels* is a conversionary protest of white supremacy, the African slave trade and its attendant atrocities, and a defense of "real" Christianity, to which its purpose is to convert; it digs up the foundations of western civilization that produced white supremacy, the African slave trade and other atrocities against black people.

Gulliver's Travels is religious in form and content, and by the form or structure the content can be known. In a nutshell: Each of the four parts begins and ends with allusions to the African slave trade, accompanied by a date which alludes to Scripture for that date in the *Queen Anne Book of Common Prayer*; each of the four parts is framed by one of Bonaventure's four lights to human knowledge; each of the four parts represents one of the faculties of the soul of white people according to Bernard's doctrine of the soul; from beginning to end, Gulliver descends Bernard's twelve steps of pride; from beginning to end Swift exposes white people's ignorance of Bernard's three steps of truth: Knowing Yourself, Knowing Your Neighbor, and Knowing God, which are pivotal to conversion and to salvation; from beginning to end Swift depicts outrageous creatures symbolic of philosophy and pride in reason, to emphasize the outrageousness, foolishness, and inferiority, of the wisdom of this world compared to "real" Christianity; Swift retraces his art, *Gulliver's Travels*, to the theology of St. Bernard of Clairvaux (as Bonaventure later teaches in *De Reductione Artium Ad Theologiam*), following in the footsteps of Dante, Chaucer, Shakespeare, and the author of *Everyman*, to whose art Swift alludes. The outer aspect thus reveals Swift's inner purpose: to convert white people to "real" Christianity. He focuses most consistently on the African slave trade and white supremacy because they demonstrate most of all the urgency of white people's dire need of conversion to "real" Christianity.

Swift's allusions to the *Queen Anne Book of Common Prayer* by the dates of Gulliver's voyages is the discovery of L.J. Morressey:

> If we simply consult the Queen Anne *Book of Common Prayer*, the dates begin to form a significant and exciting pattern.... It is surely reasonable for Swift to have assumed that his English readers would have been aware that the dates had a significance in the lectionary of the Church of England as well as in the world of commerce.... Although few of Swift's ... contemporaries would have read the "Proper Lessons" at Morning and at Evening Prayer with their families, as Swift did with his when he was dean, they would at least have been aware that each date in the year had designated lessons.... Swift chose his dates from the lectionary calendar rather than at random ... searching for applicable groups of lessons within the appropriate period and juggled dates to fit these lessons ... choosing combinations that made significant comment on the text of *Gulliver's Travels*.[18]

It is necessary to see Gulliver's voyages as African slave trade voyages to fully understand how significant the lessons Swift chose for the dates of those voyages really are. In spite of making mention of "the world of commerce," Morressey does not see Gulliver's voyages as African slave trade voyages. The lection making the most significant commentary on the African slave trade is "The Epistle of Paul to Philemon," to which Swift alludes by the date of Gulliver's last African slave trade voyage. The fact that Swift chooses lectionary dates for Gulliver's voyages, then creates a context of allusions to African slave trade ports of call, "reasonably assuming English readers would have been aware that the dates had a significance to the world of commerce," which was dominated by the African slave trade, proves, it is reasonable to conclude, that the significant commentary he chooses these lectionary dates to make is that God supports his protest of the African slave trade.

His sermons underscore the significance of his choices, and the connection he makes between his protest and "real" Christianity; for example:

> No one human creature is more worthy than another in the sight of God, farther than according to the goodness or holiness of their lives.[19]

As Swift demonstrates, only a monster could associate the African slave trade and white supremacy with "goodness" or "holiness." In another sermon he says:

> Our want of brotherly love hath almost driven out all sense of religion from among us, which cannot well be otherwise: for, since our Saviour laid so much weight upon his disciples loving one another, that he gave it among his last instructions; and since the primitive Christians are allowed to have chiefly propagated the faith by their strict observance of that instruction; it must follow, that in proportion as brotherly love declineth, Christianity will do so, too.[20]

What better way to emphasize the absence of brotherly love and "real" Christianity than by allusions to the African slave trade at the beginning and at the end of each of Gulliver's voyages, and at the beginning and at the end of each of the four parts of the book?

Swift digs up the foundations of secularization such as the philosophies of Plato, Aristotle, and Thomas Aquinas, which are responsible for the decline and disappearance of brotherly love, and, consequently, of "real" Christianity. The root cause, which is the basis of those philosophies, is "pride in reason." One of the ways Swift demonstrates white people's need of conversion is by identifying "pride in reason" with Greek monsters, the Centaurs, depicted as Houyhnhnms, whose grand maxim is: "to cultivate reason and be wholly governed by it" (216), and who are wholly governed by (white) "superiority" and (white) "supremacy," and who animalize and enslave black people.

In depicting white people as monsters, Swift digs up an old tradition. Taking Gaul, as in "Gallia," which means "whiteness," as a microcosm, both physically and symbolically, of Europe, Swift ridicules the claim of St. Jerome (340–420), the translator of the Vulgate, that, "Gaul is the country which has not produced monsters, but has always illuminated the world by wise and learned men."[21] St. Jerome is also the authority for the claim that white people "are more readily persuaded to conduct themselves according to the rules of reason,"[22] in other words, to place themselves "under the rule of the Logos, [Reason] the conventional language enunciated by the divinity for the rational ordering of the world" [instead of the rule of Jesus, "the Word made flesh"], and thus "demonstrate a greater evolution toward the celestial order of Revelations."[23] The absurdity of such claims is emphasized in Swift's depiction of white people as monsters, for monsters can hardly be said to "demonstrate a greater evolution toward the celestial order of Revelations." Moreover, it's the fact that white people "are more readily persuaded to conduct themselves according to the rules of reason," to have pride in reason, that makes them monsters, in that "they make no other use of reason than to improve and multiply the vices of nature" (225), than to create unnatural vices, in other words, such as the African slave trade, and the animalization and genocide of black people.

Thomas Aquinas said that "what is essential for man is his intellect, which means his ability to live in meanings and structures of reason. Not the will but the intellect makes him human, and distinguishes man from animals."[24] *Gulliver's Travels*, to an extent, is a compilation of meanings and structures of reason that white people live in, especially white supremacy, held up to attack and ridicule. And through the use of Bernard's doctrine of the Will, Swift demonstrates that, contrary to the claim of Thomas Aquinas, it is the will, not the intellect, that makes man human.

Swift's depiction of white people as monsters also reflects his use of Bernard's doctrine of the First and Second Ignorance. In depicting white people as monsters, Swift makes a distinction between white people and black people based on reason, and on the First and Second Ignorance. At the climax, Swift has Gulliver come to the realization that, whereas white people use reason to create unnatural vices, black people have only the vices of human nature. This conclusion is also supported by Swift's depicting black people as guilty of the First Ignorance, the First Fall, Adam's fall, the fall of man, and white people as guilty of the Second Ignorance. In Bernard's definition, the Second Ignorance brought man to a level lower than human and lower than animal, which Swift depicts as the monster level, or "pride in reason." The Second Ignorance represents a degenerate way of life that violates the laws of human nature, such as the African slave trade, racism, the animalization and extermination of black people, so that the irony of ironies of the *Travels* is that black people are superior to white people, not the other way around, as tradition has it, because black people "have only the vices of human nature" (225), being guilty of the First Ignorance. "The second ignorance was more to be feared, to be ashamed of, than the first, for the first brought man to a level with the beasts, the second made him lower."[25] Using Bernard's definition of the Second Ignorance, and, giving white people's animalization of black people, which Swift uses as a boomerang, Swift depicts white people as lower than the animals they perceive black people to be. With Bernard in the following, Swift asks the question echoed ironically through the Houyhnhnm master in Part IV:

> Do you not think that man endowed with reason but failing to live reasonably is more of a beast than the beasts themselves? For if the beast does not control himself by reason, he has an excuse based on his very nature, for that gift was denied to him; but man has no excuse, because reason is a special prerogative of his nature. A man then in this condition is rightly judged to go forth from the company of other living creatures and drop to a lower level, since he is the only creature who violates the laws of his nature by a degenerate way of life.[26]

In being banished from Houyhnhnmland, African slave ship surgeon and captain Gulliver is "rightly judged to go forth from the company of other living creatures and drop to a lower level [the monster level]," in that, as an African slave trader, and by his profession, he violates the laws of human nature by a degenerate way of life, which is one of the reasons Swift digs up Aristotle as one of the foundations of western civilization.

Swift digs up Aristotle not only because of his philosophies of degenerate ways of life, such as slavery, supremacy, conquering, colonizing, massacre, politics, and war, but because Thomas Aquinas restructured Christianity according to Aristotle's system of knowledge, thus taking the Church in the wrong direction. Swift has Gulliver start out with Aristotle's system of knowledge that says "the soul must receive impressions from the external world,"[27] which Swift depicts as Bernard's "Curiosity, the First Step of Pride, the first step of the path that leads away from God."[28] Swift's depiction also demonstrates as true the prophetic statement of one of Bonaventure's followers:

> ... the moment you pursue the Aristotelian-Thomist method and start with the external world, you will lose the principles. You will gain the external world ... but you will lose the wisdom which is able to grasp intuitively the ultimate principles within yourself [the knowledge of God].[29]

Gulliver ends on the "Twelfth Step of Pride, Habitual Sinning," on which "The fool saith in his heart, 'There is no God.'"[30] Thomas Aquinas said that "the knowledge of God, like all knowledge, must begin with sense experience and reach God on this basis in terms of rational conclusions"[31] (Tillich, 186). Bonaventure says, "God is most truly present to the soul and immediately knowable."[32] Augustine had said, "...the place of God is in the soul."[33] Bernard says, "God is the 'soul' of the soul," and that, "the soul may acquire its own 'life' (knowledge) and its own 'sensitivity' (love) by being animated by its own 'soul'"[34] (God). Swift defines "real" Christianity as pre–Thomas Aquinas, as following the line of Augustine, Anselm, Bernard, Francis, and Bonaventure but mostly, and primarily, Bernard of Clairvaux.

The basis of most of the satire and irony in the *Travels* is white people's ignorance of the Three Steps of Truth (Bernard): "Knowing Yourself, Knowing Your Neighbor, and Knowing God."[35] Swift elaborates on these subjects in his sermons in ways that provide insight into their significance in the *Travels*. The sermon titles are an obvious clue: "On the Difficulty of Knowing Oneself"; "On Brotherly Love"; "On Mutual Subjection"; "On the Trinity"; "On the Testimony of Conscience." In the *Travels* the three steps of truth are pivotally situated. The climax is the focus of the first step, when Gulliver looks into a mirror that flatters not. Gulliver's being an African slave trader, and the allusions to the African slave trade at the beginning and the end of each of the four parts of the Travels, conspicuously emphasize white people's ignorance of the second step of truth. After Gulliver's arrival home, following his last African slave trade voyage, Swift ingeniously exposes Gulliver's ignorance of the third step of truth. Implicit overall is Swift's projection that the first step would eliminate "white superiority" and "white supremacy"; the second step would eliminate the African slave trade, racism, menticide, the oppression, animalization, and extermination of black people; the third step would enable the pure in heart to see God, the ultimate goal in life, which involves "not a movement from place to place but from brightness to brightness, not in the body but in the spirit, as by the Spirit of the Lord,"[36] not like Gulliver, who travels from place to place, but like Dante, who moves from brightness to brightness.

> The brighter one becomes, the nearer is the end; and to be absolutely bright is to have arrived. For those thus arrived in his presence, to see him as he is means to be as he is, and not to be put shame by any form of unlikeness.[37]

The Steps of Truth are a blueprint for the satiric depiction of Gulliver as a white supremacist. The Steps of Truth are the key to characterization, plot, climax, denoument, and catastrophe. Moreover, the Steps of Truth are projected as knowledge far more crucial than anything philosophy has to offer. It's obvious from Bernard's definition that Gulliver is ignorant of the Steps, and Swift emphasizes their sine qua non salvational value to dramatically expose not only Gulliver's ignorance, but also the fatal consequences of such ignorance. In defining The First Step of Truth, Knowing Yourself, Bernard exhorts:

> Observe what you are, that you are wretched indeed, and so learn to be merciful, a thing you cannot know in any other way. For if you regard your neighbor's faults but do not observe your own, you are likely to be moved not to ruth but to wrath, not to condole but to condemn, not to restore in the spirit of meekness but to destroy in the spirit of anger ... truth is to be sought in ourselves before we seek it in our neighbors; "Consider thyself, how easily tempted, how liable to sin." But if you will not observe what the disciple commends, heed what the Master commands: "Thou hypocrite, first cast out the

> beam out of thine own eye; and then shalt thou see clearly to cast out the mote out of thy brother's eye." The great thick beam in the eye is pride in the mind. By its great size, although empty, not sound, swollen, not solid, it dims the mind's eye and overshadows truth in such a way that, when pride fills your mind, you can no longer see yourself, you can no longer feel yourself such as you are actually or potentially; but you either fancy that you are or hope you will become such as you would love to be.... He, therefore, who wants to know truth in himself fully must first get rid of the beam of pride, which prevents him from seeing the light, and then erect a way of ascent in his heart by which to seek himself in himself; and thus after the twelfth step of humility he will come to the first step of truth ... we may consider Paul to have said as follows: "When I did not yet know truth, I thought myself to be something, whereas I was nothing; but after I learned the truth by believing in Christ, that is, imitating his humility, it was itself exalted in me by my confession; but I was greatly humbled, that is, I became in my own sight extremely contemptible as a result of my self-examination."[38]

The climax of *Gulliver's Travels* is Gulliver's becoming, in his own sight, extremely contemptible as a result of his self-examination. But the difference between Gulliver's self-contempt and Paul's is Christ, the key to the climax. Things would have been vastly different for Gulliver could he have cried out to God at that point.

In defining The Second Step of Truth, Knowing Your Neighbor, Bernard exhorts:

> See how the proud Pharisee felt about himself: "God, I thank thee that I am not as other men are." He exalts in himself exceedingly; he insults all others arrogantly.... The Pharisee deludes only himself when he excludes only himself and condemns all others. The Pharisee disdains mercy when he disclaims misery.... He gives thanks, not that he is good, but that he is different; not so much because of his own virtues as because of the vices which he sees in others. He has not yet cast out the beam out of his own eye, yet he points out the motes in his brothers' eyes.... And this is the second step of truth, when they seek it in their neighbors, when they learn others' wants from their own, when they know from their own miseries how to commiserate with others who are miserable.[39]

Through Swift's allusion, the Pharisee becomes an exemplar for the white supremacist, and black people become exemplars for "Your Neighbor," added to which is Swift's depicting Gulliver in postures and predicaments similar to those of African slaves to signify how and why white people are to commiserate with them who are obviously miserable. Keeping in mind also Jesus's parable of the Good Samaritan, Swift makes a clearly powerful condemnation of white supremacy and the African slave trade as heresies. The Parable of the Good Samaritan is an especially pertinent example because of the racism involved, "the antipathy of Jews for Samaritans."[40]

In defining The Third Step of Truth, Knowing God, Bernard states:

> Those who persevere, therefore, in these three things, the remorse of repentance, desire of justice, and works of mercy, may then pass through contemplation to the third step, having purged the spiritual vision of the three obstacles arising from ignorance and weakness and willfulness. For these are the ways which seem good to men, to those at least "who rejoice to do evil and delight in the frowardness of the wicked," and cover themselves with weakness or ignorance to plead as excuses in sinning. But they plead weakness or ignorance without avail who choose to be ignorant or weak in order to sin more freely.[41]

Gulliver is cast in this mold. "Insatiable desire" (64) proves his willfulness and "rejoicing to do evil and delight in the frowardness of the wicked." His "Having been condemned by nature and fortune to an active and restless life" proves he "covers himself with weakness to plead as an excuse in sinning." Bernard goes on to warn those like Gulliver:

> If they do not know truth needy, naked, and weak as it is now—[African slaves]; they may shamefacedly recognize it too late when it comes with great power and strength, terrifying and accusing, and may in vain answer trembling, "When saw we thee in need and did not minister unto thee? The Lord shall be known when he executeth judgments," if he is not known when he seeketh mercy. When "they shall look on him whom they pierced," and likewise the avaricious on him whom they despised. From every blemish, therefore, arising from weakness or ignorance or willfulness the eye of the heart is purified by weeping, hungering for justice, and devotion to works of mercy. To such a heart Truth promises to appear in his splendor: "Blessed are the pure in heart: for they shall see God." Since there are therefore three steps or states of truth, we ascend to the first by the toil of humility, to the second by the emotion of compassion, to the third by the ecstasy of contemplation. In the first, truth is found harsh; in the second, loving; in the third, pure. Reason, by which we examine ourselves, leads us to the first; love, by which we sympathize with others, entices us to the second; purity, by which we are lifted to invisible heights, snatches us up to the third.[42]

In the warning regarding "truth needy, naked, and weak," the allusion is to Christ's description of the last judgment: "As ye do unto the least of these my brethren, you do unto me," the "least of these my brethren," intended by Swift to mean African slaves, so that whatever is done to black people via the African slave trade is done to Christ. This is more than a clue that Gulliver is doomed.

Gulliver's catastrophe is the result of his ignorance of The Steps of Truth. He is characterized as symbolic white supremacist, so the emphasis is on pride, which broadcasts loud and clear he does not know himself. To drive home the point, Swift takes Gulliver down Bernard's twelve steps of pride, one of the organizing motifs of the novel. The twelfth step is "Habitual Sinning," in which "the fool saith in his heart, There is no God." The impact of The Steps of Truth on *Gulliver's Travels* is enormous.

In *Gulliver's Travels*, Swift digs up the foundations of western civilization that cause white people's ignorance of The Steps of Truth. He thus agrees with Bernard that "Particularly useless and frivolous is philosophy. Its subject-matter is foolish; its doctrines are false...."[43] In his sermon "On the Wisdom of This World," Swift attacks the philosophies that are the foundation of western civilization, and demonstrates how "Christianity itself has very much suffered, by being blended up with Gentile philosophy."[44] For example:

> The Platonick system, first taken into religion, was thought to have given matter for some early heresies in the church. When disputes began to arise, the peripatetick forms were introduced by Scotus, as best fitted for controversy. And, however this may now have become necessary, it was surely the author of a litigious vein, which has since occasioned very pernicious consequences, stopped the progress of Christianity, and been a great promoter of vice.[45]

And that "this high opinion of Heathen wisdom, is not very ancient in the world ... that"

> Our Savior had but a low esteem of it, as appears by his treatment of the Pharisees and Saducees, who followed the doctrines of Plato and Epicurus. St. Paul likewise, who was well versed in all the Grecian literature, seems very much to despise their philosophy, as we find in his writings; cautioning the Colossians to "beware lest any man spoil them through philosophy and vain deceit." And in another place, he advises Timothy to "avoid profane and vain babblings, and oppositions of science falsely so called.[46]

In another attack on philosophy, "A Tritical Essay Upon The Faculties of the Mind," which is more closely symbolized in the *Travels*, Swift emphasizes the absurdity of philosophy, as well as its dangerousness as the precipitant of the schizophrenic despair that plagues Gulliver in the end. Swift says, for example:

> ... the various opinions of philosophers, have scattered through the world as many plagues of the mind, as Pandora's box did those of the body; only with this difference, that they have not left hope at the bottom.[47]

But Christianity, Swift is implying, does leave hope at the bottom, and that hope is Christ. "Hope thou in Christ," the Scripture says.

In the following from "A Tritical Essay," Swift demolishes philosophy from beginning to end in one fell swoop, again prefiguring Gulliver's consequent schizophrenic end: "separat[ing] and break[ing] in pieces":

> Philosophers say, that man is a microcosm, or little world, resembling in miniature every part of the great: and, in my opinion, the body natural may be compared to the body politick: and if this be so, how can the epicurean's opinion be true, that the universe was formed by a fortuitous concourse of atoms: which I will no more believe, than that the accidental jumbling of the

letters of the alphabet, could fall by chance into the most ingenious and learned treatise of philosophy. This false opinion must needs create many more; it is like an errour in the first concoction, which cannot be corrected in the second; the foundation is weak, and whatever superstructure you raise upon it, must of necessity fall to the ground. Thus men are led from one error to another, until with Ixion they embrace a cloud instead of Juno.... For such opinions cannot cohere; but like the iron and clay in the toes of Nebuchadnezzar's image, must separate and break in pieces.[48]

Gulliver holds forth in the style of the foundations of philosophy and science, and ends up "trotting like a horse," imitating Centaurs, the offspring of Ixion and the cloud, obviously separating and breaking in pieces. As a testimony to Swift's genius for prophecy, a twenty-first century scientist says virtually the same thing, that "the foundation is weak, and whatever superstructure you raise upon it, must of necessity fall to the ground":

> When I first went into geology, we all thought that in science you create a solid layer of findings, through experiment and careful investigation, and then you add a second layer, like a second layer of bricks, all very carefully, and so on. Occasionally some adventurous scientist stacks the bricks up in towers, and these towers turn out to be insubstantial and they get torn down, and you proceed again with the careful layers. But we now realize that the very first layers aren't even resting on solid ground. They are balanced on bubbles, on concepts that are full of air, and those bubbles are being burst today, one after another.[49]

Francis Bacon had said that, "With science we don't need God." Gulliver holds forth in that style, like Ixion, embracing a cloud or "air" (philosophy/science) instead of God.

One of Swift's purposes in creating *Gulliver's Travels* as a mirror held up to white people is to dramatize their urgent need of conversion to "real" Christianity, especially since all that is depicted, the African slave trade and white supremacy, in particular, is acceptable in "nominal" Christianity. So Swift's intention is to project a clear distinction between "real" Christianity and "nominal" Christianity. He is said to have been reading "Against Heresies" by Irenaeus when he started *Gulliver's Travels*. Irenaeus was also intensely concerned to protect Christianity against heresies. He "struggled against the heresies that came in like locusts to devour the harvests of the Gospel."[50] Although Swift is more concerned to demonstrate the inferiority of Greek and Roman philosophy, "the wisdom of this world that is foolishness with God," compared to Christianity; and "to show that the humanist preference of Heathen wisdom and virtue, before that of the Christian, is every way unjust, and grounded upon ignorance or mistake" ("error"),[51] it's very easy to hear in Swift's sermon "On the Wisdom of This World" echoes from the following from "Against Heresies":

Inasmuch as certain men have set the truth aside, and bring in lying words and vain genealogies, which, as the apostle says, "minister questions rather than godly edifying which is in faith," and by means of their craftily-constructed plausibilities draw away the minds of the inexperienced and take them captive. These men falsify the oracles of God, and prove themselves evil interpreters of the good word of revelation.[52]

Swift speaks of "some who highly exalt the wisdom of those Gentile sages, thereby obliquely to glance at, and traduce Divine Revelation, and more especially that of the Gospel."[53] In at least two other sermons, Swift echoes Irenaeus's concern about "evil interpreters" who "overthrow the faith of many, by drawing them away, under a pretence of superior knowledge...."[54] Irenaeus "sets forth the opinions of those who are now promulgating heresy."[55] Likewise, Swift sets forth the opinions of philosophers as if they were heresy. Irenaeus's statement below applies to both:

Error, indeed, is never set forth in its naked deformity, lest, being thus exposed, it should at once be detected. But it is craftily decked out in an attractive dress, so as, by its outward form, to make it appear to the inexperienced (ridiculous as the expression may seem) more true than the truth itself. One far superior to me has well said, in reference to this point, "A clever imitation in glass casts contempt, as it were, on that precious jewel the emerald ... unless it come under the eye of one able to test and expose the counterfeit.[56]

In addition, it applies to white supremacy. Swift illustrates "error" in defining a white supremacist as one who "imitates humanity so abominably."[57] For example, Gulliver is "craftily decked out in an attractive dress" so as to appear superior. His is a "clever imitation" of humanity that "casts contempt on that precious jewel," the human being, until, in his naked deformity, he "comes under the eye of one able to test and expose the counterfeit." Swift has Gulliver tell the reader: "I had hitherto concealed the secret of my dress in order to distinguish myself as much as possible from that cursed race of yahoos [black human beings]" (191). But he "comes under the eye of one able to test and expose the counterfeit," his master, who, when he sees Gulliver in his "naked deformity," says, Gulliver tells us, "it was plain I must be a perfect yahoo; but that I differed very much from the rest of my species in *the whiteness and smoothness of my skin*" (191–192). (emphasis added). "He desired to see no more, and gave me leave to put on my clothes again, for I was shuddering with cold" (191–192). Gulliver goes on to say:

I expressed my uneasiness at his giving me so often the appellation of "yahoo," an odious animal, for which I had so utter an hatred and contempt; I begged he would forbear applying that word to me, and take the same order in his family, and among his friends whom he suffered to see me. I requested likewise, that the secret of my having a false covering to my body ["craftily decked out in an attractive dress"] might be known to none but himself, at least as long as my present clothing should last [192].

The Houyhnhnms call their naked black slaves "yahoos" (with a lower case "y"), which means "human being" to them. Gulliver is the first "white" human being the Houyhnhnms have ever seen, and they see that Gulliver resembles their yahoos except for the whiteness of his skin, so they call him "yahoo." But to racist Gulliver, a black slave or black yahoo is not of the same species as white people, is not of the human species, but an animal. So Gulliver does not want to be called "yahoo," does not want to be considered of the same species, and he wears "a false covering" (192), his clothes, obviously a false symbol of civilization or superiority, as is his white skin.

In Gulliver's "hatred and contempt" (192) of black people and of being considered of the same species as black people, Swift is merely recording history, and exposing the fact that it was "nominal" Christians, who, "making no other use of reason than to improve and multiply the vices of human nature," in the middle of the seventeenth century, legalized and institutionalized the racist claim that black people are not of the same species as white people as the "excuse for transforming indentured servitude into chattel slavery."[58] This "racial justification for slavery," which "condemned all Negroes to bondage," was based on a text from the Old Testament that claimed that "Negroes were children of Ham, or Canaan, on whom Father Noah had laid his famous curse (Genesis 9:25): 'Cursed by Canaan; a servant of servants shall he be unto his brethren.'" Some slave-owners argued that "the Negro was not a human being and therefore could not become a Christian":[59]

> One pious lady said, when asked if her Negro maid was to be baptized, "You might as well baptize my black bitch." Bishop Berkeley put the same idea into philosophical language. Negroes, he said, were "creatures of another species who had no right to be included or admitted to the sacraments."[60]

It was this kind of outrage, and Swift was acquainted with Bishop Berkeley, that provoked the fierce indignation that lacerated Swift's heart and motivated him to demonstrate the irony of the racist claim by exposing white people as not human beings but monsters; and motivated his digging up the foundations of "white supremacy," foundations that "laid the groundwork for metaphorical and metaphysical constructions" that transformed whiteness of skin from "an externally distinguishing trait to a metaphor for inner qualities which assert a special relationship of white people with the Logos,"[61] which was touted to mean white people are superior, Logos being the Greek word for "reason," the controlling principle in the universe, according to Greek philosophy. So, for the promotion and entrenchment of white supremacy, "Logos" was used to usurp the place of Christ, "the Word made flesh," who made "love," *not* reason, the controlling principle of the universe because of being the Will of God.

Finally, Swift digs up foundations for the purpose of converting white people to "real" Christianity, and he has only one kind of conversion in mind as the consummate antidote to white supremacy and the brutalization and destruction of black people. The conversion Swift has in mind is stated clearly and definitively in a work printed in London in 1677, which, judging by its imprint in *Gulliver's Travels*, Swift must have read. The work is "A Mirror That Flatters Not: Certain Sermons of St. Bernard translated into English...." The anonymous translator exhorts:

> ... the Conversion to which eternal life is promised by Almighty God, is the Conversion which is most excellently described by St. Bernard in the following Sermons. Get that, and you are eternally happy; want that, and the being of whatsoever Persuasion, never so holy, or never so good, will not be able to hinder you from being eternally miserable.[62]

"Eternally miserable" is Gulliver in the end, in the manner and for the reason described in the above mentioned sermons. This is demonstrated plot-wise through Swift's depiction of the soul of white people according to Bernard's concept of the soul. "The soul is a trinity of memory, reason, and will,"[63] says Bernard. Contrary to critics of Swift's Christianity, Landa being one, Swift adhered to Bernard's epistemology in believing there is no enmity between body and soul, and that the soul cannot desire to be freed from the body. Each of the four parts of *Gulliver's Travels* represents one of the faculties of the soul of white people, the Will (I and II), the Memory (III), the Reason (IV), in need of Conversion:

> God's will is our Conversion. In fine, hear himself. "Is the death of the impious my will, says the Lord, and not rather that he should be converted, and live? (Ezek. 18:23)" ... Our Lord telling us plainly; "Unless ye be converted, and made like little ones, ye shall not enter the Kingdom of Heaven" (Matt. 18:3). I ask then, what voice is that which the dead hear, and when they have heard it, live? for perhaps it is necessary to Preach the Gospel even to the dead.[64]

Through the rest of this sermon, Swift speaks to those who trust in philosophers "as if they had something more excellent and sublime to reveal, than that God who created the heaven and the earth, and all things that are therein."[65]

> For you dare compare what God has said to the sayings of men ... the conversion of Souls is the work of God's Voice, and not of man's ... although we speak the truth of God, and seek the glory of God, we must even then from him alone hope the effect, and of him ask it: that he would please to accompany

his own Voice with a Voice of power. To this internal Voice therefore I exhort you to listen with the ears of your heart; and that you would make it your business rather to hear God speaking within you, than man speaking without you. For that is a voice of magnificence and power ... shaking off the stupid "torpor" of Souls.[66]

But Gulliver's beginning, and the end is in the beginning, is just the opposite from "God speaking within him." He starts with the external world, with Aristotle's system of knowledge depicted as Bernard's, "Curiosity, the first step of pride," which includes the warning: "Hearken to Solomon, thou curious fellow; hearken to the wise man, thou fool." "Keep thy heart," he says, "with all diligence; let all thy senses be alert for keeping that out of which 'are the issues of life.'"[67] Gulliver does not do this.

Swift makes the most pivotal use of Bernard's conversionary sermons at the climax, when he has Gulliver look into a mirror that flatters not. Indeed, the book itself is "a mirror that flatters not" held up to white people. Following Gulliver's last African slave trade voyage, and final return home, Swift ingeniously exposes the fact that Gulliver does not know God. And at the end he makes pivotal use of the conversionary sermons selected by the anonymous Translator, by depicting Gulliver in Bernard's hell, which could be called "Swift's Inferno," in that Dante's *Inferno* is also based on Bernard's teachings, and Swift alludes to Dante's *Inferno* in the *Travels*.

The African slave trade and its attendant atrocities, such as racism and the "extermination of black people from the face of earth," all based on "white supremacy," evince white people's need of conversion, and at the same time, evince the most obvious absence of "real" Christianity. It should therefore come as no surprise that Swift, a clergyman with the Doctor of Divinity degree, and one of the greatest satirists of all time, whom Landa calls a "Jeremiah," but I call an Isaiah, should "Cry aloud, spare not, lift up [his] voice like a trumpet and shew [his] people their transgressions"; and "Go, write it in a book, that it may be for the time to come for ever and ever: That this is a rebellious people, lying children ... that will not hear the law of the Lord" (Is. 58–60). Fundamentally, Swift directs white people to hear this law of the Lord: "As ye do unto the least of these my brethren, ye do it unto me." The "least of these" Swift projects as African slaves.

As a constant reminder of the perversion of "real" Christianity, eighteenth-century white-everyman-Gulliver is projected as the contrary opposite to medieval Everyman. Two pivotal counsels from Bernardian *Everyman* Gulliver failed to heed, with disastrous consequences: the Doctor's words in the epilogue, "...forsake pride, for he deceiveth you in the ende,"[68] the awareness of which Gulliver's closing diatribe against pride also reveals. He fails to heed "Knowledge" (of one's sins), which promises:

> Everyman, I will go with thee, and be thy guide,
> In thy moost nede to go by thy side.[69]

Knowledge leads Everyman to Confession, who gives him repentance through which he beseeches God, in the name of Christ, to save his soul. He puts on the robe of contrition:

> Contrition it is,
> That getteth forgiveness;
> It pleaseth God passinge well.[70]

And since Everyman has gotten his wealth at others' expense, he gives half of it to charity, and bequeaths that the other half be returned to where "it ought to be."[71] From then on Everyman follows Christ. At his death he repeats the last words Christ utters on the Cross: "Into thy handes, Lorde, my soule I commende." Angels singe: "Come, excellente electe spouse to Jesu!"[72] This is an unspeakably far cry from Gulliver's words: "...the groom is my favorite; for I feel my spirits revived by the smell he contracts in the stable" (234).

By the time Gulliver utters those words it is too late for conversion because he has no knowledge of God. He has for too long "resisted the promptings of the Holy Spirit, and thus has made himself incapable of repentance, and therefore of pardon."[73] The climax was the crucial turning point, when Gulliver's condition could have been remedied if he had known God and had turned to God. But he proves true the prophecy of one of Bonaventure's followers, that "the moment you pursue the Aristotelian-Thomist method and start with the external world ... you will lose the wisdom which is able to grasp intuitively the ultimate principles within yourself, the knowledge of God."[74] To demonstrate this, Swift has Gulliver start with the external world, with Curiosity, and pursue rationalism, so that, at the climax, he turns to the Houyhnhnms, symbols of Greek philosophy, instead of turning to God. At the climax, his coming to self-knowledge and knowledge of white people in general ("my family, my friends, my countrymen, or human race in general" [224]) (he does not consider black people human) results in justifiable self-hatred and justifiable hatred of white people, the human race in general, because of their abominations and atrocities against black people via white supremacy and the African slave trade, which he symbolizes. White people's hatred of themselves is prescribed by Swift as the first step in their conversion. It ended Gulliver's career in the African slave trade. White people *should* hate themselves "for all of the evils which they have committed in all of their abominations" against black people, Swift is saying, echoing Ezekiel: "they shall loathe themselves for the evils which they have committed in all their abominations" (6:9). In other words, Swift is advocating misanthropy of white people by white people.

There is no understanding of *Gulliver's Travels* as a whole without understanding the meaning Swift attaches to misanthropy and its pivotal importance to the *Travels'* conversionary purpose, which is motivated by, at least in part, the truth James Baldwin articulates, at some point, on the subject of white racism: "Not everything that is faced can be changed, but nothing can be changed until it is faced."[75] Swift's urgent advocacy of white self-hatred emphasizes the pivotal cruciality, as he sees it, of Bernard's Three Steps of Truth. Gulliver's tragedy is his ignorance of the Third Step, "Knowing God." His self-hatred and hatred of white people in general suggest his hatred of white supremacy and his acknowledgment that white people are unnatural and inferior to black people (The First Step Of Truth, Knowing Yourself), and that black people possess only human nature (The Second Step Of Truth, Knowing Your Neighbor) and are therefore superior to white people. Gulliver says, for example, that, "[white people] make no other use of reason than to improve and multiply those vices whereof their brethren in this country [black people] had only the share that nature allotted them" (225). Swift's criterion is: "No one human creature is more worthy than another in the sight of God, farther than according to the goodness or holiness of their lives,"[76] and he does not consider white supremacy nor the African slave trade examples of either goodness or holiness, but, rather, unnatural abominations, examples of using reason to improve and multiply the vices of human nature, that is, to make evil more evil and more plentiful.

As "we can know our neighbor only by love,"[77] Gulliver only approaches the Second Step of Truth. He goes back and forth as to whether or not black people are human or of the same species as white people. He does this only in the company or environment of the root cause of such horrifically evil thoughts, symbolized by the Houyhnhnms. In this way, Swift, at the same time, has Gulliver demonstrate cause and effect in "the great power of habit and prejudice" (121); or, what it is "to sin out of custom," and the necessity of "tracing a habit into the very first rise and imperfect beginnings of it," in order "to be able to tell by how slow and insensible advances it creepeth upon the heart; how it worketh itself by degrees into the very frame and texture of it, and so passeth into a second nature."[78] This will give "just sense of the great difficulty for him to learn to do good, who hath been long accustomed to do evil."[79] In other words, white-everyman-Gulliver symbolizes "the result of a complete acceptance of "traditional racist attitudes," as Wole Soyinka describes "the pathology of the average white South African's self-analysis," and adds, "it captures a mind's racial tabula rasa,"[80] which is the perfect example of Swift's definition in "A Tritical Essay Upon the Faculties of the Mind":

> The mind of man is a first (if you will pardon the expression) like a "tabula rasa," or like wax, which, while it is soft, is capable of any impression, till time has hardened it. And at length death, that grim tyrant, stops us in the midst of our career. The greatest conquerors have at last been conquered by death, which spares none, from the sceptre to the spade.[81]

With respect to Gulliver's time-hardened complete acceptance of traditional racist attitudes, Swift seems to have taken a clue from Shakespeare in choosing the name "Gulliver," to suggest the same source of malignancy as Emilia's assaulting Othello with "O gull!"[82]—that of gullibility, with regard to traditional racist attitudes, which caused the downfall of Othello *and* Gulliver. And like Othello, Gulliver throws away "the pearl of great price," the kingdom of heaven (Matt. 13:46).

Swift's urgent advocacy of the misanthropy of white people has a deeply rooted conversionary motive, inspired by the heinousness of the African slave trade and white supremacy, which is the basis of the profundity of his statement in a letter to Alexander Pope dated September 29, 1725:

> I hate and detest that animal called man, although I heartily love John, Peter, Thomas, and so forth. This is the system upon which I have governed myself for many years (but do not tell) and so I shall go on till I have done with them. I have got materials towards a treatise proving the falsity of that definition "animal rational" [a rational animal]; and to show it should be only "rationis capax" [capable of reason]. Upon this great foundation of misanthropy (though not Timon's manner), the whole building of my Travels is erected; and I never will have peace of mind till all honest men are of my opinion: by a consequence you are to embrace it immediately and procure that all who deserve my esteem may do so too. The matter is so clear that it will admit little dispute. Nay, I will hold a hundred pounds that you and I agree in the point.[83]

It *is* beyond dispute, that Gulliver, as the symbol of white people in general, *should* hate himself and them, just judging by his being a white supremacist, racist, intimately involved in the African slave trade and the dispossession, oppression, animalization, enslavement, menticide and genocide of black people by white people. Any other posture would mean condoning the cover-up and perhaps the excusing of such evils, which Swift will not allow for, especially given the fierce indignation that lacerated his heart because of them (as his tone and use of irony reveal), justifying his projection of white people as "lumps of deformity and diseases both in body and mind, smitten with pride" (239), in Gulliver's diatribe in the end against white supremacy, which his self-knowledge tells him is the cause of his pain, and which his self-consciousness tells us the same, as he writhes in the memory of past sins (hell) against black people. His self-consciousness, and Swift's use of the irony of self-betrayal, tell us that the "lumps of deformity and diseases both in body and mind, smitten with pride" are white people, in keeping with Swift's stated intentions in "Epistle Dedicatory to His Royal Highness Prince Posterity," prefatory to *A Tale of a Tub* (December 1697):

> Why should I go upon farther particulars, which might fill a volume with the just elogies [here, characterizations] of my contemporary brethren? I shall bequeath this piece of justice to a larger work, wherein I intend to write A Character of the Present Set of Wits in our nation; their persons I shall describe particularly and at length, their genius and understandings in miniature.[84]

Presumably, the "Character of the Present Set of Wits in our nation" (England), is symbolized by Gulliver, in the "larger work," *Gulliver's Travels*. That "Set of Wits" would be white. In white Gulliver, as in a mirror, white people are to see themselves, having, like Gulliver, completely accepted traditional racist attitudes; or the enormity of the African slave trade and its attendant atrocities, could not have existed, nor its legacy, which exists even in the twenty-first century.

In other words, to "make it plain,"[85] Swift wants white people, as a first step, to hate themselves as much as Gulliver hates himself and them, in order, hopefully, to begin to experience a metamorphosis through brotherly love and mutual subjection toward their black brethren, which is "real" Christianity. This metamorphosis Gulliver cannot experience, and Swift demonstrates why, as a warning to white people. The irony, which Swift would not have wanted missed, given the traditional racist stereotypes he has Gulliver use against and about the black yahoos in Part IV, is that white supremacy taught black people to hate themselves unjustifiably; now, Swift wants white people to hate themselves, justifiably, because of white supremacy, as Gulliver demonstrates in the end.

In defense of "real" Christianity, *Gulliver's Travels* is a fiercely indignant protest not only of the African slave trade and white supremacy as heresies but also of the foundations of these heresies, foundations Swift digs up as heresies; such as Plato's *The Republic*; Aristotle's *Politics* and system of knowledge; Thomas Aquinas; racism; Humanism; politics; law; war; rationalism; science; and pride in reason. These heresies white-everyman Gulliver embraces in the Lilliputians, the Brobdingnagians, the Laputans, and the Houyhnhnms, all of which monsters he personifies, Swift's point being, the fact that these heresies do not fit the definitive definition of "heresy" is what makes them heresies. In other words, the fact that they are *not* dissents or deviations from the dominant opinion and practice, but are generally accepted beliefs is the problem, in that they are all perverse deviations and dissents from what *should* be the dominant belief and practice: "real" Christianity. Swift defines "real" Christianity mainly through allusions to Bernard of Clairvaux. *Gulliver's Travels* is a mirror held up to white people, to the end that self-knowledge will produce self-hatred, and move them to "real" Christianity and its path to salvation, *instead of* the path (the first step being Aristotle's system of knowledge) to the Hell that white supremacist, African slave trader Gulliver travels.

1

The African Slave Trade

Whoever is born anywhere as a human being, that is, as a rational mortal creature, however strange he may appear to our senses in bodily form, or colour, or motion, or utterance, or in any faculty, part, or quality of his nature whatsoever, let no true believer have any doubt that such an individual is descended from the one man who first existed.[1]

The first major acceleration of the African slave trade occurred during the period 1602–1611, when Shakespeare wrote his major plays *Hamlet, Othello, King Lear, Macbeth,* and *The Tempest* about unnatural evil. From the 1590s to 1617, "28,000 slaves were being ship ped annually from Angola and the Congo."[2] "During this era of the High Renaissance in Europe, the pattern for the entire history of the Atlantic slave trade was set."[3] The second major acceleration of the African slave trade occurred from 1680 to 1688, during which period Swift was at least at work on *Gulliver's Travels,* which is also about unnatural evil.

> From 1680 to 1700, 300,000 slaves were shipped in English vessels alone. From 1680 to 1688 the Royal African Company had 249 slavers in operation, and these embarked 60,783 slaves, only 46,396 of whom survived the voyage.[4]

It is inconceivable Shakespeare and Swift did not know what was going on:

> Supplying, shipping and disposing of this vast number of human chattels became a gigantic international operation and one that favored the growth of new industries in England especially, but also in France and the Netherlands. There was no such industrial growth in Africa, but only a vast disruption of native culture ... the slave trade was so enormously profitable that nothing else could compete with it.[5]

Taking more than one cue from Shakespeare, Swift "tweaks the conscience" of his time by thrusting the embodiment of his time, his main character, Gulliver, actively and prominently into the African slave trade as surgeon and captain of African slave ships. From the clues Swift provides, we *have* to assume that Gulliver is an African slave ship surgeon and captain.

First of all, he trained and studied to be both, "being bound apprentice to an eminent surgeon; learning navigation, and other parts of the mathematics, useful to those who intend to travel, as I always believed it would be ... my 'fortune' to do; studying physic ... knowing it would be useful in long voyages;" and immediately after his return he is recommended "to be surgeon to the *Swallow*," the name of an authentic African slave ship, "Abraham Pannell commander, with whom he continued three years and a half..." (15). Approximately two years after returning home, he says: "I determined to go again to sea. I was surgeon successively in two ships, and made several voyages, for six years, to the East and West Indies [African slave trade ports], by which I got some addition to my 'fortune'" (16). We have to assume, then, that by profession he is a surgeon on the voyages in Parts I and II. In Part III, he is "invited to be surgeon [of another ship bearing the name of an authentic African slave ship]," with "another surgeon under me besides our two mates; my salary should be double to the usual pay" (123). The Captain also says that, having experienced Gulliver's "knowledge in sea-affairs to be at least equal to his, he would enter into any engagement to follow [Gulliver's] advice, as much as if [Gulliver] had share in the command" (123). It's an offer he can't refuse. In Part IV, Gulliver "accepts an advantageous offer made [him] to be captain of the *Adventure*, a stout merchantman of 350 ton," and says, "for I understood navigation well, and being grown weary of a surgeon's employment at sea, which however I could exercise upon occasion..." (179). More authentic African slave ships were given the name "Adventure" than any other name, no doubt in tribute to the first English African slaving company, "The Company of Royal Adventurers of England Trading to Africa." "It was chartered in 1663 under the Duke of York, brother of Charles II, to supply a minimum of three thousand slaves yearly to the new colonies. As a tribute to the duke, its slaves were branded with the letters *DY*."[6]

Since Gulliver himself says he is surgeon and captain on ships named for authentic African slave ships, on which he makes "prosperous" voyages only to African slave trade ports of call, during periods of the rapid acceleration of the African slave trade, when there would be no other reason for Gulliver's travels to African slave trade ports of call except for African slave trade business, what other conclusion can we come to but that Gulliver is surgeon and captain on African slave ships, even though no other scholar has so stated in the almost 300 years of criticism on *Gulliver's Travels*. And the fact that Gulliver is obsessed with money, and connects his "fortune" with his travels, coupled with the fact that "the African slave trade was so enormously profitable that nothing else could compete with it,"[7] should remove all doubts about his African slave ship employments.

1. The African Slave Trade

If *Gulliver's Travels* has nothing to do with the African slave trade, since noted Swift scholars never even mention the African slave trade, certain questions *have* to be asked. Why does Swift, at the beginning and at the end of each of the four parts of the *Travels* which comprise the four legal voyages, mention African slave trade ports of call which are solidly, deeply, famously, and historically entrenched in the African slave trade, a fact which can be authenticated? Why not just stick to fictitious names of places which can't be found on a map, if the book is "embedded in fantasy"[8] as scholars claim? Why even use fictitious names if Gulliver is not meant to be seen as covering up the fact that he travels *only* to African slave trade ports of call? Swift is also exposing lying and fraud as salient character traits of white people. Why does Swift give each of Gulliver's ships the name of a historically authentic African slave ship? Why does Swift have Gulliver repeatedly state that his voyages are "very prosperous" but he won't "trouble the reader with the details," if not to cover up the fact that all of his voyages are African slave trade voyages, and the trade was "so enormously profitable that nothing could compete with it"?[9] That's the "fortune" he refers to when he says he "always believed it would be some time or other his fortune" to "travel," with a double entendre on "fortune" as the clue. Also, if Gulliver just intends to travel, why does he feel the need to learn surgery, navigation, mathematics, and physic, the precise combination of expertise required on an African slave ship, unless he *plans* to become an African slave ship surgeon with ambitions to become "captain" of an African slave ship? It is no coincidence that both of these ambitions are realized, which is proof in itself that plans and preparations and intentions are indicated. Moreover, as the title indicates, the book is about symbolic white Gulliver's "travels," so that his itinerary is of utmost symbolic significance as representing white people's "gigantic international operation"[10] known as the African slave trade. In this regard, no travel is of greater symbolic significance than travels to African slave trade ports of call, which is why Swift mentions them satirically and consistently.

It was my discovery in the early eighties that *Gulliver's Travels* was a protest of the African slave trade, and after much arduous research, finding no other scholar coming even close to the same conclusion, that prompted the present undertaking. But my discovery and project were shot down. It so happens, however, that a scholar in the early nineties, Deborah Wyrick, seems to have said what I said, in part at least, without really saying it, that is, she alludes to the African slave trade by a different name, "mercantile capitalism."[11] One wonders why. A cover-up? Leading up to *Gulliver's Travels* in this regard, Wyrick first mentions Aphra Behn's *Oroonoko*, and that it takes place in Suriname immediately before it was ceded by England to

Holland, "and the book's narrative concerns the slave trade, slave rebellion, and the ambivalent attitude of colonizers to the colonized and the conquered."[12] Wyrick goes on to say that "Robinson Crusoe was actually engaged in the slave trade, having signed on 'on board a vessel bound to the coast of Africa ... a voyage to Guinea,' as was another protagonist of Defoe, Captain Singleton."[13] She makes no mention of the fact that Gulliver goes to Guinea. She does not by direct statement connect *Gulliver's Travels* to the "African slave trade." Instead, Wyrick says:

> Before launching into the adventures in Lilliput, Swift sketches Gulliver's earliest travels: to "the Levant, and some other Parts" and "several Voyages, for six Years, to the East and West-Indies; by which [he] got some Addition to [his] fortune." The enterprise from which Gulliver hopes to make his fortune, that enterprise that is submerged beneath the textual surface, is mercantile capitalism and its enactment through colonial imperialism. Ships went to the West Indies as part of the slave-and-sugar trade, to the East Indies in the service of the East India Company, to further commercial interests.... When the recorded journeys began, Gulliver lands in Lilliput after being wrecked "North-west of Van Diemen's Land" during a "Voyage to the South-Sea." His ship's destination suggests affiliation with the South Sea Company and (from Swift's time perspective if not from Gulliver's) the disastrous South Sea Bubble.[14]

(Wyrick does not mention the connection between the South Sea Company and the African slave trade, that the Tory party created "a great South Sea Company which was to take over a part of the National Debt, and add to the revenues by importing African slaves and merchandise into South America").[15]

> The reference to Van Diemen's land suggests the Southern Hemisphere navigation projects of Sir Edmund Halley and the Australian hydrographic surveys of Gulliver's "cousin" William Dampier. Such scientific expeditions served clear economic purposes: improved navigation facilitates expansion of trade.[16]

I think Swift mentions Van Diemen's land to protest the Dutch involvement in the African slave trade. The Dutch controlled most of the East Indies. Van Diemen's Land is now Tasmania, named after Abel Tasman, the Dutch navigator who discovered it and named it after the governor of the Dutch East India Company.[17] Wyrick continues with the following:

> Gulliver's further journeys are motivated by the same, but unspecified, economic interests. The voyage to Brobdingnag begins aboard "the Adventure, a Merchant-Ship of three Hundred Tons, bound for Surat," in other words, a vessel engaged in the India trade. The third voyage takes Gulliver again to the East Indies via India; his misfortunes commence in the Gulf of Tonkin, where his captain engages in ad hoc buying and selling while waiting for delivery of previously contracted cargo. Again, Swift's language is extremely vague about

the exact nature of the ship's commercial mission, but he does indicate that Gulliver has received additional authority, becoming a full participant in the mercantalist enterprise.[18]

Presumably, Gulliver's becoming "a full participant in the mercantalist enterprise" means he's become a full participant in the African slave trade. But actually, by the time indicated in Wyrick's statement above, Gulliver's been a full participant, as African slave ship surgeon, in the African slave trade for seventeen years. Wyrick's proof of Gulliver's "becoming a full participant" is the following explanation by Gulliver:

> Many of the [Goods the captain] intended to buy were not ready ... therefore in hopes to defray some of the charges he must be at, he bought a Sloop, loaded it with several Sorts of Goods ... appointed me Master of the Sloop, and gave me Power to traffick, while he transacted his Affairs at Tonquin [124].

Wyrick goes on to say:

> And on his fourth voyage, Gulliver attains the status of "Captain of the Adventure, a stout Merchant-man ... [employed to] trade with the Indians in the South-Sea." Thus the destinations of Gulliver's merchant ships show a pattern of involvement with the most powerful instruments of colonialism, and his rise in responsibility and title discloses his rise through the ranks of — and his deepening implication in — the network of politico-economic activities institutionalized in the South Sea and East India Companies.[19]

Gulliver's Travels was written in the wake of the South Sea Bubble, a paper-credit scheme that Swift despised not only because of the financial ruination it brought but also because it symbolized the ascendency of money interests over landed interests. Swift's attitude toward Gulliver's mercantile peregrinations would necessarily be skeptical, even disapproving; one suspects that Gulliver is being set up to act, in some ways, as an embodiment of the imperialist spirit. His literal displacements, then, are necessary conditions for him to function as avatar and interrogator of mercantile capitalism. Yet the textual silences about Gulliver's involvement in the practices he ultimately condemns suggest the existence of what Machery identifies as the inevitable "conflict between text and ideological content."[20]

Other significant statements by Wyrick are that "At times *Gulliver's Travels* attacks colonialism and slavery, but at other times its stance toward these institutions is profoundly ambivalent."

> This ambivalence is nowhere more apparent that in part 4. The Houyhnhnms are both a caste-defined society and a slaveholding one. They have hunted down the Yahoos and bound them into servitude; the main subject of the Houyhnhnm Assembly is the Yahoo question, solutions ranging from genocide to castration (the latter refinement having been suggested inadvertently by Gulliver). They treat Gulliver as an exotic curiosity, albeit one who might lead his fellow Yahoos into a slave revolt in the manner of Oroonoko.[21]

From the aforesaid, as I try to prove, there is little or no doubt that the Houyhnhnms' yahoos are black, African slaves. Wyrick goes on to say: "Throughout his dialogues with the Houyhnhnm master, Gulliver denounces the colonialist system of which he has been a part. He brings the colonialist subtest to the surface, but he admits his own complicity only through the weak and generalizing device of the first-person plural."[22] Wyrick mentions a "silenced critique of the oppression of Ireland," and that it "suggests the hidden and contradictory ideology of Swift's novel, an ideology dependent on imperialist capitalism and complicitous in its "naturalization" through science, leisure, and individual entrepreneurship."[23]

The latter statement in no way applies to Swift, the novel's being a fiercely indignant protest of the African slave trade and white supremacy in which Swift is nowhere "ambivalent." It does, however, apply to Gulliver up until the climax, when he arrives at self-knowledge and, consequently, self-hatred.

By all indications and implications concerning Gulliver's "mercantile peregrinations," Wyrick is saying, without saying, what I long ago discovered, that Gulliver is an African slave ship surgeon and captain who has, with "insatiable desire" (64), spent most of his life in the African slave trade, representing the character of white people ironized.

Evidence of Gulliver's African slave trade intentions, and his obsession with money, are indicated from the beginning. At seventeen he is "bound apprentice" to "an eminent surgeon in London," with whom, he says:

> I continued four years; and my father now and then sending me small sums of money, I laid them out in learning navigation, and other parts of the mathematics, useful to those who intend to travel, as I always believed it would be some time or other my fortune to do [15].

He goes on to say:

> I went down to my father; where, by the assistance of him and my uncle John, and some other relations I got forty pounds, and a promise of thirty pounds a year to maintain me at Leyden: there I studied physic two years and seven months, knowing it would be useful in long voyages [15].

Gulliver is minutely precise about everything but the truth. It's one of the ways we know he's lying or perpetrating fraud. It is immoral, as well as disingenuous, for him to deliberately give the impression that he studied physic because he knew it would be "usefull" for travel, when he knew it was *necessary* for such "long voyages" as African slave trade voyages. Anyone training to become an African slave ship surgeon in Swift's day would have known the following bit of history:

1. The African Slave Trade   31

> Along with their human cargoes, crowded, filthy, undernourished, and terrified out of the wish to live, the ships also carried an invisible cargo of microbes, bacilli, spirochetes, viruses, and intestinal worms from one continent to another; the Middle Passage was a crossroads and marketplace of diseases. From Europe came smallpox, measles ... gonorrhea, and syphilis.... The African diseases were yellow fever ... dengue, blackwater fever, malaria ... the bloody flux, Guinea worms, hookworm, yaws, elephantiasis, and leprosy.[24]

Leyden could very well have provided the best training at the time for aspiring African slave ship surgeons, for the slave trade was still in the hands of the Dutch, "who exceeded all other Europeans in the careful management of their slave ships as to cleanliness and neatness."[25] "They also created the largest merchant marine in the world. With its ten thousand ships, and its merchants, it was becoming the world's greatest center of finance and insurance. To a great extent the trade was directed by Sephardic Jews. The Sephardim also became a factor in the spread of sugar cultivation from Brazil to the West Indies and in the development of Dutch overseas plantation colonies."[26] "Another religious group that contributed to the economic growth of the Dutch Republic were the Calvinists, "an influential minority of the population, many of them merchants. The Dutch were attracted to Calvinism because of its tolerance of capitalistic practices." Also, "Calvinist theologians accepted slavery as a legitimate human institution, justifying it on the so-called curse of Ham theory."[27]

Soon after completing his study of physic, Gulliver goes directly into the African slave trade, moving right along as planned, but making no mention of the trade. He says:

> Soon after my return from Leyden, I was recommended, by my good master Mr. Bates, to be surgeon to the Swallow, Captain Abraham Pannell, commander; with whom I continued three years and a half, making a voyage or two into the Levant, and some other parts [15].

Through his use of the irony of self-betrayal, Swift lets Gulliver expose himself. With the names *Swallow*, Abraham, and the Levant (Cyprus, Israel, Jordan, Lebonon, Palistine, Syria), Swift protests the involvement of Arabs and Jews in the African slave trade. He also relies on history in the naming of *all* of Gulliver's African slave ships, the first being the *Swallow*. There are documented historical records of at least five African slave ships named the *Swallow*. In her four-volume collection, *Documents Illustrative of the History of the Slave Trade to America*, Elizabeth Donnan cites the following bill of lading:

London the 31st March 1681

Nevis. Received from Mr. Henry Carpenter and company the sum of Two

Hundred Sixty-two pounds in Negroes at Sixteen pounds per head and is full payment for two-thirds parts of Freight of eighty-seven Negroes brought to this island in the ship *Swallow* and for which I have given three receipts by this tenour and date.
Dated the 17th day of January 1680.
F262   Evan Seys.

All of Gulliver's ships are named after authentic African slave ships.

When Gulliver returned from the Levant, and some other parts, he "took part of a small house in the Old Jury," (15) a Jewish section of London, which is meant to identify Gulliver with the prominent roll the Jews played in the African slave trade; with "the proud Pharisee" who said: "God, I thank thee that I am not as other men are" (Luke 18:11); with the crucifying of Christ; and with the worship of money (the golden calf, Exodus 31). The very next thing Gulliver does is marry for money.

Notwithstanding all of these allusions to the African slave trade on the first page, scholars seem not to have seen these allusions as clues to the meaning of *Gulliver's Travels*. This is certainly indicative of the suggestion made by noted Swift scholar Louis Landa that "we rob Swift a little of his uniqueness":

> ... it may help us to assess Swift more competently if we rob him a little of his uniqueness though not of his literary greatness in viewing the age. Envision him as one of a collective body of eighteenth-century Jeremiahs whose lamentations were filling the air. The Tory wits, as Professor Louis Bredvold has so persuasively shown in his excellent essay, "The Gloom of the Tory Satirists," reflected, even generated, their fair share of the gloom-thickened atmosphere of the period of Queen Anne and the first Georges. But in this limited respect there was nothing singular, except their talents, about Swift and his friends — Pope, Gay, Arbuthnot, and Parnell. "We are doomed to be undone," wrote Bishop George Berkeley in 1721, in his tract significantly titled, "An Essay Towards Preventing the Ruin of Great Britain," one of numerous dark pictures of character and destiny of the British. Many looked about and saw widely prevailing infection, a culture losing its vigor and its better values, under the impact of bribery, luxury, political faction, deteriorated education, an immoral stage, ostentatious fashions, a dissolute and slothful poor, an irresponsible aristocracy, loss of public spirit, imitation of French and Italian fopperies, the vulgarization of the arts, and a dozen other such evils.[28]

Every evil complained of except the worst evil, the African slave trade. And yet, when Bishop George Berkeley wrote his essay, mentioned above, in 1721, by modest estimates, "40,000 slaves a year were being shipped from Africa, and the English were supplying more than half of these."[29] But then, it is this same Bishop George Berkeley, whom Swift knew, who put the new Christian apologetics condemning all Negroes to bondage into "philosophical language": "Negroes," he said, were "creatures of another species,"[30] in support of the new racial justification for slavery, and that "the Negro was not a human being...."[31] Swift cannot, therefore, be robbed, even a little, of his uniqueness. He *is* unique in being the only one who cried aloud, and showed his people their worst transgression: the African slave trade.

Another noted Swift scholar, Donald Greene, also does not mention the African slave trade while simultaneously painting Gulliver as "dangerous" and more than capable of atrocities. After introducing Gulliver as "a decent, sober, solid Englishman, a representative of the best that western European civilization (English brand) has produced up to the time of his adventure,"[32] Donald Greene adds:

> Swift significantly bestows on him the name "Gulliver." He knows of no values beyond those he has absorbed from his own cultural environment, one of the chief being a profound complacency that his own modern white Anglo-Saxon Protestant culture is the acme of human achievment, and any mode of thinking and behaving that differs strikingly from it is *a priori* inferior. It is to him, to us, that Swift and Eliot and a thousand other prophets and preachers, from Job and Jeremiah and Ezekiel, through Paul and Augustine and Francis of Assissi and Savonarola and the author of *Everyman* and Donne and Wesley, down to certain "radical" novelists and poets of today, address their message: decency, respectability, conformity, unquestioning acceptance of the norms of the "civilized" society around us is not enough. For Gulliver is dangerous. The proof of this is the history of the vaunted "western civilization" which he and his fellows constitute — which we constitute — a history which, as the King of Brobdingnag tells him has hitherto consisted of "a heap of conspiracies, rebellions, murders, massacres, revolutions, banishments, the very worst effects that avarice, faction, hypocrisy, perfidiousness, cruelty, rage, madness, hatred, envy, lust, malice, and ambition could produce...." This, let it be repeated, is what we get when we scratch the pleasant surface of the decent, considerate, "civilized" Gulliver — the man who is responsible for the history of the modern western world, which in the twentieth century has produced atrocities, Passchencaele, Auschwitz, Buchenwald, Hiroshima, Biafra, that would have been beyond Swift's darkest imagination. What is wrong with Gulliver? The King of Brobdingnag states it clearly: He was amazed how so impotent and groveling an insect as I (these were his expressions) could entertain such inhuman ideas, and in so familiar a manner as to appear wholly unmoved at all by the scenes of blood and desolation which I had painted...." The trouble is an inadequacy of emotional response toward his fellow creatures, a lack of feeling, a callous heart.... The "inoffensive," "harmless" ordinary member of society who uncritically accepts what he is told by those around him, is, in history, responsible for an incredible, horrifying amount of harm; Eliot's "decent, godless people" are desperately in need of re-education, both for their own sake and the sake of those who come in contact with them...."[33]

Inasmuch as Swift, in *Gulliver's Travels*, fiercely protests the fifteenth-, the sixteenth-, the seventeenth-, and the eighteenth-century atrocities of the African slave trade, the twentieth-century atrocities that Greene mentions would hardly have been beyond Swift's darkest imagination. It is surprising that, although it ran the gamut of horrors in Swift's own day, Greene, in speaking of atrocities, does not even mention the African slave trade, let alone see Gulliver as responsible for it, as Swift does.

In seeing Gulliver through Greene's eyes, as "decent, considerate, civilized," we are seeing Gulliver's white supremacist facade, which he believes is all he needs. He is a phoney, a hypocrit, a liar, and a fraud. It is true, as Greene points out, that Gulliver has "a lack of feeling," "a callous heart" (typical of an African slave trader), and that he is "responsible for an incredible, horrifying amount of harm," via the African slave trade. But it is because he "holds forth in the style of the masters he has learned from,"[34] Plato and Aristotle, whose philosophies, among others, are the foundations of western civilization that Swift is digging up, and because Gulliver is "godless" in Swift's context of "real" Christianity. Gulliver starts out with Aristotle's system of knowledge, (depicted as Bernard's "Curiosity, that first step of Pride") and ends up a schizophrenic genocidal monster: "The fool saying in his heart, "There is no God.""[35] Gulliver is a Humanist proponent of Aristotle's philosophy of "superiority" and "supremacy" and slavery, and of Plato's philosophy of genocide, deception, and fraud. When Greene says of Gulliver that "He knows of no values beyond those he has absorbed from his own cultural environment, one of the chief being a profound complacency that his own modern white Anglo-Saxon Protestant culture is the acme of human achievement, and any mode of thinking and behavior that differs strikingly from it is *a priori* inferior,"[36] he gives Gulliver the characteristics of a white supremacist and an African slave trader, both reflecting Aristotle. The introduction to Aristotle's *Politics*, for example, states the following:

> "Humanity is divided into two: the masters and the slaves; or, if one prefers it, the Greeks and the barbarians, those who have the right to command; and those who are born to obey." That seemed to imply that, to an Athenian, everyone who was not Greek could be captured and enslaved — even should be. Aristotle also said: "A slave is property with a soul. Thus he accepted slavery as an institution. He also declared that "the use of domestic animals and slaves is about the same; they both lend us their physical efforts to satisfy the needs of existence." He noted that some had argued that "the rule of a master over slaves is contrary to nature, and that the distinction between master and slave exists only by law ... and, being an interference with nature, is thus unjust." These ambiguous propositions would have importance in the sixteenth century, when Aristotle was looked upon as the guide to almost everything.[37]

Swift projects the African slave trade as an unnatural evil, a degenerate way of life that violates the laws of nature, by depicting the enslavers as Greek monsters (Centaurs), including Gulliver, who delights in imitating them even to the extent of "trotting like a horse" (225). It was not only in the sixteenth century that Aristotle was looked upon as the guide to almost everything, it was throughout the African slave trade, especially in America, the last country to end the trade. As Aristotle continues his notoriously arrogant and audacious definition of a slave, it's not difficult to see how his philosophy was used as a guide for justifying and establishing the African slave trade as an institution, and why his philosophy is one of the foundations, both of the African slave trade and white supremacy, Swift is digging up:

> ... a slave is a sort of living piece of property ... any human being that by nature belongs not to himself but to another is by nature a slave; and a human being belongs to another whenever, inspite of being a man, he is a piece of property ... those whose condition is such that their function is the use of their bodies and nothing better can be expected of them, those, I say, are slaves by nature. It is better for them to be ruled thus. For the slave by nature is he that can and therefore does belong to another, and he that participates in reason so far as to recognize it but not so as to possess it (whereas the other animals obey not reason but emotions). The use made of slaves hardly differs at all from that of tame animals; they both help with their bodies to supply our essential needs. It is, then, nature's purpose to make the bodies of free men to differ from those of slaves, the latter strong enough to be used for necessary tasks, the former erect and useless for that kind of work, but well suited for the life of a citizen of a state, a life which is in turn divided between the requirements of war and peace.... It is clear then that by nature some are free, others slaves, and that for these it is both just and expedient that they should serve as slaves.[38]

Aristotle is more of a barbarian than a Greek. His statement above, that "The use made of slaves hardly differs at all from that of tame animals," can be seen as the foundation of the practice of animalizing African slaves, which Gulliver demonstrates. Swift also attacks the practice with scathing irony in the following echo from Aristotle. Speaking of African slaves as "yahoos," while debating exterminating them from the face of the earth (shades of Plato), Gulliver says of the Houyhnhnms, who are symbolic of Plato and Aristotle:

> ... the Houyhnhnms, to get rid of this evil [the yahoos], made a general hunting, and at last enclosed the whole herd; and destroying the older, every Houyhnhnm kept two young ones in a kennel, and brought them to such a degree of tameness, as an animal so savage by nature can be capable of acquiring; using them for draught and carriage.... That [the Houyhnhnms] taking a fancy to use the service of the yahoos [African slaves], had very imprudently neglected to cultivate the breed of asses, easily kept, more tame and orderly, without any offensive smell, strong enough for labour, although they yield to the other in agility of body; and if their braying be no agreeable sound, it is far preferable to the horrible howlings of the [African slaves] yahoos [219].

Now, the foregoing comes after it has already been well established by Swift's clues, that these yahoos are black human beings animalized by white supremacy, the African slave trade, and racism. The "general hunting" of them, as well as the animalizing of them, is also a practice straight from Aristotle, who says:

> The knowledge of how to "acquire" slaves is different from the knowledge of statecraft or philosophy. The just method of acquisition, for instance, being a kind of military or hunting skill.[39]

The ironic similarities between Swift's depiction of the animalization and enslavement of black Africans (A.K.A. "yahoos") and Aristotle's philosophy of slavery, the foundation and model for the African slave trade, should indicate that Swift is protesting the African slave trade, and doing so as further justification for digging up the Aristotelian foundations of western civilization. *Gulliver's Travels* also contains other attacks upon Aristotle's philosophy, as expressed by Aristotle in the following:

> ... anything which conquers does so because it excels in some good. It seems therefore that force is not without virtue.[40]

Swift, as we have seen, puts "conquering" in the context of the African slave trade and colonizing, to be condemned, as one of the Four Horsemen of the Apocalypse, who "went forth conquering, and to conquer" (Rev. 6:2). Swift also condemns Aristotle's "art of war" (a phrase Gulliver uses) as justified and encouraged in the following:

> If then nature makes nothing without some end in view, nothing to no purpose, it must be that nature has made all of them for the sake of man. This means that it is according to nature that even the art of war, since hunting is a part of it, should in a sense be a way of acquiring property; and that it must be used both against such men as are by nature intended to be ruled over but refuse; for that is the kind of warfare that is by nature just.[41]

Swift may have had Aristotle's morally despicable arrogance (above) in mind when he says through Gulliver that, although vilely arrogant white supremacists had the audacity to decide that black Africans are by nature intended to be ruled over, *they* "do not appear to have any desire of being conquered, and enslaved, murdered or driven out by colonies..." (237). But, following Aristotle, that is exactly what happened and why it happened, lack of "desire" being an understatement for "refuse." For example, "The slaves flung themselves on the beach, clutching handfuls of sand in a desperate effort to remain in Africa. Some tried to strangle themselves with their chains."[42] Again, Aristotle is one of the foundations Swift is digging up.

After his maiden African slave trade voyage on the *Swallow*, Gulliver returns to the trade, telling the reader: "I was surgeon successively in two ships, and made several voyages, for six years, to the East and West Indies, by which I got some addition to my fortune" (16). The six years Gulliver speaks of would be from 1688 to1694, a period of an astonishing increase in the immensity of the traffic in slaves. "Liverpool slavers made 878 voyages to the Guinea Coast, each lasting an average of nine or ten months and yielding an average cash return of 14,002 pounds per voyage, the profit from slaves alone, not including extra revenue from the cargoes of sugar and ginger carried from the West Indies to Liverpool."[43]

> The Guinea trade was "three-cornered." It consisted in carrying Manchester goods to Africa, where they were exchanged for slaves; then carrying slaves to the West Indies, where they were exchanged for cash or three-year notes-of-hand bearing six-per-cent interest; the buying sugar, cocoa, coffee, indigo, and ginger to carry home — and sell to buy Manchester goods and repeat the process. A ship ... had to show a profit for every leg of the voyage — though of course the profit was highest on the run from Guinea to the West Indies, which was known as the Middle Passage.[44]

Swift also has Gulliver travel to the West Indies to expose the historical fact that "two innocuous crops, sugar and cotton, had a profound effect on the slave trade and so have been responsible for the death and suffering of millions of human beings."[45]

Gulliver travels to Barbadoes, and the Leeward Islands, "by the direction of the merchants who employed me" (179), he says. If "merchants" *employed* him to voyage to these West Indies islands, it could only have been for African slave trade business:

> It was in 1605 that the English laid claim to Barbadoes, their first possession in the Caribbean area; later it would be called "the mother of the West Indian sugar islands." Barbadoes was rapidly transformed ... into eight hundred sugar plantations.... Even before the intensive cultivation of sugar began to exhaust the soil of Barbadoes, the plantation system spread to other islands, beginning with those of the Leeward chain....[46]

Also significant in Swift's mention of the West Indies in his protest of the African slave trade is the fact that "It was widely admitted that slaves in the West Indies were treated more harshly than those in the English colonies on the mainland."[47]

> There was little room for human regard between master and slaves ... the slaves were regarded as work units, not as men, women, and children. "Kindliness and comfort, cruelty and hardship, were rated at balance-sheet value; births and deaths were reckoned in profit and loss.... The fact seems to be that brutality was often profitable.[48]

A horrific example, Sir Hans Sloane's description of the treatment of slaves in the West Indies, parallels Swift's description of the analytical reason as "officious with tools for cutting, and opening, and mangling, and piercing," which Swift "takes to be the last degree of perverting nature."[49] Not only does the treatment of the slaves constitute "the last degree of perverting nature," Swift suggests a cause and effect connection between the analytical reason and science and the perception of, the enslavement of, and the treatment of African slaves:

> Slaves were kept in a state of terror. After a tour of the islands in 1688, Sir Hans Sloane reported that they were punished for major crimes by "nailing them down to the ground with crooked sticks on every Limb and then applying the Fire by degrees from the feet and the hands, burning them gradually up to the head, whereby their pains are extravagant; for Crimes of a lesser nature Gelding or chopping off half of the foot with an Ax. Their punishments are suffered by them with great Constancy. For running away they put Iron rings of great weight on their ankles or Pottochs about their Necks which are iron rings with two long Necks rivetted to them or a Spur in the mouth. They are whip'd till they are Raw; some put on their skin Pepper and Salt to make them smart, at other times their Masters will drop melted wax on their Skin and use several very exquisite Torments." Sir Hans was not tender-hearted, for he adds: "These punishments are sometimes merited by the Blacks, who are a very perverse Generation of People, and though the punishments appear harsh, yet are scarce equal to some of their crimes and inferior to what Punishments other European Nations inflict on their Slaves in the East-Indies."[50]

Considering white people's heinously perverse treatment of black people, Swift would have us see the irony in a white person calling black people "a very perverse Generation of People." The "not tender-hearted" Sir Hans, president of the scientific society, The Royal Academy, which Swift ridicules as the Grand Academy of Lagado in Part III, is a good example of Professor Greene's criticism of white-everyman-Gulliver: "The trouble is an inadequacy of emotional response toward his fellow creatures, a lack of feeling, a callous heart."[51] Moreover, if the punishment of slaves in the West Indies is "inferior" to the punishment of slaves in the East Indies, that would explain Swift's calling attentions in protest of this fact by having Gulliver voyage to the East Indies, in protest also of the involvement in the African slave trade of European nations other than England. For example:

> The Portuguese had explored the Guinea Coast and rounded the Cape of Good Hope, and their claim to exclusive rights in the whole African continent had been confirmed by two papal bulls issued in 1493. By that time they had already begun to build forts on the coast ... as depots in which slaves could be held for shipment.[52]

Gulliver travels to the first of these forts, Fort St. George, at Elmina on the Gold Coast, which was started in 1481.

The Dutch took control of much of the Portuguese overseas empire, such as most of the East Indies, or Indonesia, several other commercial strongholds in southern and eastern Asia, much of the western coast of Africa, northeastern Brazil, and a number of Caribbean islands. "By 1648 the Dutch were indisputably the greatest trading nation in the world, with commercial outposts and fortified 'factories' scattered from Archangel to Recife and from New Amsterdam to Nagasaki."[53] The Dutch also had trading stations in India, Japan, Formosa (Taiwan), and Ceylon (Sri Lanka). Gulliver travels to India, Japan (Nagasaki), Brazil, and three times to the East Indies. All English merchants were taxed 10 percent for the benefit of The Royal African Company. Gulliver tells the reader:

> I accepted an advantageous offer from Captain William Prichard, master of the *Antelope*, who was making a voyage to the South Sea. We set sail from Bristol May 4th, 1699, and our voyage at first was very prosperous [16].

The *Antelope* was the name of an actual African slave ship owned by England's Royal African Company. It was seized by the French in 1693.[54] The South Sea is in the East Indies. Setting sail from Bristol is also significant as indicative of Swift's protest of the African slave trade:

> London was the headquarters of the Royal African Company and hence, until the end of the seventeenth century, it was the principal English slaving port. After the trade was thrown open to independent vessels, or "ten percenters," in 1689, Bristol outdistanced London.[55]

Swift has Gulliver continue, with further evidence he's on an African slave trade voyage and is defrauding the reader as to that fact. He calls hunting and catching human prey an "adventure," recalling the first English company, "The Company of Royal Adventurers of England Trading to Africa." Historically, more African slave ships were given the name "Adventure" than any other name. Swift gives two of Gulliver's ships the name "Adventure" to emphasize the morally despicable practice of referring to hunting and enslaving human beings as an "adventure." Gulliver says:

> It would not be proper, for some reason, to trouble the reader with the particulars of our adventures in those seas: let it suffice to inform him, that in our passage from thence to the East Indies we were driven by a violent storm to the northwest of Van Dieman's Land. By an observation, we found ourselves in the latitude of 30 degrees 2 minutes south. Twelve of our crew were dead by immoderate labour, and ill food, the rest were in a very weak condition. On the fifth of November, which was the beginning of summer in those parts, the weather being very hazy.[56]

We get a wealth of information about the African slave trade from Gulliver's above narration. He certainly doesn't want the reader to know what he is doing in "those seas," or what actually are his "adventures." That should tell us a lot, or at least arouse our suspicions. In his mention of "Van Diemen's Land," Swift is protesting the Dutch involvement in the African slave trade.

Gulliver also says they find themselves in the "latitude of 30 degrees 2 minutes south," which is South Africa, where, "on the fifth of November, it is the beginning of summer in those parts." The fact that "twelve of his crew were dead by immoderate labour" suggests that the ship is in the "horse latitudes," a region of subsiding dry air and high pressure which results in weak winds, becalming the ship in the doldrums. "Fearful of running out of food and water, sailors threw their horses and slaves overboard to save on provisions."[57] The "horse latitudes" was the most dangerous leg of the Middle Passage, but the shortest leg of the triangular trade.

Of the "particulars" Gulliver says "It would not be proper, for some reason, to trouble the reader" with, one would surely be the details of his job, which Swift *would* want the reader troubled with, as integral to his protests of the African slave trade: "On all English and European voyages, the ship's surgeons usually played an essential part in the selection of the slaves. Indeed, his was the decisive voice in advising captains whether or not to buy. Much the same procedure was followed, whatever the nationality of the purchaser."[58] Very often the surgeons stowed the slaves. One English African slave ship surgeon tells of "making the most of the room in stowing the slaves, and wedged them in. They had not so much room as a man in his coffin either in length or breadth."[59] Another surgeon documented the following on a ship the usual size of Gulliver's slave ships:

> *The Brookes* ... was permitted by law to carry 454 slaves, although by the chart, it was impossible to fit more than 451. Dr. Trotter, surgeon on *The Brookes*, tells that she had carried 600 slaves on one voyage and 608 on another.[60]

"So great was the profit on each slave landed alive in the East Indies that hardly a captain refrained from loading his vessel to her utmost capacity ... sometimes leaving only twenty inches of headroom for the slaves; they could not sit upright during the whole voyage."[61] Some captains "left their slaves to wallow in excrement during the whole Atlantic passage."[62]

Gulliver's ship is driven by a strong wind directly upon a rock and immediately splits. He and six of the crew made a shift to get clear of the ship and the rock" (16). One is left to wonder how the slaves fared. "A major cause of unusually high mortality among the slaves is storms at sea,"[63] with hundreds of slaves chained together and "tightly packed" in the hold of the slave ship. During one storm, "702 slaves were left to drown,"[64] in another, 820 slaves.

One of Swift's conversionary objectives is to arouse compassion for African slaves (The Second Step of Truth). So, assuming white people's incapacity for empathy with African slaves—presumably if they could empathize there'd have been no African slave trade—Swift places Gulliver, with whom white people can identify with and thus empathize with, into African slave postures. For example, Gulliver wakes in Lilliput nailed to the ground, like the African slaves in Sir Hans's description of such punishment. But Gulliver sees no relationship; he is incapable of empathy. The same is true when his lodging in Lilliput suggests the size of an African slave's allotted space in the hold of a slave ship.

After his shipwreck in "the latitude of 30 degrees 2 minutes south," which is most likely Tasmania, Gulliver swims to the shores of a land to which he gives the fictitious name of "Lilliput," as a cover-up for his true location and its African slave trade connection. But the coinage gives him away. Taking "Lilli" to mean lily white; and giving "put" its medieval meaning of "to launch persons, a boat, a fleet" (*OED*), and "to carry or cause to be taken across a body of water" (*MW*), the name "Lilliput" becomes a protest in itself: Lily-white men launching ships across oceans to capture innocent black human beings to forcefully carry across an ocean.

In keeping with his pattern of beginning and ending each of the four parts of *Gulliver's Travels* with historically verifiable allusions to the African slave trade, Swift, here at the end of Part I, has Gulliver again mention Van Diemen's Land, 30 degrees south, and has him picked up by an English African slave ship returning from Japan by the North and South Seas, about which he says: "I shall not trouble the reader with a particular account of this voyage, which was very prosperous for the most part."

Once back home, all Gulliver talks about is money. Referring to the miniature souvenir livestock from Blefuscu, he says: "The short time I continued in England, I made a considerable profit by showing my cattle to many persons of quality, and others: and before I began my second voyage, I sold them for six hundred pounds" (64). Swift is emphasizing the profit-and-loss mentality of white people, and their obsessive propensity to do anything for money. After being away from home and family for three years, on African slave trade voyages, he says: "I stayed but two months with my wife and family; for my insatiable desire of seeing foreign countries would suffer me to continue no longer" (64). What he means is his insatiable desire for the enormous profits from the African slave trade. The only foreign countries he sees are African slave trade ports of call. His greed is all the more pronounced by his being already in good shape financially, by his own admission:

> I left fifteen hundred pounds with my wife, and fixed her in a good house at Redriff. My remaining stock I carried with me, part in money, and part in goods, in hopes to improve my fortunes. My eldest uncle John had left me an estate in land, near Epping, of about thirty pounds a year; and I had a long lease of the Black Bull in Fetter Lane, which yielded me as much more: so that I was not in any danger of leaving my family upon the parish.... I took leave of my wife, and boy and girl with tears on both sides, and went on board the *Adventure*, a merchant-ship of three hundred tons, bound for Surat.... But my account of this voyage must be referred to the second part of my *Travels* [64].

(Swift says elsewhere that white people think "they can never have enough money to spend or to save, as they find themselves inclined from their natural bent either to profusion or avarice" (203).

Swift begins the second part of *Gulliver's Travels* using the irony of self-betrayal in Gulliver's opening statement, "Having been condemned by nature and fortune to an active and restless life ... I again left my native country, and took shipping ... in the *Adventure*, Capt. John Nicholas, a Cornish man, commander, bound for Surat," a trading station under the management of the Dutch East India Company. In having Gulliver mention, at the very end of Part I, that his captain is from Liverpool, Swift chooses a city upon which the African slave trade had a major impact. One historian states that "The rise of Liverpool is a remarkable history, in which the slave trade played an important perhaps even a decisive part." Another historian states:

> Liverpool made no secret of the source of its sudden wealth. The town hall was covered with reproductions of elephants' teeth and blackamoors. Shop windows were full of handcuffs, leg irons, collars, and slave chains for outgoing vessels. Goldsmiths advertised "Silver locks and Collars for Blacks and Dogs," and ladies of fashion appeared in public each with a little black slave boy wearing a turban and baggy silk pantaloons. "Young bloods of the town deemed it fine amusement to circulate handbills in which Negro girls are offered for sale," reported one shocked observer. The famous actor George Frederick Cooke appeared drunk on the stage of the Theater Royal in Liverpool and was booed by the audience. Reeling to the footlights, he shouted, "I have not come here to be insulted by a set of wretches, every brick in whose infernal town is cemented with an African's blood."[65]

At the beginning and at the end of each part of the *Travels*, Swift's allusions to the African slave trade include the mention by name of each of the captains of each of the African slave ships on which Gulliver makes his voyages. We have to assume that Swift has an implicit satiric purpose in mind, such as to expose the gigantic international scope of the trade, to which the names are a clue, suggesting Jewish, Dutch, Portuguese, and mostly British involvement, the latter having "inflicted more suffering on the Negroes than any other nation."[66] Also, needless to say, the slave ship captains played an indispensable role, and Gulliver becomes an African slave ship captain in Part IV. Swift, in addition, would have us know what recorded accounts have to say about African slave ship captains:

> The Guinea trade brought out the worst in master and seamen alike.... There were some captains who had been absolutely corrupted by the absolute power they exercised. After first being heartless for the sake of profits, they had learned to enjoy cruelty for its own sake, even when it cost them money by leading to the needless loss of slaves.[67]

As mentioned, Gulliver takes shipping in the *Adventure*. He says: "We had a very prosperous gale till we arrived at the Cape of Good Hope, where we landed for fresh water," signifying Swift's calling attention to the cruciality of the Cape of Good Hope to the African slave trade, which is a clue to Swift's repeated mention of the Cape. The Cape was named "The Cape of Good Hope" by Portuguese navigator Bartolomeu Dias because "its discovery was a good omen that India could be reached by sea from Europe."[68] Gulliver, at this time, is bound for India. The Cape of Good Hope had long been a strategic concern to European nations. With his mention of the Cape, Surat, the Straits of Madagascar, the Molucca Islands, navigation, and the southern monsoon, Swift brings into focus several related historical aspects of the African slave trade.

For example, Gulliver's ship is bound for Surat, "the emporium of India,"[69] via the Cape of Good Hope. "The British established their first Indian trading post in Surat in 1612, essentially made possible by Bartolomeu Dias. In 1487, Dias set off on the famous journey from Lisbon to find India. His fleet was blown round the Cape of Good Hope. Only on his way back did they see that 'for so many ages unknown promontory,' the southern cone of Africa."[70] The spice trade was the major prize at the time, which is why Swift mentions Molucca, one of the spice islands.

In 1497 Vasco da Gama was sent out on his voyage to India and back via the Cape of Good Hope and the East African coast. Da Gama convinced the Portuguese authorities that "the major aim of the enterprise begun nearly three quarters of a century earlier by Henry the Navigator was within their grasp." ("Circumnavigation of Africa and entry into the Indian Ocean and its trading system was the aim of Henry's enterprise from the beginning.")[71] This bit of information on the subject of the Cape of Good Hope and navigation explains Swift's satiric purpose in having Gulliver winter at the Cape and focus outrageously on navigation. He thus exposes, in a historical context, Gulliver's aim as contrary not only to the aim of Henry the Navigator but also to the intended purpose of navigation defined in Bonaventure's First Light, the light of mechanical skill, both aims demonstrating the better uses to which navigation can be put, rather than slave trading. This is exposed in the onerous, obscure details Gulliver uses to impress the reader with his navigational skills, the description of which is a smokescreen to cover up his aim of slave trading, while audaciously (the Seventh Step of Pride) representing himself as a sort of Henry the Navigator. He broaches the subject by referring to his captain as "a man well experienced in the navigation of those seas," who "bid us all prepare against a storm, which accordingly happened the day following: for a southern wind, called the southern monsoon, began to set in":

> Finding it was like to overblow, we took in our spritsail, and stood by to hand the foresail; but making foul weather, we looked the guns were all fast, and handed the missen. The ship lay very broad off, so we thought it better spooning before the sea, than trying or hulling. We reefed the foresail and set him, we hauled aft the foresheet; the helm was hard a weather. The ship wore bravely [67–68].

Gulliver goes on and on and on in esoteric language which serves as an allusion to historical difficulties in those very same seas, and their ultimate African slave trade connection.

There was a problem which slowed the maritime expansion of the Portuguese, beginning with the monsoon winds Gulliver refers to:

> The Portuguese were aware that in the Indian Ocean there was both a set pattern of navigation based on the monsoon winds, and also a long-established and maritime trading system linking the Near East and East African coast with India, and India with the East Indies and the Far East. The Portuguese must have realized that they could not simply thrust forward into the Indian Ocean.[72]

At the same time, the Dutch sought to create "national overseas companies [the East Indian Company and the West India Company] strong enough to engage directly in commercial ventures on the Atlantic and Indian Oceans and to attack and destroy Spanish and Portuguese naval power on them."[73]

> The Portuguese scheme to exploit this hinged on the possession of a base in India from which it sought to dominate the whole monsoon-based Indian Ocean trading system. But with better ships and techniques of sailing and navigation than the Portuguese had possessed, the Dutch were able to ignore the monsoon winds altogether. Their ships sailed with the trade winds from the Cape of Good Hope until they had made enough easting to turn north, and to arrive directly in the East Indies through the Sundra Strait between the islands of Sumatra and Java.[74]

The historical significance of all of this, which explains Swift's allusions to it, is his leading up to the following:

> In the first decade of the seventeenth century, the Dutch East India Company destroyed Portuguese power in the Indian Ocean, and between 1637 and 1642,

the Dutch West India Company seized all the major Portuguese establishments on the western coast of Africa. It was these iniatives ... which led to the incorporation of tropical Africa into a dynamic world trading system dominated by western Europeans. Ultimately this system was to generate sufficient power and momentum to lead to European political control of the whole of the continent.[75]

Thus, Gulliver's ship's landing at the Cape of Good Hope "for fresh water" has historical significance confirmed by Swift's allusions to the history cited above and by the following:

> The first European settlement in southern Africa was established in 1652 by the Dutch East India Company at Table Bay, 30 miles north of the Cape. The settlement at Table Bay became Cape Town, whose purpose was to supply fresh food and water to Dutch trading ships rounding the Cape of Good Hope on their voyages to and from Dutch East Indies (now Indonesia).... Slaves were imported at first from West Africa, and later in larger numbers from Madagascar, Ceylon (now Sri Lanka), and the Dutch East Indies.[76]

After wintering at the Cape of Good Hope, Gulliver says they set sail again and have a good voyage until they pass the Straits of Madagascar; "but having got northward of that island ... the winds begin to blow with much greater violence for twenty days together, during which time they are driven a little to the east of the Molucca Islands." They go into the storm previously mentioned. Gulliver says:

> During this storm, which was followed by a strong wind west-southwest, we were carried by my computation about five hundred leagues to the east, so the oldest sailor on board could not tell in what part of the world we were [68].

They soon discover land that fits the description of Africa:

> On the 16th day of June, 1703, a boy on the topmast discovered land. On the 17th we came in full view of a great island or continent (for we knew not whether) on the south side whereof was a small neck of land jutting out into the sea, and a creek too shallow to hold a ship of above one hundred tons. We cast anchor within a league of this creek, and our captain sent a dozen of his men well armed in the longboat, with vessels for water if any could be found [68].

Although Gulliver's description fits the description of Africa, it also fits the description of South America, which was discovered knowingly as a new continent by traveller, discoverer, and navigator Amerigo Vespucci, whom Gulliver impersonates from time to time as part of his cover-up. Although Vespucci readily speaks of his trafficking in African slaves, Gulliver never does. Since the oldest sailor on board could not tell what part of the world they were in, and they'd already been to South Africa, this is most probably South America that they've discovered. This would also explain why

Gulliver mentions "New Holland" when he is rescued on his way back to England from so-called Brobdingnag. Vespucci would also be a target of Swift's attack on audacious "discoverers" of land for their crown, land already inhabited by indigenous people who don't wish to be enslaved or colonized.

Gulliver goes ashore with the men looking for water. The name he gives this newly discovered land "blows his cover." "Brobdingnag" is a coinage exposing the treatment of African slaves: "Brob" means to goad, prod, prick; "ding" means to deal heavy blows; to beat, thrash, flog, to dash or violently drive a thing away, down, in, out, over; "nag" means to badger, irritate, provoke, find fault with incessantly (OED). For example:

> After the slaves were branded with a red hot iron, they were marched toward the beach. Many of them, coming from the interior, had never seen or even heard of the sea.... When they saw the Atlantic, the great mountains of white-crested breakers, and beyond them the waiting ship, this was the critical moment when even the hippopotamus-hide whips ... and ... the cat-o'nine-tails sometimes proved useless. The slaves flung themselves on the beach, clutching handfuls of sand in a desperate effort to remain in Africa. Some tried to strangle themselves with their chains.... The slaves were beaten, pushed, dragged, and even carried to the big canoes.[77]

Captain Thomas Phillips says:

> The negroes are so wilful and loth to leave their own country, that they have often leap'd out of canoes, boat and ship, into the sea, and kept underwater till they were drowned, to avoid being taken up and saved.[78]

It is also the case that "Many more slaves died during the often long time of waiting for shipment than did so in rebellions or protests. Sometimes, the time spent waiting to be shipped was as long as five months."[79] A certain Captain William Blake "bought for James Rogers and Co. of Bristol (England) 939 slaves, of whom 203 died, 'of natural causes,' while still on the West African coast."[80]

There are numerous other documented examples of "the cycle of suffering and death."[81] Relatedly, there are numerous allusions to the African slave trade and the treatment of African slaves, in Brobdingnag, mainly having to do with Gulliver's treatment suggestive of the treatment of an African slave, to expose his lack of empathy and compassion for them. Perhaps the example which best speaks for itself occurs when Gulliver's master sells him to the Queen:

> The frequent labors I underwent every day made in a few weeks a very considerable change in my health: the more my master got by me, the more unsatiable he grew. I had quite lost my stomach, and was almost reduced to a skeleton. The farmer observed it, and concluding I soon must die, resolved to

make as good a hand of me as he could ... an usher came from court, commanding my master to bring me immediately thither for the diversion of the Queen.... She asked whether I would be content to live at court. I bowed down to the board of the table, and humbly answered that I was my master's slave, but if I were at my own disposal, I should be proud to devote my life to her Majesty's service. She then asked my master whether he were willing to sell me at a good price. He, who apprehended I could not live a month, was ready enough to part with me, and demanded a thousand pieces of gold, which were ordered him on the spot.... I made bold to tell her Majesty that I owed no other obligation to my late master, than his not dashing out the brains of a poor harmless creature found by chance in his field; which obligation was amply recompensed by ... the price he now sold me for. That the life I had since led was laborious enough to kill an animal of ten times my strength [81–82].

Gulliver's being treated like an animal, and being a slave, did not one thing to arouse empathy and compassion within him for the Africans he continued to enslave and animalize.

Another example of his situation and an African slave's situation being analogous but not vicarious, occurs when his travelling box, in which he is shut up, it picked up and dropped into the sea by an eagle. He says obtusely, even using the word "hold," where slaves are kept in a slave ship:

Perhaps many travellers have not been under greater difficulties and distress than I was at this juncture, expecting every moment to see my box dashed in pieces, or at least overset by the first violent blast, or a rising wave.... I saw the water ooze in at several crannies.... I was not able to lift up the roof of my closet, which otherwise I certainly should have done, and sat on top of it, where I might at least preserve my self from being shut up, as I may call it, in the hold [115].

He later begs to be delivered out of the "dungeon" he is in, like the slaves held in the dungeon of Fort St. George, awaiting shipment on African slave ships. Gulliver voyages to Fort St. George and stays three weeks, so his choice of words is ironic.

The allusions to the African slave trade that end the second part of *Gulliver's Travels*, are Tonquin, a Dutch East Indies trading station in the South Pacific; New Holland, the Dutch colony in Brazil, the acquisition of which got the Dutch involved in the Atlantic slave trade on a systematic basis[82]; and, the Cape of Good Hope, which, the slave ship that rescued Gulliver, doubled. Another allusion of the African slave trade, is Gulliver's statement: "Our voyage was very prosperous, but I shall not trouble the reader with a journal of it."

The third part of *Gulliver's Travels* begins with Gulliver's being made an offer he can't refuse, although he's only been home ten days. Captain William Robinson, commander of the Hope-well, a stout ship of three hundred tons, the usual size of an African slave ship, visits Gulliver to inform him of his intentions to make a voyage to the East Indies. Gulliver says:

> ... he ... plainly invited me ... to be surgeon of the ship; that I should have another surgeon under me besides our two mates; that my salary should be double to the usual pay; and having experienced my knowledge in sea-affairs to be at least equal to his, he would enter into any engagement to follow my advise, as much as if I had share in the command [123].

Captain Robinson is a disingenuous in the manner in which he makes his offer, as Gulliver is in accepting it, saying:

> I could not reject his proposal; the thirst I had of seeing the world, notwithstanding my past misfortunes, continuing as violent as ever [123].

It's his avaricious thirst for money that continues as violent as ever. He has already seen the East Indies, and he goes only to other African slave trade ports of call; although, there are so many of those ports all over the world, it is tantamount to seeing the world by just going to them. The alarm is, he'd already been traveling to these ports for four years, since his last return home, and now he's off again to West Africa after being home for only two months. That's a violent lust for money by the lowest means possible, and Swift is exposing it as it is.

Gulliver sets out in August 1706, arrives at Fort St. George in April 1707, and stays there three weeks. Now, anyone would be hard put to come up with a reason for going to Fort St. George in 1707 other than African slave trade business. Moreover, he sets out on a ship named after a historically documented African slave ship, the *Hope-well*, with a captain named after an authentic African slave ship captain.

> One of the most ambitious undertakings of the Portuguese was the erection of Fort St. George at Elmina in West Africa, begun with great ceremony in 1481. It was a center of Negro trade till the end of the eighteenth century. It was the first of the forts built as depots in which slaves could be held for shipment.[83]

Fort St. George was captured by the Dutch in 1637. They retained it, with some interruptions, for more than two centuries.[84] The Dutch did not possess adequate bases in Africa until the capture of Elmina. In 1612 the Dutch had acquired a small trading station at Mori on the Gold Coast, modern-day Ghana, but it was not until they captured the chief Portuguese stronghold at Elmina, Fort St. George, in 1637 that they could engage in the slave trade in earnest.[85] So it is possible to see a telling transition from Gulliver's mention of "New Holland" in Brazil at the end of Part II, to his voyage to Elmina at the beginning of Part III, it that, "With the establishment of the Dutch in New Holland, Brazil and their capture of Elimina, a boom in their exportation of slaves from Africa occurred."[86]

1. The African Slave Trade 49

From Fort St. George at Elmina on the Gold Coast in West Africa we have "A Slave-Ship Consignment" to further authenticate what went on there, and the reason Swift, in protest of African slave trade, would have Gulliver travel there in a ship the usual size of an African slave ship, with the name of a historically documented African slave ship, at a time when there was no other reason except African slave trade business to go there in such a ship:

CONSIGNMENT

I, the undersigned, Jan Pietersz. Gewelt, Captain under God on the Noble ship *Sonnesteyn*, presently prepared to sail from here [Elmina] to St. Eustatius in America, acknowledge to have received into the ship just mentioned, from the hands of the Honorable Lord Director-General Pieter Valkenier, the total of 627 head of slaves, consisting of 410 men, 112 women, 39 boys at two-thirds, 32 boys at one-half, 7 boys at one-third, 19 girls at two-thirds, and 8 girls at one-half, altogether consisting of 583 "piezas de India," all healthy and in good condition.

All the slaves mentioned are to cross the Atlantic at the risk of the Honorable General Chartered Dutch West India Company, which I promise and accept to deliver — if God almighty grants me a safe voyage — at St. Eustatius, into the hands of the Lord Commander, Joannes Lindezaay, in order to be sold by him and for me, and of which I shall give an accounting to the Lord Directors on my return to the fatherland.

To the fulfillment of this charge, I pledge my whole being and all my goods, actions, credits, and integrity, nothing excluded, especially my already earned and still to be earned salary and premiums, and according to regulations I shall not draw on this.

As evidence of the truth of this, four identical affidavits are written, one is signed and the others are of no value. Enacted at the Chief Castle St. George d'Elmina, this 6th of March, 1726.
(Signature)

(The above is an affidavit of transfer of responsibility for a cargo of slaves, from West India Company authorities in Africa to the captain of a WIC slave ship. Captains signed such documents just prior to leaving Africa and starting the middle passage. This particular consignment paper is located in WIC, vol. 488, p. 799. The document has been translated almost verbatim in order to preserve the original style. For the sake of clarity and brevity, the numerical figures of the original long hand have been changed into numerals in this English translation.)[87]

Gulliver departs Fort St. George, "a true castle" with "room in its dungeons for a thousand slaves,"[88] and goes to Tonquin (East Indies) "where Captain Robinson resolved to continue some time...." He buys a sloop, appoints Gulliver master of the sloop, and gives him "power to traffic" (buy and sell slaves) while he transacts his affairs at Tonquin (124). After he is out ten days, Gulliver's sloop is chased by two pirates, who soon overtake him; "for," says Gulliver, "my sloop was so deep laden, that she sailed very slow, neither were we in a condition to defend ourselves" (124). This is, in essence, what history says of Captain Robinson, whose African slave ship, the *Avarilla*, was seized by the French in the same year, 1694, that the *Hopewell*, Gulliver's Captain Robinson's ship, was seized:

> In all probability, had he had his complement of men, he might have escaped, the two privateers not exceeding him together in number or guns, but were encouraged to assault him by his insufficiency to defend himself.[89]

As history tells us, "Often it is difficult to say whether some of the vessels that took part in the trade were slavers, pirates, or privateers," and that "...capturing merchantmen on the high seas was a lucrative profession."[90] Swift's depiction of Gulliver's experience emphasizes that fact and its significance in the history of the African slave trade he is alluding to in protest of every aspect:

> At times pirate groups become so powerful that they established land bases, such as at Dunkirque and on the Algerian coast. Slave ships often carried a so-called Turkish pass, which had been purchased from pirates operating from Algeria, and made the Atlantic waters to the west of Algeria dangerous for slave ships leaving and returning to Europe. In 1687 a large Dutch West India Company slave ship, on its way to Africa, was attacked and sunk near the Canary Islands by an Algerian pirate, apparently because it did not carry such a pass.
> Occasionally, the Dutch WIC also had to contend with pirates on the African coast. In 1685–6 two powerful pirate ships appeared on the Slave Coast and captured two WIC slavers at Ouidah, while a third company ship barely escaped. And again, in 1719 pirates made the West African coast unsafe and captured or grounded several merchant ships of various nationalities ... commerce stagnated along the entire Guinea coast, because merchant vessels did not dare leave the protection of the European forts.... Again, in 1721–2 a team of four large pirate ships made the Guinea coast unsafe.[91]

"Captain William Verney, having been slaving on the coast of Guinea and thence set sail for Virginia, turned pirate, the negroes being thrown overboard."[92] One of the pirates who commandeers Gulliver's sloop is a Dutchman whom Gulliver appeals: "I begged him in consideration of our being Christians and Protestants of neighboring countries, in strict alliance, that he would move the captains to take pity on us" (124). The obvious irony in a slave trader calling himself a "Christian" is not to be overlooked. The strict alliance Swift has Gulliver refer to had African slave trade historical significance in 1707:

> In 1669 tensions between the Dutch West India Company and the English Royal African Company rose to the brink of war, even though the two nations

they represented were allies during most of the war period of 1674–1713.... An agreement between the two companies was reached in 1701, and two years later they negotiated a defensive pact, which was aimed at keeping the French from gaining a foothold on the Gold Coast.[93]

Ultimately, Gulliver is set adrift in a small canoe, with paddles, a sail, and four days' provisions.

Part III of *Gulliver's Travels* ends with an apparent focus on Swift's attitude toward the Dutch impact on the African slave trade. It's to be expected in a protest of the African slave trade that "the greatest trading nation in the world, indisputably,"[94] as the Dutch were at the time, would be the prime target. Noted scholars think otherwise without even mentioning the African slave trade. Ehrenpreis says, for example, that "Swift had particular reasons for loathing the Dutch. In commerce they remained a rival ... to British trade around the globe, the bitterest rival."[95] Another scholar sees the particular reason in Gulliver's journey to the Dutch commercial outpost in Nagasaki, where soon after his arrival he falls into the company of some Dutch sailors belonging to the *Amboyna* of Amsterdam. The historical significance of "Amboyna" is its being one of the spice islands in the East Indies, and its calling to mind the Dutch brutality toward the English over control of Amboyna, in that "ten Englishmen were tortured and executed."[96]

Victoria Glendinning mentions that "Swift disliked the Dutch."[97] And, although she states that "The Dutch were a major sea power and trading group, importing wine, tea and coffee, controlling the East European grain trade, and Baltic shipping,"[98] and that "The Dutch ... were England's main commercial rivals,"[99] she doesn't mention the African slave trade. But if rivalry were the "particular reason," the implication would be that Swift approved of the African slave trade but just wanted England to control it, which would be a blatant contradiction, not only because of all of the evidence to the contrary, but also because I don't think he would be capable of it.

Other allusions to the African slave trade that end Part III are the Cape of Good Hope, where, according to African slave ship tradition, they "stayed only to take in fresh water":

> The Dutch East India Company supplied Cape Colony at the southern tip of Africa with slaves from Eastern Africa. Approximately 4000 slaves were shipped to the Cape of Good Hope during the period 1652 to 1795.[100]

Gulliver also mentions losing one of his seamen, "who fell from the foremast into the sea, not far from the coast of Guinea" (176), which tells us where Gulliver's ship has been and why. "Amsterdam," which he mentions twice, has African slave trade historical significance as well: "...during the West India Company monopoly, Amsterdam played the leading role in the slave trade."[101]

Part IV of *Gulliver's Travels* opens with Gulliver's having reached the pinnacle of his aspirations from the beginning: to be "captain" of an African slave ship. He accepts "an advantageous offer to be captain of the *Adventure*, a stout merchantman of 350 tons." What he adds is no coincidence: "for I understood navigation well," having "laid out small sums of money in learning navigation, and other parts of the mathematics, useful to those who [intend to become an African slave ship captain], as I always believed it would be some time or other my fortune [plan] to [be]," (15) all of which introduced us to Gulliver in the very beginning.

Gulliver sets sail from Portsmouth, a naval port important to the African slave trade because of the role the British navy played in ending the pirate attacks on the African coast. He meets up with Captain Pocock of Bristol (a center of the African slave trade), at Tenerife (one of the Canary Islands), who was going to the bay of Campechy, to cut logwood" (179). Campechy is an old town in Mexico, founded in 1540, and a leading port under Spanish rule.[102]

According to a February 1, 2006, *New York Times* "Science Times" article by John Noble Wilford, archaeologists believe they have discovered the some of the earliest known remains of African slaves in the New World. The skeletal remains were found in Campeche, in a cemetery in use since 1550. Colonial Campeche "was an important Spanish gateway to the Americas and would have had substantial traffic in slaves." Moreover, "the fact that the burials were found in the ruins of a colonial church could mean that these slaves had some kind of status or were converted to Christianity." They "appeared to have come from the area around Elmina, Ghana, a major West African port in the slave trade." Gulliver travels to Fort St. George in Elmina. This was also the region of origin of some of the slaves found in the 17th and 18th century African Burial Ground, uncovered in 1991 in Lower Manhattan." Included in Wilford's article is a map showing the "approximate route of transport" from Elmina to Campeche.

The Canary Islands were important to the African slave trade from the beginning:

> The difficult relations between Spain and Portugal ended in a peace treaty in 1480, the conditions of which "permanently affected the history of Africa and the slave trade." One of the conditions was that "Portugal would leave the Canary Islands...." Sometimes, thenceforward, Portuguese captains would stop at the Canary Islands on the way home despite their Spanish administration; and a few black slaves previously taken to those islands entered the Portuguese

dominions in that way.... One consequence of importing these slaves was to inspire the Canary Islands to grow sugar ... especially in Tenerife....[103]

The first sugar mill was set up in 1484, the Canary Islands began to produce as much sugar as Madeira in the early sixteenth century, and African slaves were soon used there on a large scale.[104]

From Tenerife Gulliver goes to Barbados, and the Leeward Islands, "where," he says, "I touched by the direction of the merchants who employed me" (179). That's certainly an unequivocal admission of involvement in the African slave trade. Why else would Swift have "merchants" employ an experienced African slave ship surgeon who "understood navigation" well enough to be captain of a 350 ton merchantman given the most chosen name of authentic African slave ships, the *Adventure*, to sail in 1710 to the West Indies, the second leg of the triangular trade, if not for African slave trade business? Especially considering what's been previously cited concerning Barbados and the Leeward Islands. Other clues Gulliver is conducting African slave trade business is his being forced to get recruits out of Barbados and the Leeward Islands because he "had several men [who] died in his ship of calentures," which is an African fever, which proves he'd already been to Africa via the triangular trade, and also the mutiny on his ship, initiated by his new recruits, who debauch his other men:

> There are fairly detailed accounts of fifty-five mutinies on slavers from 1699 to 1845, not to mention passing references to more than a hundred others. The list of ships "cut off" by the natives ... is almost as long.[105]

The most conspicuous clue is Gulliver's mention of the South Sea, which brings his travels full circle, his first legal African slave trade voyage having been to the South Sea. Add to this his "orders to trade" with the Indians in the South Sea." Most importantly, however, is that this is an attack on the English South Sea Company, having to do with "the plans of the Tory party to create a great South Sea Company which was to take over a part of the National Debt, and add to the revenues by importing slaves and merchandise into South America."[106] None of the previously mentioned Swift scholars connect the South Sea Company with the African slave trade. Glendinning mentions that "Swift had invested one thousand pounds in the company...."[107] It seems Swift "held stock in the company ten years before starting *Gulliver's Travels*, which could account for the self-satire and self-irony that noted Swift scholar Irvin Ehrenpreis cited in the *Travels*.[108] It is certainly reasonable to conclude, given the tone of fierce indignation in the *Travels*, that Swift had a change of heart, and made himself, as well as England, the target of his own scathing satire.[109] Ehrenpreis does not make a connection between Swift's self-irony and self-satire and the African slave trade, but I do. The impact of the South Sea Company is not to be minimized. It gained England the "Asiento," but it caused "England's first great stock market panic."[110]

> Defoe wrote a powerful pamphlet in favor of setting up the Company: "There has not been in our memory an undertaking of such consequence," he said, though he did not mention the main purpose of the enterprise once in his forty pages.
> A torchlight procession through London greeted the news of the grant. Happy days had, it seemed, come again! The moment had been foreshadowed in Queen Anne's speech to Parliament of June 6, 1712: "I have insisted and obtained that the 'asiento' or contract for furnishing the Spanish West Indies with negroes shall be made with us for thirty years."[111]

Imagine, a torchlight procession to celebrate the destruction of the lives of millions of innocent black human beings, past, present, and, at least thirty years into the future! Enthusiasm was so high it caused a panic!

> One hundred pounds shares were run up to over then times that sum. The South Sea Company at times rivaled in influence even the Bank of England (incorporated in 1698); but the highly inflated value of its stock caused, in 1720, England's first great stock-market panic in which thousands were ruined [ReadEncy].[112]
> Banks, directors, great insurance companies, statesmen, noblemen saw their imagined fortunes collapse. Some of the most powerful men in the country were ruined; at their head, the duke of Portland, son of William III's favorite, who was afterwards forced to seek a colonial governorship. His move to Jamaica, the main South Sea slave entrepot, seemed a suitable "denoument" to this affair. Britain's other main slaving center, Barbados, equally appropriately, went to another lord who had lost a fortune: Lord Bellhaven who lost his life, too, when the South Sea ship the "Royal Anne," taking him to his new office, sank off the Scilly Islands. Sir Isaac Newton lost $20,000 and, it is said, could not bear to hear the words "South Sea" for the rest of his distinguished life. The playwright John Gay and the fashionable portraitist Kneller were also hard his....

"Still, the South Sea Company survived and, between 1715 and 1731, sold altogether about 64,000 slaves.... Despite the disappointment caused by the South Sea Company, the British slave trade grew immeasurably in the early eighteenth century."[113]

We left Gulliver chained to his bed following the mutiny on his African slave ship. The "design" of the mutineers "was to turn pirates, and plunder the Spaniards ... then go to Madagascar" (180). The mention of "Madagascar" signifies two allusions to the history of the African slave trade:

> The English New Yorkers ... established, in the first year after the capture of Manhattan, a fruitful relation with the pirates who infested the East India route and had their headquarters at Madagascar. How many slaves were thereby brought by the formidable journey from there may never be known.[114]

The South Sea Company, inadequately supplied by the Royal African Company, dispatched slaves to the Americas from Madagascar, in considerable numbers.[115]

Gulliver is forced into a longboat, and rowed to where he is set down on a strand. Even in these dire straits his concern is the false covering of white supremacy, that he may "appear" superior, not "be" superior. He says:

> They forced me into the long-boat, letting me put on my best suit of clothes, which were as good as new, and a small bundle of linen [180].

Being an African slave ship captain, he's the real savage. Yet he says, after he is upon firm ground, and a little refreshed:

> I went up into the country, resolving to deliver myself to the first savages I should meet, and purchase my life from them by some bracelets, glass rings, and other toys, which sailors usually provide themselves with in those voyages, whereof I had some about me [180].

The country he goes up into is Houyhnhnmland. In this fourth part, although beginning and ending with allusions to the African slave trade, like the other three parts, the middle is taken up by allusions to African slavery, white supremacy, and racism, personified by the symbols of the foundations of the African slave trade, white supremacy and racism. Gulliver says, as if coming upon African slaves for the first time (Swift's clue that they are human is in "many tracks of human feet," exposing Gulliver's racist description):

> I fell into a beaten road, where I saw many tracks of human feet, and some of cows, but most of horses [181].

He goes on to animalize black African human beings:

> At last I beheld several animals in a field, and one or two of the same kind sitting in trees. Their shape was very singular and deformed, which a little discomposed me, so that I lay down behind a thicket to observe them better. Some of them coming forward near the place where I lay, gave me an opportunity of distinctly marking their form. Their heads and breasts were covered with a thick hair, some frizzled and others lank; they had beards like goats, and a long ridge of hair down their backs, and the foreparts of their legs and feet, but the rest of their bodies were bare, so that I might see their skins, which were of a *brown buff color*.... They would often spring, and bound, and leap with prodigious agility.... Upon the whole, I never beheld in all my travels so disagreeable an animal, or one against which I naturally conceived so strong antipathy. So that thinking I had seen enough, full of contempt and aversion, I got up and pursued the beaten road, hoping it might direct me to the cabin of some Indian [181].

The above description, Gulliver's animalization of black people, is symbolic of the seventeenth-century justification for the African slave trade: that "the Negro was not a human being."[116]

Gulliver's supremacist preference of "some Indian" rather than the Negroes he describes above is also an allusion to the African slave trade:

> That the Negroes unquestionably made better slaves than the Indians — who either "died like fish in a bucket," as one indignant Spanish planter complained, or else were intractable — is a fact often quoted to prove that the Negroes are a naturally servile race. The Indians, so the argument runs, were too "noble" to bend their necks to the white man's yoke.[117]

Gulliver reflects the racism of the Houyhnhnms, who are symbolic of the philosophies of Plato and Aristotle, which are the foundations Swift is digging up. Animalized black people are called "yahoos" by the Houyhnhnms, who hold themselves "superior" to "human beings," which yahoos means. But they distinguish between black yahoos and white yahoos, themselves representing the origins of such distinctions. Gulliver, then, "holds forth in the style of the masters he has learned from"[118] when he says that the "natural awe" he bears them "was mingled with a respectful love and gratitude, that they would condescend to distinguish me from the rest of my species" (224). By the latter, he means black human beings, but at least he's admitting that black human beings are of the same species as white human beings.

As further proof that the creatures that racist Gulliver describes as "animals with brown buff colored skin" are black human beings (African slaves), Swift incorporates traditional racist stereotypes, as used against Othello, for example, to expose the egregiousness of white supremacy. Perhaps the oldest traditional racist stereotype for black people as a race is "cursed," manufactured from the Biblical curse of Ham. Gulliver says, for example: "I had hitherto concealed the secret of my dress, in order to distinguish myself as much as possible from that cursed race of yahoos" (191).

The Houyhnhnms call their African slaves "yahoos," meant as a demeaning term for human being, to which species they hold themselves "superior," echoing Socrates in Plato's *Republic*, who held up horses for the imitation of human kind. Other foundations of racism, also reflecting the *Republic*, Swift parodies in the following:

> ... among the Houyhnhnms, the white, the sorrel, and the iron-grey were not so exactly shaped as the bay, the dapple-grey, and the black; nor born with equal talents of the mind, or a capacity to improve them; and therefore continued always in the condition of servants, without ever aspiring to match out of their own race, which in that country would be reckoned montrous and unnatural [207].

Also for the imitation of mankind, which white mankind imitates:

> In their marriages they are exactly careful to choose such colours as will not make any disagreeable mixture in the breed [217].

By demonstrating in the above two examples the absurdity of Plato's utopian ideal of mankind imitating horses, Swift condemns white people for using such an absurdity to justify racism, white supremacy, and the African slave trade. He thus justifies digging up the foundations of western civilization, chief of which are Plato and Aristotle. Swift demonstrates how the above examples are used as a model for the treatment of black people, as symbolized by the treatment of the black yahoos. The first example is demonstrated in the racist stereotype that the black yahoos "are the most unteachable of all brutes ... their capacities never reaching higher than to draw or carry burthens" (214). The second example is demonstrated in the distinguishing of "color." In his first description Gulliver says the skin of the black yahoos is of a "brown buff color" (181). Gulliver is the first "white" yahoo the Houyhnhnms have ever seen, and, for as long as he can get away with it, he denies that the black yahoos are of the same species as white yahoos like himself, although the Houyhnhnms have their doubts. For a comparison, they take Gulliver to the kennel of the black yahoos, who are "all tied by the neck with strong withes, fastened to a beam" (186), suggestive of lynching. Gulliver says:

> The beast and I were brought close together, and our countenances diligently compared, both by master and servant, who thereupon repeated several times the word "yahoo." My horror and astonishment are not to be described, when I observed, in this abominable animal, a perfect human figure; the face of it was flat and broad, the nose depressed, the lips large, and the mouth wide.... The forefeet of the yahoo differed from my hands in nothing else but the ... *the browness of the palms*.... There was the same resemblance between our feet ... except as to hairiness and *colour*... [186].

When Gulliver's master sees Gulliver naked, he says that Gulliver is "an exact yahoo in every part, only of a *whiter colour*" (219), in other words, white Gulliver is of the same species as the black human beings that he and the Houyhnhnms animalize. At another time Gulliver's master says "it (is) plain Gulliver must be a perfect yahoo; but that (he) differed very much from the rest of (his) species, in the *whiteness* and smoothness of (his) skin..." (192). And, Gulliver tells us, his master

> desired to know whether those among whom I lived resembled me or the yahoos of his country. I assured him, that I was as well shaped as most of my age: but the younger and the females were much more soft and tender, and the skins of the latter generally as white as milk [195].

Surely the most alarming example of racism as a degenerate way of life that violates the laws of nature is the Houyhnhnm debate, the only debate they ever have, "whether to exterminate the black people from the face of the earth" (218). The idea or ideal for such a debate has its origins in Plato's utopian *Republic*, where it is proposed that leaders lie to their subjects while orchestrating the mysterious disappearance of people considered undesirable. Swift's genius for prophecy is given twentieth-century relevance in the white South African apartheid plan to exterminate black people from the face of the earth by documented scientific means.[119] Gulliver recommends castration:

> That this invention might be practiced upon the younger yahoos [blacks] here, which, besides rendering them tractable and fitter for use, would in an age put an end to the whole species without destroying life [220].

Castration is another racist tradition stereotypically perpetrated upon black men, even when they are in the process of being lynched. Could anyone really believe that Swift would depict and allude to all of the above racist justifications for the African slave trade, the extermination of black people, and white supremacy, if he were not protesting such racism and its foundations? And what other purpose could the Houyhnhnm's yahoos serve, but as racism's black victims?

The criticism in a Norton Critical Edition of Swift's writings reveals just how misunderstood the yahoos have been. One critic makes the claim that "The most powerful single symbol in all Swift is the Yahoos. They do not represent Swift's view of man, but rather of the bestial element in man.... The seeds of human society and of human depravity, as they exist in Europe, are clearly discerned in the society and conduct of the Yahoos ... and the sight drives him mad."[120] This critic does, however, say, speaking of the Houyhnhnms: "Their society is an aristocracy, resting upon the slave labor of the Yahoos and the work of an especially-bred servant class."[121] Another critic states: "Swift has taken everything that was connected with the passionate or erotic nature and made a kind of trash heap from it, which he calls the Yahoos."[122] Still another critic says: "The Yahoos represent a critique of the anal function, the raw core of human bestiality.... Swift's vision of the Yahoos as excrementally filthy beyond all other animals is comprehensively metaphysical."[123] Yet another critic says: "Gulliver commits the error ... of equating human beings with the Yahoos."[124]

Since the early eighties I've never had any doubts about the Houyhnhnms' yahoos being black people, African slaves, and that Gulliver's description of them, suggestive of monkeys, was symbolically the white supremacist perception of black people. Surprisingly, in the nineties two scholars came close to agreeing with my exegesis of the yahoos. When Deborah Wyrick says, for example, that the Houyhnhnms "treat Gulliver as an exotic curiosity, albeit one who might lead his fellow Yahoos into a slave revolt,"[125] we have to assume the Yahoos are the slaves. Laura Brown provides compelling white supremacist models in a cultural overview of the period. She says, for example: "Gulliver begins at a seemingly unbridgeable distance from the yahoos, which are represented as some species of monkey, perhaps, having little in common with the human."[126] Of course, Gulliver doesn't "begin" where Brown is saying. He's been involved in the African slave trade as a profession for almost twenty-five years when he first sees the Houyhnhnms' African slaves, the likes of whom he is certainly not seeing for the first time. And it's not that the Houyhnhnms' yahoos, the black Gulliver describes, "are represented as some species of monkey,"[127] it's that they are represented as the racist distortions of a white supremacist. The reader sees them through the eyes of Gulliver, not Swift, who is attacking white supremacy, and Gulliver as eighteenth-century white-everyman.

Brown goes on to document "the eighteenth-century accounts of racial difference focusing on the Negro,"[128] beginning with the accounts of "travellers, naturalists, and colonialists of the nature and society of the Negro in what they describe as his native habitat in Africa or under slavery in the colonies of the New World."[129] She says:

> Unlike *Gulliver's Travels*, of course, this fiction was accepted as objective testimony in the travel literature and ultimately encoded as science in the most widely read volumes of travel and natural history through the middle of the next century. At stake was the status of the Negro on the chain of being, his proximity to man or ape. And those two standards of deviation determined the definition of the Negro race.[130]

Swift would consider such writers, such literature, such a chain, such defining, as demonstrative of presumptuous human deviants arrogantly perverting nature. He could very well be attacking such deviants and deviations, while at the same time, with the use of the irony of self-betrayal, portraying Gulliver as protesting too much such writers, while being one himself:

> I could heartily wish a law were enacted, that every traveller before he were permitted to publish his voyages, should be obliged to make oath before the Lord High Chancellor that all he intended to print was absolutely true to the best of his knowledge; for then the world would no longer be deceived as it usually is, while some writers, to make their works pass the better upon the public, impose the grossest falsities on the unwary reader. I have perused several books of travels with great delight in my younger days; but having gone over most parts of the globe, and been able to contradict many fabulous accounts from my own observation, it hath given me great disgust against this part of reading, and some indignation to see the credulity of mankind so impudently abused [235].

Gulliver's Travels may not have been accepted as "objective testimony,"[131] although Gulliver presents it as such, but Swift is certainly exposing such writings so called by Laura Brown, as anything but "objective testimony," but, rather, deeply subjective, in fact, racist.

Brown's first example of "objective testimony" reminds us of Gulliver's description of the Houyhnhnms' yahoos as if seeing black people for the first time: "Janet Shaw, in her journal of a voyage to the West Indies, and North Carolina (1774) spontaneously reproduces, in her account of her first sight of Negro children upon her arrival in Antiqua, an association quite typical of the period":

> Just as we got into the lane, a number of pigs ran out at a door, and after them a parcel of monkeys. This not a little surprised me, but I found what I took for monkeys were negro children, naked as they were born [*Journal of a Lady of Quality*].[132]

(Gulliver speaks often of "the quality," being most impressed.)

Brown goes on to say:

> If we juxtapose the details of two prominent contemporary accounts which served as compendia of seventeenth and eighteenth century observations of the inhabitants of Africa, we can set the context for Janet Shaw's predictable mistakes. George Louis Leclerc Buffon's massive and influential *Natural History* and Edward Long's *History of Jamaica*, both summarize accounts of the Negro from earlier writings ... dating from the early seventeenth century on.[133]

A case could well be made for Gulliver's descriptive reaction to the black yahoos being a compendium of Buffon and Long's descriptions of black people, which is why Gulliver qualifies as racist-white-everyman, a symbol of centuries past, present, and future. And, although it would be impossible to find the first clue in Buffon, we are told that "Buffon, unlike Long, ultimately dismisses the argument that apes and Negroes are of the same species."[134]

Although Part IV, the most important Part of *Gulliver's Travels*, is a cause-and-effect culmination resisting isolation, Laura Brown makes the following statement:

> In short, Book IV of *Gulliver's Travels* is pervasively connected with — indeed essentially compiled from — contemporary evidence of racial difference derived from accounts of the race that was in this period most immediately and visibly the object and human implement of mercantile capitalist expansion [the African slave trade]. This is not to say that the Yahoos are meant to stand for African blacks in any straightforward allegorical fashion.... What we have observed in Book IV of the *Travels* is not allegory, but a pervasive contextualization in which the shifting status of the male observer, the dynamic of aversion and implication, difference, and incorporation, that we have already observed in Swift's satire is given a specific historical referent: English imperialism and the trade in slaves.[135]

1. The African Slave Trade 61

Swift would be outraged by the phrase, "contemporary evidence of racial difference," in that racist distortions cannot, in truth, be considered "evidence," which is the thrust of his attack on white supremacy in this regard, and his strategic use of Bernard. Brown is very much mistaken in implying that the yahoos are not meant to stand for African blacks. Even given her "contextualization" and "specific historical referent," what other purpose could the Houyhnhnms' yahoos serve, but that of symbols of enslaved African blacks, the prime victims of "English imperialism and the trade in slaves"?

Swift would be fiercely outraged at what he would consider a white supremacist perception mirroring Gulliver's perceptions, in Brown's statement that "the fourth voyage brings Gulliver into contact with an absolutely alien and hideous other, in the face of which all the brutality of colonialism, repression — genocide included — must seem justified."[136] Such a statement is a tribute to Swift's prophetic genius, and more than justifies his devoting his masterpiece to exposing such a horrific, inhuman consideration justifying white supremacy, for which there is no justification, as he broadcasts loud and clear. He would have us see innocent, vulnerable black humans beings brought into contact with "an absolutely alien and hideous other," an execrable, brutal, oppressive, repressive, genocidal white monster. Swift, as Edward Albee says of the dramatist, "holds up a mirror [*Gulliver's Travels*]" to white people, "and says, 'Hey, this is you. If you don't like what you see — change it.'"[137]

My research forces me to challenge one of Brown's closing statements:

> Contemporary readers — steeped in the racist images associated with English colonialism in that period — would have been much more ready than modern ones to register the crucial evocations of racial difference in Book IV, and much quicker than we are to pick up that text's pervasive playing with ideas of racial superiority and its perverse leveling of whites and nonwhites to one common depravity. Indeed, the vitality and cultural power of *Gulliver's Travels* — and perhaps even its longevity in the canon of English literature — may be explained in part by the fact that it represented a challenge to an ideology that itself had a vital and powerful current function.[138]

If either eighteenth century or modern readers "registered the crucial evocations of racial difference in Book IV," there's certainly no indication of it in the abundant criticism of *Gulliver's Travels*, even by noted Swift scholars, who never even mention "racist images," as I have tried to point out. Swift does not "play" with ideas of racial superiority, far from it. He fiercely condemns such ideas as heretical, unnatural, absurd and perverse. It is to have missed the irony and satire to say there is a "perverse leveling of whites and non-whites to one common depravity." First of all, there is no such leveling. Part IV clearly projects black people as superior to white people, in the climactic statement that white people "make no other use of reason than to multiply and improve those vices whereof their brethren in this country [black people] had only the share that nature allotted them." White supremacy, the African slave trade and its attendant atrocities, are examples of multiplying and improving the vices of human nature which Swift projects as degenerate ways of life that violate the laws of nature. The perversion and depravity Brown speaks of is clearly and solely associated with white people as characteristic, and *not* as she claims.

Moreover, Swift would be aghast to have it thought, in what reads like parallel praise by Brown of two contrary ideologies, that the "vitality, cultural power, and longevity" of *Gulliver's Travels*[139] was on a competitive track as an equal with "the vital and powerful ... function"[140] of white supremacy and the African slave trade. I am aghast that anyone in the twenty-first century, or in any century, would consider white supremacy and the African slave trade "vital."

The prestigious status of *Gulliver's Travels* in world literature cannot be explained, even in part, by Brown's claim that *Gulliver's Travels* represents a challenge to white supremacy and the African slave trade, because for almost three centuries no one else has understood it in that light, by all indications.

Finally, regarding the "politics of political criticism," Laura Brown's closing statement proves she has missed Swift's irony and has profoundly misunderstood his satire: "Let's say that Swift's travesty of true consciousness is the true radical criticism."[141] It would be more accurate to say that *Gulliver's Travels* is a travesty of political consciousness that exposes politics as "nothing but corruptions,"[142] targeting white supremacy, the African slave trade and attendant atrocities from racism to genocide as indisputable proof. *Gulliver's Travels* as radical criticism urges the replacement of political consciousness with religious consciousness, for which white supremacy, the animalization of black people, and other unnatural political abominations against black people prove an urgent necessity, as the novel demonstrates. Religious consciousness is rooted in "Humility" and the "Three Steps of Truth."

It's not what Samuel Monk *says* drives Gulliver mad that drives Gulliver mad. It's *not* seeing white people as yahoos, it's seeing white people as white people that drives Gulliver mad. It's like what Toni Morrison says in her Pulitzer Prize winning *Beloved*:

> It wasn't the jungle blacks brought with them to this place from the other (livable) place. It was the jungle whitefolks planted in them. And it grew. It spread.[143]

It's the realization Gulliver shares with Morrison's main character that drives Gulliver mad: "That anybody white could take your whole self for anything that came to mind. Not just work, kill, or maim you, but dirty you. Dirty you so bad you couldn't like yourself anymore. Dirty you so bad you forgot who you were and couldn't think it up."[144]

References to the African slave trade and the planting of colonies necessary to the trade are significant focuses in Gulliver's leave-taking of the reader for the last time. Remaining quite in character, he makes these references through lies and fraud, revealing what he intends to conceal, through Swift's use of the irony of self-betrayal, which allows Gulliver to unwittingly expose his guilt. He seeks to cover up his being an African slave trader by claiming to travel to "remote countries which are seldom visited by Englishmen or other Europeans," when the real countries he travels to, which Swift makes known, are African slave trade ports of call which thousands of Englishmen and other Europeans relentlessly travel to for some three centuries as part of the "gigantic international operation"[145] known as the African slave trade, and not with any "aim of making men wiser and better," as Gulliver claims was his chief aim. He claims to "relate only plain facts that happened in distant countries, where we have not the least interest with respect to trade or negotiations," but he goes only where England has enormous interests with respect to trade and negotiations via the African slave trade. By a hypocritical confession (The Ninth Step of Pride) he exposes British colonialism. He says:

> I confess, it was whispered to me that I was bound in duty, as a subject of England, to have given in a memorial to a secretary of state, at my first coming over; because, whatever lands are discovered by a subject belong to the crown [236].

Swift's condemnation of the practice is felt through his depiction of Gulliver's hypocrisy. Swift's condemnation of the African slave trade is felt through Gulliver's guilt in the following nutshell rendition suggestive of England's entry into the African slave trade. Swift sees symbolic Gulliver, and Gulliver at this point sees himself, as a member of the "execrable crew of butchers," while feigning scruples:

> But I had another reason which made me less forward to enlarge his Majesty's dominions by my discoveries. To say the truth, I had a few scruples with relation to the distributive justice of princes upon those occasions. For instance, a crew of pirates are driven by a storm they know not whither, at length a boy discovers land from the topmast, they go on shore to rob and plunder, they see an harmless people, are entertained with kindness, they give the country a new name, they take formal possession of it for the king, they set up a rotten plank or a stone for a memorial, they murder two or three dozen of the

> natives, bring away a couple more by force for a sample, return home, and get their pardon. Here commences a new dominion acquired with a title by "divine right." Ships are sent with the first opportunity, the natives driven out or destroyed, their princes tortured to discover their gold, a free license given to all acts of inhumanity and lust, the earth reeking with the blood of its inhabitants: and this execrable crew of butchers employed in so pious and expedition, is a modern colony sent to convert and civilize an idolatrous and barbarous people [237].

The irony is not to be missed in an execrable crew of butchers converting and civilizing an idolatrous and barbarous people. Swift is here projecting the utter absurdity of white supremacy, the implication being who is more uncivilized, in need of conversion, idolatrous, and barbarous than execrable white people claiming superiority? And it is a scathing condemnation of the African slave trade, and its perpetrators and perpetuators.

Gulliver's next statement, a hypocritical confession, is so profoundly the opposite of truth, of the real situations, that Swift's intent is not so far below the surface it can't be known and felt. Swift's use of irony is so effective we are made to feel the vehemence, again, and perhaps more so, of his condemnation of the African slave trade, colonizing, white people and the lies and fraud they use to cover up the trade and colonies. Referring to his nutshell description of the trade and "a modern colony," Gulliver states:

> But this description, I confess, doth by no means affect the British nation, who may be an example to the whole world for their wisdom, care, and justice in planting colonies; their liberal endowments for the advancement of religion and learning; their choice of devout and able pastors to propagate Christianity; their caution in stocking their provinces with people of sober lives and conversations from this the mother kingdom; their strict regard to the distribution of justice, in supplying the civil administration through all their colonies with officers of the greatest abilities, utter strangers to corruption; and to crown all, by sending the most vigilant and virtuous governors, who have no other views than the happiness of the people over whom they preside, and the honour of the king their master [237].

Swift is exposing the historical truth: that "the English were not in the least concerned with the souls of their "black cargoes," and, unlike the Portuguese, they did not even send missionaries to Africa until the end of the eighteenth century; they sent only drygoods, gin, and firearms. In their practical way, and with their genius for large-scale undertakings, they probably inflicted more suffering on the Negroes than any other nation."[146]

Swift next has Gulliver tell the truth but disingenuously apply it to fictitious countries rather than to the countries to which that truth does apply, and which constitute Gulliver's real travels. Gulliver says:

> But as those countries which I have described do not appear to have any desire of being conquered, and enslaved, murdered or driven out by colonies, not abound either in gold, silver, sugar or tobacco; I did humbly conceive they were by no means proper objects of our zeal, our valour, or our interest [237–238].

In other words, Swift is saying that the "real" countries, countries in Africa, for example, and countries made colonies, to which Gulliver travels but does not describe, certainly have *no* desire of being conquered, enslaved, murdered, or driven out by colonies, even though they *do* abound either in gold, silver, sugar or tobacco, which is why the British, the Europeans, and the Americans conceive those "real" countries proper objects of their zeal, their valour, and their interest.

With Gulliver's self-incriminating diatribe against white supremacist pride, Swift had Gulliver expose the hell he suffers ("...the memory of past sins is what constitutes the torment of hell..." (Bernard)[147] as the result of his lifetime African slave trade profession. Swift thus uses Gulliver to demonstrate white people's need for conversion to "real" Christianity. Gulliver says, speaking of white people:

> ... when I behold a lump of deformity and diseases both in body and mind, smitten with pride, it immediately breaks all the measures of my patience; neither shall I be ever able to comprehend how such an animal and such a vice could tally together ... and therefore I here entreat those who have any tincture of this absurd vice, that they will not presume to appear in my sight [239].

This Hell is the denouement, the culmination of Gulliver's self-hatred and hatred of white people in general, the product of his self-knowledge and knowledge of other white people, which is the climax of the *Travels*, when he says, for example, speaking of white people: "When I thought of my family, my friends, my countrymen, or human race in general [by which he means white people] ... [they] make no other use of reason than to improve and multiply those vices whereof their brethren [black people] in this country had only the share that nature allotted them" (224–225). Swift emphasizes the fact that white supremacy and the African slave trade are unnatural atrocities, for which white people should hate themselves, as Gulliver does immediately upon the above realization:

> When I happened to behold the reflection of my own form in a lake or fountain, I turned away my face in horror and detestation of myself, and could better endure the sight of a common yahoo, than of my own person [225].

This is the kind of misanthropy Swift is proposing to white people, which is echoed in his labeling them "lumps of deformity and diseases both in body and mind, smitten with pride," and in his letter to Pope, previously quoted, "Upon this great foundation of misanthropy (though not Timon's manner) the whole building of my *Travels* is erected...."[148]

Fundamental in this is Swift's belief that white people's hatred of black people shows their hatred of God. Therefore, white people should hate themselves and be hated. According to Bernard:

> Sinners, who do not love God, are not to be loved. Having withdrawn from God, who is their being, they are nothing; and that which is nothing is not a proper object of love. Curable sinners are actually nothing but potentially something; they should be loved only in order that they may love. That is, you should have benevolence but not sympathy for them, for sympathy would be malevolence in the case of those who will their own evil. Only in this way can you love your enemies, whose hatred for you shows their hatred for God. Incurable sinners are absolutely nothing; they should not be loved at all, but rather hated. Sympathy for them would be to join yourself to their sin; benevolence for them would be to oppose God's justice and so be out of sympathy with God. Therefore you should have no compassion for the damned.... This applies equally to incurable sinners still living, but in practice this fact is unknowable.

With irrefutable evidence, Swift projects Gulliver as one who not only does not love God, but who doesn't even know God. Gulliver calls himself a Christian, but, being an African slave trader, it's obvious he has withdrawn from God. He certainly willed his own evil, with "insatiable desire," and is and represents the damned. In *Inferno*, Dante demonstrates the lack of compassion for the damned prescribed by Bernard, and similarly, in this, Swift's depiction of hell, we are to have no compassion for Gulliver, symbolic of white people, who *should* hate themselves, as Gulliver demonstrates.

2

Malignant Aggression

We learn a great deal about Gulliver, right from the start, from Swift's clues. Significantly the prologue opens with, "My father" instead of "Our Father (which art in heaven)," which tells us Gulliver does not start with God, in the Augustinian/Bernardian way, but with the external world, in the Aristotelian/Thomist way. He says his father "had a small estate in Nottinghamshire," which is ironically significant in that Nottinghamshire is the town famous for the folk hero Robin Hood, who robbed the rich to give to the poor. White-everyman-Gulliver, hardly a folk hero, is studying and training to consummately rob the poor, African slaves, to give to the rich. And this is ironic because in Glubbdubdrib, after having "melancholy reflections to observe how much the race of human kind was degenerate among us within these hundred years past," he says, "I descended so low as to desire that some English yeomen of the old stamp might be summoned to appear" (163). Another clue he doesn't start with God is his father's sending him to "Emanuel College in Cambridge." "Emanuel" is one of Christ's names, but Emanuel College is not known for Christ, but for its scientific rather than humane learning. "Emanuel" means "God with us." But because Gulliver starts out with Aristotle's system of knowledge, and prepares for a career in the African slave trade, serving Mammon, he is not "with God" in the beginning, and God is not with him in the end in fulfillment of the Last Judgment prophecy (Matt. 25:31–46), alluded to by Bernard in the Third Step of Truth, Knowing God. Emanuel College is also significant because it had been the center for Puritanism when John Calvin was in power. As previously mentioned, Calvinism accepted, encouraged, and justified the African slave trade. Calvinism's Pharisaic obsession with outer rather than inner cleanliness; its compulsive association of purity with whiteness and evil with blackness; its idealization of the merchant, who saw to the flourishing of the African slave trade, from which he derived his wealth; and its doctrine of predestination qualified it as heresy. Swift also attacks Calvinism in "A Tale of a Tub," in the characterization of "Jack."

At Emanuel College Gulliver "applied himself close to his studies" (15), like Chaucer's Clerk, who "Of study took he most care and most heed," and would rather have "twenty books clad in black or red, of Aristotle and his philosophy, than rich robes, fiddle, or psaltery."[1] Swift's depiction of Aristotle in Glubdubdrib resembles Chaucer's Clerk in "looking hollow and sober":

> Aristotle stooped much, and made use of a staff. His visage was meager, his hair lank and thin, and his voice was hollow [159].

We can assume that at Emanuel College, Gulliver, like Chaucer's Clerk, studied Aristotle, in keeping with the College's reputation for scientific learning.

Gulliver leaves Emanuel to become an apprentice to an eminent surgeon in London, so that, by seventeen, he knows what he wants to do in his life: he wants to make a fortune in the African slave trade. He tells us:

> ... my father now and then sending me small sums of money, I laid them out in learning navigation, and other parts of the mathematics, useful to those who intended to travel, as I always believed it would be some time or other my fortune to do [15].

Taken together, "intend" and "fortune," as used here, are oxymoronic. Travel on an African slave ship as surgeon aspiring to captain will make him a fortune, in money, as he always believed it would. He goes to Leyden (the best scientific institution in Europe) to study physic, "knowing it would be useful in long voyages" (15). After these studies he takes a long voyage on an African slave ship as surgeon. So we know this has all been a setup, and Gulliver has all along been preparing for a career in the lucrative African slave trade, which he begins at age twenty-three. After slave trading for three years and a half, Gulliver marries for money and settles in an old Jewish section of London, where he practices surgery for two years.

His callousness extends to calling the practice of surgery a "business," speaking of which, he can add "hypocrisy" to callousness and lack of a conscience, when he says: "...my business began to fail; for my conscience would not suffer me to imitate the bad practice of too many among my brethren" (16). Presumably he means performing unnecessary surgery for money. But his conscience *does* suffer him to make black human beings his prey. Swift is here alluding to his sermon "On the Testimony of Conscience" to give us deeper insight into white-everyman-Gulliver's character. He did say, in "A Tale of A Tub":

> Why should I go upon farther particulars, which might fill a volume with the just elogies [here, characterizations] of my contemporary brethren? I shall bequeath this piece of justice to a larger work, wherein I intend to write A Character of the Present Set of Wits in our nation; their persons I shall describe particularly and at length, their genius and understandings in miniature.[2]

Gulliver is the symbol of that Character, and his understanding of "conscience" is "in miniature." As Swift says, conscience "is a word extremely abused by many people, who apply other meanings to it, which God Almighty never intended."[3] He prefaces his sermon with Scripture: "For our rejoicing is this, the testimony of our conscience" (2 Cor. 1:12). Gulliver's rejoicing is not the testimony of his conscience, as he says, being an African slave trader. Obviously he is "applying other meanings to it, which God Almighty never intended." This is an extremely important sermon in understanding the Travels. It is the basis of Swift's protest of white supremacy and the African slave trade in defense of "real" Christianity. It confronts the issue of how the conscience of white people, like Gulliver's, could suffer them to persist in so many egregious abominations against black people, and still believe themselves to be good, decent, not to mention superior, people, how they can go on not being what they think they are for so long. It's an issue that justifies the sermon, and proves the need of conversion. Swift states straightforwardly:

> The word Conscience properly signifies that knowledge which a man hath within himself of his own thoughts and actions. And because if a man judgeth fairly of his own actions, by comparing them with the law of God, his mind will either approve or condemn him, according as he hath done good or evil; therefore this knowledge or conscience may properly be called both an accuser and a judge. So that whenever our conscience accuseth us, we are certainly guilty; but we are not always innocent, when it doth not accuse us: for very often through the hardness of our hearts, or the fondness and favour we bear to ourselves, or through ignorance or neglect, we do not suffer our conscience to take any cognisance of several sins we commit.[4]

Swift proceeds to prove "that there is no solid, firm foundations for virtue, but on a conscience which is guided by religion."[5] He begins by exposing the "weakness and uncertainty of two false principles, which many people set up in the place of conscience, for a guide to their actions."[6] Here he emphasizes the crucial difference between moral honesty and religion:

> The first of these false principles is what the world usually calls moral honesty. There are some people, who appear very indifferent as to religion, and yet have the repute of being just and fair in their dealings; and these are generally known by the character of good moral men. But now, if you look into the grounds and motives of such men's actions, you shall find them to be no other

than his own ease and interest. For example: you trust a moral man with your money in the way of trade, you trust another with the defense of your cause at law, and perhaps they both deal justly with you. Why? Not from any regard they have for justice, but because their fortune depends upon their credit, and a stain of open publick dishonesty must be to their disadvantage. But let it consist with such a man's interest and safety to wrong you, and then it will be impossible you can have any hold upon him; because there is nothing left to give him a check, or put in the balance against his profit. For if he hath nothing to govern himself by but the opinion of the world, as long as he can conceal his injustice from the world he thinks he is safe.[7]

Gulliver is a good example. As far as he is concerned he conceals his injustice against black people, and he thinks he is safe. Swift goes on:

Besides, it is found by experience, that those men who set up for morality without regard to religion, are generally virtuous but in part; they will be just in their dealings between man and man; but if they find themselves disposed to pride, lust, intemperance, or avarice, they do not think their morality concerned to check them in any of these vices; because it is the great rule of such men, that they may lawfully follow the dictates of nature, wherever their safety, health, and fortune are not injured. So that upon the whole there is hardly one vice, which a mere moral man may not, upon some occasion, allow himself to preactice.[8]

As we have seen, Gulliver's morality is not concerned to check him in his zeal for the African slave trade, because, in his white supremacist pride, his lust for money, and his avarice, he is only following the dictates of his nature, actually, of his Will. Swift is here, as elsewhere, satirizing Humanism in its promotion of the moral philosophy of the ancient Greek and Roman philosophers, which, it was thought, "had the ability to make man a fully realized human creature, elevated and distinct from the lower animals," and "could teach Christians how to attain the perfections of life."[9] Swift demonstrates the ironic contrary, that the moral philosophy of Plato, Aristotle, et al., made the white man a fully realized monster, lower than the lower animals.

Swift goes on to explain the "other false principle, which some men set up in the place of conscience to be their director in life. It's what those who pretend to it call honour."[10] He depicts a good example in African slave ship captain Pedro de Mendez, in Part IV, when Gulliver says: "Don Pedro ... put it upon me as a point of honour and conscience..." (233). In his sermon, Swift says:

The word honour is often made the sanction of an oath; it is reckoned to be a great commendation to be a strict man of honour; and it is commonly understood, that a man of honour can never be guilty of a base action. This is usually the style of military men, of persons with titles, and of others who pretend to birth and quality. 'Tis true indeed, that in ancient times it was universally understood, that honour was the reward of virtue; but, if such honour as is nowadays going will not permit a man to do a base action, it must be allowed, there are few such things as base actions in nature.[11]

Swift's irony is well taken in his employment of such words as "honour and conscience" in a conversation between two perpetrators of the most base action, the African slave trade by two African slave ship captains, Gulliver and Don Pedro:

> No man of honour, as that word is usually understood, did ever pretend that his honour obliged him to ... be useful to his country, to do good to mankind ... or if he had any of these virtues, they were never learned in the catechism of honour; which contains but two precepts, the punctual payment of debts contracted at play, and the right understanding the several degrees of an affront, in order to revenge it by the death of an adversary.
>
> But suppose the principle of honour ... did really produce more virtues than it ever pretended to do; yet, since the very being of that honour depended upon the breath, the opinion, or the fancy of the people, the virtues derived from it could be of no long or certain duration. For example: suppose a man, from a principle of honour ... thought he could gain honour by the falsest and vilest action (which is a case that very often happens), [African slave trading, for example] he would make no scruple to perform it. And God knows, it would be an unhappy state, to have the religion, the liberty, or the property of a people lodged in such hands: which however hath been too often the case.[12]

And *is* the case as Swift writes, and *is* what he is saying as he writes, in the midst of "7,000,000" slaves being shipped from all parts of Guinea to the New World in the eighteenth century, with the English shipping more than half. And white people *did* gain honor by these vilest of actions, and the religion, the liberty, and the property of a people *are* lodged in such hands. Swift goes on to say:

> Having thus shown you the weakness and uncertainty of those principles, which some men set up in the place of conscience to direct them in their actions; I shall now endeavour to prove to you, that there is no solid, firm foundation of virtues, but in a conscience directed by the principles of religion.[13]

He proceeds to explain why:

> There is no way of judging how far we may depend upon the actions of men, otherwise than by knowing the motives, and grounds, and causes of them; and if the motives of our actions be not resolved and determined into the law of God, they will be precarious and uncertain, and liable to perpetual changes.... No earthly interest can ever come in competition to balance the danger of offending his Creator, or the happiness of pleasing him.
>
> Secondly; Fear and hope are the two greatest natural motives of all men's actions, but neither of these passions will ever put us in the way of virtue, unless they be directed by conscience. For, although virtuous men do sometimes

accidentally make their way to preferment, yet the world is so corrupted that no man can reasonably hope to be rewarded in it merely upon account of his virtue. And consequently the fear of punishment in this life will preserve men from very few vices, since some of the basest do often prove the surest steps to favour; such as ingratitude, hypocrisy, treachery, malice, subornation ... and many more, which human laws do little concern themselves about....

Lastly, Conscience will direct us to love God, and to put our whole trust and confidence in him. Our love of God will inspire us with a detestation for sin, as what is of all things most contrary to his divine nature: and if we have an entire confidence in him, that will enable us to subdue and despise all the allurements of the world.[14]

Before concluding, Swift emphasizes not only that "a religious conscience is the only true solid foundation upon which virtue can be built," but demonstrates "how necessary such a conscience is, to conduct us in every station and condition of our lives."[15]

> It was the advice of Jethro to his son-in-law Moses, to "provide able men, such as fear God, men of truth, hating covetousness," and to place such over the people; and Moses, who was as wise a statesman at least as any in this age, thought fit to follow that advice. Great abilities, without the fear of God, are most dangerous instruments, when they are trusted with power....
>
> And the reason why we find so many frauds, abuses, and corruptions where any trust is conferred, can be no other, than that there is so little conscience and religion left in the world....
>
> Therefore, to conclude: It plainly appears that unless men are guided by the advice and judgment of conscience founded on religion, they can give no security that they will be either good subjects, faithful servants of the publick, or honest in their mutual dealings; since there is not other tie, through which the pride, or lust, or avarice, or ambition of mankind, will not certainly break one time or other.[16]

And Swift provides numerous examples in *Gulliver's Travels*, starting with Gulliver's pride, lust, avarice, and ambition, insatiably focused on the African slave trade. Moreover, the sermon serves as a frame of reference for the pride, lust, avarice, and ambition of white people as Lilliputians.

As his excuse for returning to the slave trade, Gulliver chooses the worst of two evils: making millions of black people his prey, imitating the bad practice of too many among his brethren, which his conscience does suffer him to imitate, the lesser evil being, presumably, performing unnecessary surgery:

> ... my business began to fail; for my conscience would not suffer me to imitate the bad practice of too many among my brethren.... I determined to go again to sea [16].

Calling surgery a "business" doesn't say much for his conscience, to begin with, but to not even mention conscience in connection with the African slave trade constitutes the nadir of unconscionable, which proves the point of Swift's sermon. Also proving the point is the motive behind Gulliver's leaving his surgery "business" to return to the African slave trade: "The African slave trade was so enormously profitable that nothing else could compete with it,"[17] which he doesn't fail to imply:

> I was surgeon successively in two ships, and made several voyages, for six years, to the East and West Indies, by which I got some addition to my fortune [16].

In the context of the next clue Swift alludes to, we learn even more about Gulliver's lack of spirituality, sensitivity, and religiousness: He says:

> My hours of leisure I spent in reading the best authors ancient and modern, being always provided with a good number of books; and when I was ashore, in observing the manners and disposition of the people, as well as learning their language, wherein I had a great facility by the strength of my memory [16].

It's Gulliver's lack of a scale of values in what he reads and in the knowledge he possesses that Swift exposes allusive of Bernard, who says we should "give precedence to all that aids spiritual progress"; that we should "pursue more eagerly all that strengthens love more"; and that we should not pursue knowledge for the purpose of "vain-glory or curiosity or any base motive" [like the African slave trade,] but for the goodness of oneself or one's neighbor.[18] As we shall see, just by being an African slave trader, a white supremacist rooted in Aristotle, Plato, and Thomism, and characterized by all twelve of Bernard's Steps of Pride, it becomes obvious that Gulliver gives precedence to *nothing* that aids spiritual progress; that he pursues *nothing* that strengthens love more; and that he pursues knowledge for the base motive of buying and selling human beings for the love of money, and for vainglory (white supremacy). Because of these realities, his mention of having "a great facility by the strength of my memory" signifies that the Memory of the soul of white people is dead. Each Part of *Gulliver's Travels* exposes one of the faculties of the soul of white people, according to Bernard's doctrine of the soul. The Memory is "the most essential faculty," without which the soul would fail to be a soul at all. It is the "thinking faculty."[19] "In the state of spiritual death the memory is devoted to thoughts which are not thoughts of truth,"[20] such as Aristotle's system of knowledge and philosophy of slavery, politics, war, and supremacy; Plato's thoughts in *The Republic*; Thomas Aquinas's Aristotelian system of Christianity or "nominal" Christianity; white supremacy, legalism, the worship of money, and the African slave trade, all of which foundations white-everyman-Gulliver embodies, foundations Swift is digging up. In Parts I and II, Swift emphasizes the outrageously unlimited thoughts white people devote to the necessities of the body, which is further proof their thinking faculty, their memory, is in the state of spiritual death. Necessities of the body cannot be neglected "but should be limited,"[21] according to Bernard. More importantly, however, is Bernard's definition of hell, according to which Swift depicts Gulliver's end and his suffering from the climax to the end: "Sins exist in the memory even when past; and the memory of past sins is what constitutes the torment of hell, which is everlasting because the sins cannot be eradicated from the memory."[22] There is a preponderance of evidence of white people's memory in the state of spiritual death, but nowhere do we see evidence of their memory in the state of spiritual life: "...in the state of spiritual life the memory is devoted to thoughts of God."[23] Swift emphasizes this absence by exposing, in the end, Gulliver's stark lack of knowledge of God.

Gulliver's reference to the strength of his memory ends the prologue. The faculty of the soul of white people that Swift is condemning in Part I of the novel proper is the Will, the emotional faculty, epitomized by Gulliver's "insatiable desire" for the African slave trade, desire being of the Will. That is, as Bernard would say, Gulliver's "will is moved to the sin the [African slave trade], by an emotional desire for it."[24] He accepts "an advantageous offer" to be surgeon of the *Antelope*, the name of an authentic African slave ship, traveling to the South Sea. The novel proper thus begins with the first dated voyage. Gulliver sets sail from Bristol May 4, 1699, and he makes his first reference to money without revealing what he is doing to earn it: "...our voyage at first was very prosperous. It would not be proper, for some reason, to trouble the reader with the particulars of our adventures in those seas" (16).

With the date of this first voyage, we are introduced to the major covert theme of faith in God, exposing Gulliver's lack of it, and demonstrating as a statement how faith in God is related to the other frames of reference pivotal to understanding Part I, such as the Memory and Will of the soul; Curiosity, the First Step of Pride; Bonaventrue's First Light, Samson, and the Twenty-Third Psalm.

One designated lesson in the *Queen Anne Book of Common Prayer* for the date of Gulliver's first dated African slave trade voyage is one of the most powerful affirmations of faith, the Twenty-Third Psalm:

> The LORD is my shepherd; I shall not want.
> He maketh me to lie down in green pastures
> He leadeth me beside the still waters.
> He restoreth my soul: he leadeth me in the paths
>   of righteousness for his name's sake.

> Yea, though I walk through the valley of the shadow
> of death, I will fear no evil: for thou art with me;
> thy rod and thy staff they comfort me....
> Surely goodness and mercy shall follow me all the
> days of my life: and I will dwell in the house
> of the LORD for ever.

The LORD is never Gulliver's shepherd or master. Goodness and mercy do not follow him because all the days of his life are spent in the African slave trade, so he won't dwell in the house of the LORD but in hell forever, according to Swift's depiction.

In addition to his African slave trade profession, his lack of faith in God is demonstrated after his ship is driven by the wind directly upon a rock and immediately splits, and instead of trusting in the mercy of God he says: "We trusted ourselves to the mercy of the waves.... For my own part, I swam as fortune directed me," (16), unlike Dante, who is "not the friend of Fortune."[25] Swift draws many ironic analogies between Gulliver and Dante in Part II.

As soon as Gulliver makes it ashore, his lack of faith is made even more conspicuous by the ironic analogy drawn between him, a giant of no faith, and Samson, a giant of faith, as the Apostle Paul calls him. For example: What with Gulliver's extreme fatigue, the heat of the weather, and the "half a pint of brandy he drank as he left the ship," he falls asleep on the grass. The mention of brandy is an allusion to the Nazarite prohibition against strong drink, by which Samson is bound. Both Samson and Gulliver are captured while they sleep. When Gulliver wakes he finds his arms and legs strongly fastened on each side to the ground; and his hair, "which was long and thick," like Samson's, was tied down in the same manner. Also, just as Samson was bound with "fetters of brass," Gulliver is bound with "several slender ligatures," which could have been "brass" wire. He says, "I could only look upwards, the sun began to grow hot, and the light offended my eyes," suggestive of Jesus Christ, the "Son," the "Light of the world," who said, "Blessed is he whosoever shall not be offended in me." Similarly, when Samson wakes "he wist not that the Lord was departed from him." Samson's eyes are offended by the Philistines, who put them out, which proves to be no impediment to his bodily strength. The Lilliputians threaten to put out Gulliver's eyes, telling him, "the loss of your eyes will be no impediment to your bodily strength...." In the end, Samson achieved more by faith when blind than he achieved when sighted: "So the dead which he slew at his death [when blind] were more than the dead which he slew in his life [when sighted]." But Samson had repented and cried out to God: "O Lord God, remember me, I pray thee, and strengthen me...." and God returned to him. Gulliver never cried out to God, so he is forever left alone by God. This punishment is alluded to when Gulliver complains that the light of the sun/Son offended his eyes, and when he is threatened with being blinded by the Lilliputians as Samson was by the Philistines, but most significantly at the climax. Of course, Gulliver has already been blinded by philistinism. The punishment Swift alludes to is the following:

> God hath blinded their eyes, and hardened their heart; that they should not see with their eyes, nor understand with their heart, and be converted, and I should heal them [John 12:40].

This punishment has already been visited upon Gulliver, from which there is no resurrection in the end, as we shall see. So that when Gulliver, tied down, says, "I could only look upwards," Swift alludes to Bernard's voice from Curiosity, the First Step of Pride, and the first step of pride Gulliver has taken:

> How dost thou dare lift thy eyes to heaven, when thou hast sinned against heaven? Look at the earth in order to know thyself. Only it will show thee an image of thyself, "for dust thou art, and unto dust shalt thou return."[26]

As if in response, Gulliver says

> ... bending my eyes downward as much as I could, perceived it to be a human creature not six inches high, with a bow and arrow in his hands, and a quiver at his back.

Thus, Gulliver is identified with a six inch philistine Lilliputian moving on his left leg, advancing over his breast, and coming almost up to his chin. Gulliver is identified with the Philistines because of his worship of money and his love of violence and sorcerers and magicians. It is also significant the connection Swift makes between the African slave trade and the Philistines. Gulliver sets sail on his African slave trade voyage on the *Antelope* on May 4.

The Philistines worship the god, Dagon, who is the father of Baal. May 4 is the date of one of the most important yearly festivals of the Druidic worship of Baal. Swift seems to project the lust for violence characteristic of those in the African slave trade, and the lust for violence characteristic of Druidic rituals, as a white racial trait. The Druids were an ancient British order of priests, teachers of religion, magicians, and sorcerers, legendary for their lust for violence. A Druidic ritual could consist of sacrificing an "honored victim by beheading, bludgeoning, cutting the throat, and drowning. The Lindow Man of 2,200 years ago, discovered in Manchester, England, in 1984, had had his throat cut, his windpipe crushed with a thong, his head bludgeoned, and his face held under water, merely for drawing the short straw of the burned bannock. It is believed that he must have been considered very valuable by his priestly order that he was so honored by such extravagant brutality."[27]

The irony in using philistine Gulliver to suggest the giant of faith Samson affords a projection of the enormous contrariety between the Philistine religion and "real" Christianity, in that Samson is a forerunner of Christ. Just as an angel of the Lord came to Mary to announce that, although she was a virgin, she was to bear a son, an angel of the Lord came to Samson's mother to announce that, although she is barren, she shall conceive and bear a son. "And the woman bare a son, and called his name Samson," which means "sunlike," as in Sonlike, and "the light of the world." Also, Samson and Christ were both Nazarenes.

One of Swift's main reasons for identifying Gulliver with the philistine Lilliputians in Part I, and as a six inch microcosm in Part II, is to emphasize the absurdity of Plato's philosophy that there is more good in the macrocosm than in the microcosm, in the state than in the individual, based on size. But Swift demonstrates by size differentials that the basis of evil or good is the same in large and small objects. There is just as little good in the six inch King of Lilliput, the state, as there is in the giant African slave trader Gulliver, or the giant farmer in Brobdingnag who enslaves the six inch Gulliver. Swift's point, which holds true for skin color as well, as he later shows, is St. Augustine's:

> ... neither beauty, nor yet size and strength, are of much moment to the wise man, whose blessedness lies in spiritual and immortal blessings, in far better and more enduring gifts, in the good things that are the peculiar property of the good, and are not shared by good and bad alike.[28]

Also to be considered is the crucial fact that we see things from Gulliver's racist perspective, which means his "troubled vision," which prevents him from seeing the "Sun of Justice" that "enlightens every man who comes into this world,"[29] and causes him to distort nature. His "spiritual condition dictates the rectitude with which his soul records the figures of nature,"[30] and since his soul is not able to subject itself to the will of Christ, it won't be free of distortion. If distortions occur, it is not that there are distortions in creation, but rather in the attitude of [Gulliver]" (Grosseteste). And we are reminded that "Man judges by appearance but God judges the heart."

The focus on appearance and size differentials brings us to a further attack on Aristotle's system of knowledge (that "the soul must receive impressions from the external world,")[31] by the introduction of Bonaventure's first light, the "external" light:

> The first light, then, since it enlightens the mind for appreciation of the arts and crafts, which are, as it were, exterior to man and intended to supply the needs of the body, is called the light of "mechanical skill." Being, in a certain sense, servile ... this light can rightly be termed "external." It has seven divisions corresponding to the seven mechanical arts enumerated by Hugh in his "Didascalicon," namely, weaving, armour-making, agriculture, hunting, navigation, medicine, and the dramatic art. That the above mentioned arts "suffice" for all the needs of mankind is shown in the following way; every mechanical art is intended for man's "consolation" or his "comfort"; its purpose, therefore, is to banish either "sorrow" or "want"; it either "benefits" or "delights," according to the words of Horace: "Either to serve or to please is the wish of the poets." "He hath gained universal applause who hath combined the profitable with the pleasing." If its aim is to afford "consolation" and amusement, it is "dramatic art" ... which embraces every form of entertainment.[32]

There's no doubt about Swift's allusion to Bonaventure's four lights, at least not to this first light, the external light, for he takes Gulliver through all seven mechanical arts, beginning with the "dramatic art." For example, while still tied down, Gulliver says:

> I saw a stage erected about a foot and a half from the ground, capable of holding four of the inhabitants, with two or three ladders to mount it: from whence one of them, who seemed to be a person of quality, made me a long speech.... He acted every part of an orator, and I could observe many periods of threatenings, and other of promises, pity and kindness.

The next of the seven mechanical arts Swift alludes to has to do with food. Gulliver is "famished with hunger, having not eaten a morsel for some hours before [he] left the ship." The reader should keep in mind, while Swift runs the gamut of the mechanical arts, that one of the reasons the memory (the thinking faculty) of the soul of white people is in the state of spiritual death is their excessive devotion to thoughts for the necessities of the body, "which cannot be neglected but should be limited. Swift uses the size differentials to call attention to the *un*limited thought devoted to the necessities of the body, to the inordinate and arrogant extent of an African slave trade. The outrageousness of the spectacle of getting food to Gulliver, is to emphasize the outrageousness of white people's inordinate attentiveness to the needs of their bodies. Gulliver says:

> I found the demands of nature so strong upon me that I could not forbear showing my impatience (perhaps against the strict rules of decency) by putting my finger frequently on my mouth, to signify that I wanted food [19].

Several ladders are applied to Gulliver's sides,

> on which above an hundred of the inhabitants mounted, and walked towards my mouth, laden with baskets full of meat.... There were shoulders, legs and

loins ... but smaller than the wings of a lark. I eat them by two or three at a mouthful, and took three loaves at a time, about the bigness of musket bullets... [19].

Two hogsheads of wine are slung up, each holding a pint, which Gulliver "drank off at a draught." This is all in keeping with Swift's allusion to Bonaventure's first light, the "exterior" light. For example, Bonaventure says:

> In the matter of "food," mechanical skill may benefit in two ways, for we derive our sustenance from "vegetables," and from "flesh meats." If it supplies us with "vegetables," it is "farming;" if it provides us with "flesh meats," it is "hunting." Or, again, as regards "food," mechanical skill has a twofold advantage: either it aids in the "production" and multiplication of crops, in which case it is agriculture, or in the various ways of "preparing" food under which aspect it is hunting, an art which extends to every conceivable way of preparing foods, drinks, and delicacies....[33]

Notice, he does not include hunting human beings. Nor does he include the navigation of slave ships. As he continues, much of what he does include Swift alludes to:

> Furthermore, as an aid in the "acquisition of each of these necessities, the mechanical arts contribute to the welfare of man in two ways either by supplying a want, and in this case it is navigation, which includes all commerce of articles of covering or food; or by removing impediments and ills of the body, under which aspect it is "medicine," whether it is concerned with the preparation of drugs, *potions*, or *ointments*, with *the healing of wounds*.[34]

Still feeling "the smart of their arrows upon his face and hands, which were all blisters, and many of the darts still sticking in them," Gulliver says the Lilliputians "daubed his face and hands with a sort of *ointment* ... which in a few minutes *removed all the smart* of their arrows." He soon falls asleep, and it was no wonder, he says, "for the physicians ... had mingled a sleeping *potion* in the hogsheads of wine." As if to shock white people into an awareness of their obsession with the necessities of the body, Swift has Gulliver relate the following:

> I felt great number of the people on my left side relaxing the cords to such a degree that I was able to turn upon my right, and to ease myself with making water; which I very plentifully did, to the great astonishment of the people, who conjecturing by my motions what I was going to do, immediately opened to the right and left on that side to avoid the torrent which fell with such noise and violence from me [20].

Still alluding to the mechanical arts, Swift makes use of Gulliver's study of mathematics and navigation not mentioned by Bonaventure, but which makes a statement about the African slave trade that calls attention to white people's lack of empathy indicative of the death of the memory, will, and reason of their soul. He has Gulliver say, for example:

> These people are most excellent mathematicians, and arrived to a great perfection in mechanics by the countenance and encouragement of the Emperor, who is a renowned patron of learning.

Gulliver goes on to describe the navigation of his bound body on a machine suggestive of a ship, and transported to a lodging suggestive of the hold in an African slave ship. The entire operation suggests a description of the African slave trade previously quoted, and the "English genius for large-scale undertakings,"[35] which Swift is ridiculing: "Supplying, shipping, and disposing of this vast number of human chattels became a gigantic international operation and one favored the growth of new industries in England especially...."[36] Gulliver says:

> Five hundred carpenters and engineers were immediately set at work to prepare the greatest engine they had. It was a frame of wood raised three inches from the ground, about seven foot long and four wide, moving upon twenty-two wheels.... It was brought parallel to me as I lay. But the principal difficulty was to raise and place me in this vehicle. Eighty poles, each of one foot high, were erected for this purpose, and very strong cords of the bigness of packthread were fastened by hooks to many bandages, which the workmen had girt round my neck, my hands, my body, and my legs. Nine hundred of the strongest men were employed to draw up these cords by many pulleys fastened on the poles, and thus, in less than three hours, I was raised and slung into the engine, and there tied fast. All this I was told, for while the whole operation was performing, I lay in a profound sleep, by the force of that soporiferous medicine infused into my liquor. Fifteen hundred of the Emperor's largest horses, each about four inches and a half high, were employed to draw me towards the metropolis, which, as I said, was half a mile distant [21].

His lodging is the largest temple in the kingdom, allowing him a space of about "four foot high, and almost two foot wide, through which he could easily creep." To emphasize his lack of empathy, he is put in the same position as he puts African slaves. He says: "The chains that held my left leg were about two yards long, and gave me not only the liberty of walking backwards and forwards in a semicircle; but, being fixed within four inches of the gate, allowed me to creep in, and lie at my full length in the temple." He complains of "as melancholy a disposition" as ever I had in my life" (23). As an African slave ship surgeon he would have known of a far worse melancholy, the "fixed melancholy," a "deadly scourge of the Guinea cargoes," which "was responsible for the loss of two-thirds of the slaves who died on the *Elizabeth*."[37] These slaves "simply had no wish to live," and willed themselves dead.[38] But Gulliver's own melancholy did not teach him how to commiserate with the "fixed melancholy" suffered by slaves, as he was completely ignorant of the Second Step of Truth, Knowing Your Neighbor.

Swift uses Bernard's definition of "Curiosity, the First Step of Pride," to attack Aristotle's system of knowledge, that of starting with the external world. As a way of emphasizing Gulliver's starting out with Aristotle's system of knowledge, and consequently losing the wisdom which is able to grasp intuitively the knowledge of God within himself, Swift has Gulliver use some form of the word "curiosity" at least eighteen times in Lilliput and Brobdingnag combined, while focusing on the Will of the soul. The "curious" man, according to Bernard, occupies himself with feeding his eyes and ears, no longer curious to know how he has left himself within. After his bout of melancholia, Gulliver says, with emphasis on the "eye" words:

> When I found myself on my feet, I looked about me, and must confess I never beheld a more entertaining prospect. The country round appeared like a continued garden.... I viewed the town on my left hand, which looked like a painted scene of a city in a theatre [23].

According to Bernard, the eyes and ears signify sin, and are windows through which death enters the mind, and they involve the Will: Lust of the flesh, lust of the eyes, worldly ambition, and philistinism, cause the spiritual death of the Will. Swift makes an abrupt shift to another aspect of external knowledge that causes spiritual death — unlimited or obsessive thoughts or concerns for the necessities of the body. He uses the outrageous to expose the outrageous:

> I had been for some hours extremely pressed by the necessities of nature; which was no wonder, it being almost two days since I had last disburthened myself. I was under great difficulties between urgency and shame. The best expedient I could think on was to creep into my house, which I accordingly did; and shutting the gate after me, I went as far as the length of my chain would suffer, and discharged my body of that uneasy load [23].

(This is not what Norman O. Brown called Swift's "Excremental Vision," or "emphasis on the anal function.") As an African slave ship surgeon, Gulliver would have been well acquainted with the following history:

> Most often the noise heard by the sailors was that of quarreling among the slaves. The usual occasion for quarrels was their problem of reaching the latrines.... It often happens that those who are placed at a distance from the buckets, in endeavouring to get to them, tumble over their companions, in consequence of their being shackled.... In this situation, unable to proceed and prevented from going to the buckets, they desist from the attempt; and as the necessities of nature are not be resisted, they ease themselves as they lie.[39]

The slaves did what they were forced to do under the circumstances, and that was that, no need to go on about it. But Gulliver gives it the wrong focus by a misplacement of values, and a misunderstanding of "cleanliness," saying, "But this was the only time I was ever guilty of so uncleanly an action." He was guilty of a far more uncleanly action when he took his first African slave trade voyage. Nevertheless, he appeals to the reader regarding "so uncleanly an action";

> for which I cannot but hope the candid reader will give some allowance, after he hath maturely and impartially considered my case, and the distress I was in. From this time my constant practice was, as soon as I rose, to perform that business in open air, at the full extent of my chain, and due care was taken every morning before company came, that the offensive matter should be carried off in wheelbarrows by two servants appointed for that purpose. I would not have dwelt so long upon a circumstance, that perhaps at first sight may appear not very momentous, if I had not thought it necessary to justify my character in point of cleanliness to the world; which I am told some of my maligners have been pleased, upon this and other occasions, to call in question [23–24].

Like Ezekiel's eating dung, Swift's dwelling on dung is prompted by the desire to raise white people into a perception of the infinite (Blake, plate 14, 39). Swift has Gulliver thus "strain at a gnat and swallow a camel," to identify Gulliver with the Pharisees as earning the reproof of Christ, the Infinite:

> Not that which goeth into the mouth defileth a man; but that which cometh out of the mouth, this defileth a man ... whatsoever entereth in at the mouth goeth into the belly, and is cast out into the draught. But those things which proceed out of the mouth come forth from the heart; and they defile the man. For out of the heart proceed evil thoughts, murders, adulteries, fornications, thefts, false witness, blasphemies. These are the things which defile a man.

As an allusion, Christ's reproof reveals a lot more about the character of white people than that of a reflection of Gulliver's obsession with external cleanliness and the "appearance" of cleanliness. It's an allusion to further reproof, with which Swift exposes the character of white people, and white superiority and supremacy as a cover-up. Christ's further reproof is also Swift's reproof of white people:

> Ye blind guides, which strain at a gnat, and swallow a camel. Woe unto you, scribes and Pharisees, hypocrites! for ye make clean the outside of the cup and of the platter, but within they are full of extortion and excess.... Woe unto you, scribes and Pharisees, hypocrites! for ye are like unto whited sepulchres, which indeed appear beautiful outwardly, but are within full of dead men's bones, and of all uncleanness. Even so ye also outwardly appear righteous unto men, but within ye are full of hypocrisy and iniquity [Matt. 23:24–28].

The King of Lilliput comes on the scene as a good example. He gives a princely impression, judging by appearance. The absurdity of "white superiority" and "white supremacy" are ridiculed in the arrogance of this six inch King. Also ridiculed is judging by appearance. Regardless of his princely outward appearance, within he is full of hypocrisy and iniquity, a "whited sepulchre," as Gulliver is later to discover. For example, the following custom was introduces by this prince:

> ... that after the court had decreed any cruel execution, either to gratify the monarch's resentment, or the malice of a favourite, the Emperor always made a speech to his whole council, expressing his great lenity and tenderness, as qualities known and confessed by all the world. This speech was immediately published through the kingdom; not did any thing terrify the people so much as those encomiums on his Majesty's mercy; because it was observed, that the more these praises were enlarged and insisted on, the more inhuman was the punishment, and the sufferer more innocent [58].

The next character trait of white people that Swift exposes is frivolousness, the Second Step of Pride, to which they devote unlimited thought, which, according to Bernard, "distracts the soul."[40] Swift emphasizes this with four pages devoted to the written inventory of Gulliver's pockets, the full page description of Gulliver's hat, and the meticulous, unlimited thoughts for the necessities of the body, such as three hundred tailors to make Gulliver a suit of clothes after the fashion of the country. In the midst of the frivolous, and easily overlooked, is the image of Gulliver on his knees begging for his liberty, an image made famous by Josiah Wedgewood of an African slave begging on his knees for his liberty. To allude, in the context of the frivolous, to an African slave on his knees begging for freedom is to emphasize through Gulliver's identical posture the inadequacy of feeling, and the incapacity for empathy on the part of white people for black people, of which Gulliver is proof.

Swift takes us from this image of slavery in the context of the frivolous (Aristotle puts slavery in the context of politics) to politics in the context of the frivolous, to his definition of politics as corruption:

> Politicks are nothing but corruptions, and are consequently of no use to a good king, or a good ministry: for which reason all courts are so full of politicks.[41]

Swift projects the court of Lilliput as an inherited racial archetypal example of the corruption and frivolity that is politics. He depicts the frivolous, which obviously includes Gulliver, according to Bernard's Second Step of Pride, in which we can see Gulliver and the politicians as men "who neglect themselves to become curious about other men," and so, "respect some as superior, reject others as inferior; see in some cause for envy, in others cause for ridicule." The soul's "love of its own excellence makes it both grieve to be surpassed and rejoice to surpass others."⁴² It's important to note that Gulliver's description is Swift's condemnation of politics, and not intended for the entertainment of the reader, except to identify the reader with Gulliver, who says:

> I was diverted with none so much as that of the rope-dancers, performed upon a slender white thread, extended about two foot, and twelve inches from the ground.... This diversion is only practised by those persons who are candidates for great employments, and high favour, at court. They are trained in this art from their youth, and are not always of noble birth, or liberal education. When a great office is vacant either by death or disgrace (which often happens) five or six of those candidates petition the Emperor to entertain his Majesty and the court with a dance on the rope, and whoever jumps the highest without falling, succeeds in the office.... But the danger is much greater when the ministers themselves are commanded to show their dexterity; for by contending to excel themselves and their fellows, they strain so far, that there is hardly one of them who hath not received a fall, and some of them two or three....
>
> There is likewise another diversion, which is only shown before the Emperor and Empress, and first minister, upon particular occasions. The ceremony is performed in his Majesty's great chamber of state.... The Emperor holds a stick in his hands, both ends parallel to the horizon, while the candidates, advancing one by one, sometimes leap over the stick, sometimes creep under it backwards and forwards several times, according as the stick is advanced or depressed.... Whoever performs his part with most agility, and holds out the longest in leaping and creeping, is rewarded with the blue coloured silk thread; the red is given to the next, and the green to the third, which they all wear girt twice round about the middle; and you see few great persons about this court who are not adorned with one of these girdles [31–32].

In other words, politics itself is a diversion or deviation from the principal concerns of government, which is why "Politicks are nothing but corruptions." Swift alludes to other examples, beginning with the Emperor, in satire of the concept of empire as a form of divine monarchy. Swift's satire is revealed loud and clear in his statement, which also includes Plato's praise of monarchy:

> Among other theological arguments made use of in those times in praise of monarchy, and justification of absolute obedience to a prince, there seemed to be one of a singular nature; it was urged, that Heaven was governed by a monarch, who had none to control his power, but was absolutely obeyed: then it followed, that earthly governments were the more perfect, the nearer they imitated the government in Heaven. All which I look upon as the strongest argument against despotick power, that ever was offered; since no reason can possibly be assigned, why it is best for the world, that God Almighty has such power, which does not directly prove that no mortal man should ever have the like.⁴³

The Scriptures in the *Queen Anne Book of Common Prayer* designated for the date chosen for Gulliver's first dated African slave trade voyage, May 4, can be seen to have been chosen for their relevance to Swift's satire of monarchy. The first Scripture alluded to for the May 4 date is I Kings 12, having to do with the cruelty and tyranny of King Rehoboam, of whom the King of Lilliput is very much a reflection. The counsel that King Rehoboam forsakes, "If you will be a servant to this people today and serve them, and speak good words for them, then they will be your servants forever," is echoed in the counsel Swift gives:

> ... so that the best prince is, in the opinion of wise men, only the greatest servant of the nation; not only a servant to the publick in general, but in some sort to every man in it. In the like manner, a servant owes obedience, and diligence, and faithfulness to his master.... This our Saviour himself confirmed by his own example; for he appeared in the form of a slave, and washed his disciples' feet, adding those memorable words, "Ye call me Lord and Master, and ye say well, for so I am. If I then your Lord and Master wash your feet, how much more ought ye to wash one another's feet?" Under which expression of washing the feet, is included all that subjection, assistance, love, and duty, which every good Christian ought to pay his brother, in whatever station God hath placed him. For the greatest prince, and the meanest slave, are not, by infinite degrees so distant, as our Saviour and those disciples, whose feet he vouchsafed to wash.[44]

In another Scripture alluded to for the morning of May 4, Swift identifies white people with King Jeroboam, and the African slave trade with the worship of money:

> Whereupon the king took counsel, and made two calves of gold, and said unto them ... behold thy gods, O Israel, which brought thee up out of the land of Egypt [I Kings 12:28].

With the Scripture alluded to for the evening of May 4th, Swift makes a blanket condemnation of white people in general and covering the book as a whole, which exposes their need for conversion. What the Scripture expresses is verifiable by the African slave trade, and the history of Europe, as related by Gulliver to the King of Brobdingnag:

> There is none righteous, no, not one ... there is none that seeketh after God ... there is none that doeth good, no, not one. Their throat is an open sepulchre; with their tongues they have used deceit; the poison of asps is under their lips: Whose mouth is full of bitterness their feet are swift to shed blood: Destruction and misery are in their ways: And the way of peace have they not known: There is no fear of God before their eyes [Rom. 3:10–18].

A Psalm alluded to appropriately serves as commentary on Swift's protest of white supremacy. David prays what the supremacist Pharisee should have prayed, instead of "God, I thank thee that I am not as other men are."

("He exults in himself exceedingly; he insults all others arrogantly.")[45] David prays otherwise, asking God to:

> Keep back thy servant from presumptuous sins; let them not have dominion over me: then shall I be upright, and I shall be innocent from the great transgression [Ps. 19:13].

From, in arrogance, divorcing himself from God's ways, the subject returns to politics when Gulliver is told about the two struggling parties in the empire: the "Tramecksan" and the "Slamecksan," so called because of the high and low heels on their shoes, by which they distinguish themselves. Politics being what it is, reasons for going to war, being political, are often frivolous, like which is the proper end of an egg to break. The two great empires of Lilliput and Blefuscu have been at war for six and thirty moons past over this question. Swift is here satirizing the Thirty Years War, which devastated Europe. Gulliver is asked to join the war effort, and he prevents an invasion of Lilliput by Blefuscu. But the King of Lilliput, not content, wants Gulliver to reduce the whole empire of Blefuscu into a virtual Lilliputian colony governed by a viceroy. In projecting white supremacy as ridiculous, Swift exposes the hypocritical absurdity of supremacist pretensions to the sublime, in Gulliver's racist boast: "I plainly protested, that I would never be an instrument of bringing a free and brave people into slavery"; and again when he presumes to do His Majesty a "signal" service. In both instances, Swift is aided in his depictions by Bernard's Fifth Step of Pride, Singularity, in which he "who vaunts himself above other men, strives, not to be but to appear superior."[46] The truth of this in the first instance speaks for itself, in Gulliver's having devoted his life to being more than an instrument of bringing a free and brave black people into slavery, whom he did not consider "people," which is confirmed when he animalizes them again in Houyhnhnmland.

In doing His Majesty "a most signal service," Gulliver shows what pretensions to superiority and supremacy amount to, by his method of putting out the fire in the palace:

> I had the evening before drank plentifully of a delicious wine.... By the luckiest chance in the world, I had not discharged myself of any part of it. The heat I had contracted by coming very near the flames, and by my laboring to quench them, made the wine begin to operate by urine; which I voided in such a quantity, and applied so well to the proper places, that in three minutes the fire was wholly extinguished.... It was now daylight, and I returned to my house, without waiting to congratulate with the Emperor; because although I had done a very eminent piece of service, yet I could not tell how His Majesty might resent the manner by which I had performed it: for, by the fundamental laws of the realm, it is capital in any person of what quality soever, to make water within the precincts of the palace [45].

He incurs the extreme displeasure of the Empress, who vows revenge.

In the meantime, he is content to gratify the "curious" reader with some general ideas about the Lilliputians, their customs, learning, etc. Many of the ideas are taken straight out of Plato's *Republic*, and ridiculed. For example, the unnatural way of caring for children, as they are sent to nurseries at twenty months of age:

> Their parents are suffered to see them only once a year; the visit is not to last above an hour. They are allowed to kiss the child at meeting and parting only; but a professor, who always stands by on those occasions, will not suffer them to whisper, or use any fondling expressions, or bring any presents of toys, sweetmeats, and the like [49].

Most of the laws reflect the fraudulence of the character of the lawmakers, including the crime of fraud, which, theoretically, is taken very seriously, while being committed by the King, as idealized in *The Republic*. Socrates says, for example:

> Our rulers will find a considerable dose of falsehood and deceit necessary for the good of their subjects: and the use of all these things regarded as medicines might be of advantage.[47]

Fraud is projected as one of the salient character traits of white people, identifying them with Satan here, and in later allusions to Milton's Satan, whom Milton calls the "Artificer of Fraud." In discussing fraud with Gulliver, the King's statement, "Honesty hath no fence against superior cunning," is an allusion to "Curiosity, the first step of pride," to define "white superiority" as "superior cunning" for the purpose of identifying white people with the superior "cunning malice" and superior "malicious cunning" of Satan who rules them, inasmuch as Satan "canst dwell only in the hearts of the proud,"[48] "white superiority" and "white supremacy" epitomizing "the proud" in whose hearts Satan dwells.

Another law mentioned is an allusion to "Curiosity" and to the punishment of both Satan and Gulliver, thereby again identifying white people with Satan. Gulliver says:

> Ingratitude is among them a capital crime, as we read it to have been in some other countries; for they reason thus, that whoever makes ill returns to his benefactor, must needs be a common enemy to the rest of mankind, from whom he hath received no obligation, and therefore such a man is not fit to live [48].

In "Curiosity," Bernard says that Satan "is ungrateful for God's gracious goodness," and that he "fallest into the pit destined for its own maker, and learnest that he whom Satan knewest to be good is also just," for God cannot "suffer his goodness to be blasphemed with impunity"[49]:

> He so softens the sentence of punishment that, shouldst thou wish to recover thyself, he will not refuse forgiveness; but after thy hardness and impenitent heart thou canst not so wish, and so thou canst not escape from thy punishment either.[50]

And this is white-everyman-Gulliver's punishment in the end. He falls into the pit he made for himself through hardness of heart, one of the hazards of the African slave trade, and impenitence, as the consequence of repeatedly ignoring the promptings of the Holy Spirit, as explained in the following definition of the "final blasphemy":

> The sin against the Holy Ghost implies a state of final and hopeless impenitence, and is committed by those who have again and again wilfully resisted the influences and warnings of the Holy Ghost, and have made themselves incapable of repentance, and consequently of pardon.[51]

In other words, if Gulliver would not have wilfully resisted the influences and warnings of the Holy Ghost ("the Voice of God preaching the Gospel to the dead") he would not have studied, trained, prepared for, and gone into the African slave trade, and would not have developed hardness and numbness of heart ("...the necessity of treating the Negroes like cattle gradually brings a numbness upon the heart")[52], and thus would not have made himself incapable of repentance, without which there is no hope of salvation. Swift projects all of this as a powerful incentive for conversion.

Gulliver is soon to learn there is not more good in the macrocosm, when he is falsely accused of treason and learns of the government's capacity for vicious and malicious tyranny, from the myriad creative schemes of torture devised by the state against him. Gulliver manages to escape to Blefuscu. Three days after his arrival there, "walking out of *curiosity* to the northeast coast of the island," he sees at a distance an overturned boat only a little damaged. In a month he makes it seaworthy. It is noteworthy that, just as after his African slave shipwreck he "swam as *fortune* (not God), directed," he tells the Emperor that, "since *fortune* (not God), whether good or evil, had thrown a vessel in my way, I was resolved to venture myself in the ocean." In other words, "Curiosity," Aristotle's approach to knowledge, comports well with the African slave trade and with "fortune," but leads away from God.

Gulliver sets sail from Blefuscu on the twenty-fourth day of September 1701. The first Scripture for that date in the *Queen Anne Book of Common Prayer*, as applied by Swift, identifies white people with "God's judgement upon the Jews," which brings Part I full circle with Gulliver's move to the "Old Jury" following his first African slave trade voyages:

Among my people are found wicked men: they lay wait, as he that setteth snares; they set a trap, *they catch men*. As a cage is full of birds, so are their houses full of deceit: therefore they are become great, and waxen rich. Shall I not visit for these things? saith the Lord shall not my soul be avenged on such a nation as this?

The companion Scripture answers the question. Both question and answer are to be understood as involving wicked Jews and white people who "catch men" via the African slave trade. Shall the Lord not visit and be avenged for this? The answer is the "Last Judgment" on them, to whom Christ will say:

Depart from me, ye cursed, into everlasting fire, prepared for the devil and his angels: For I was hungry and ye gave me no meat: I was thirsty, and ye gave me no drink: I was a stranger, and ye took me not in: naked, and ye clothed me not: sick, and in prison, and ye visited me not. Then shall they answer him saying, Lord, when saw we thee hungry or thirsty, or a stranger, or naked, or sick or in prison, and did not minister unto thee? Then shall he answer then, saying, Verily, I say unto you, Inasmuch as ye did it not to one of the least of these, ye did it not to me. And these shall go away into everlasting punishment ... [Matt. 25:41–46].

"The least of these" Swift interprets as African slaves. The first Scripture for the evening is in the same judgmental vein applicable to African slave traders and merchants:

Woe unto him that buildeth his house by unrighteousness, and his chambers by wrong; that useth his neighbour's service without wages, and giveth him not for his work ... thine eyes and thine heart are not for thy covetousness, and for to shed innocent blood, and for oppression, and for violence, to do it [Jer. 25:13, 17].

On September 26, two days after setting sail, Gulliver spies the sail of an African slave ship. He says, "my heart leapt within me to see her English colours." One of the first things he tells us once onboard, is, "We were now in the latitude of 30 degrees south," the latitude of South Africa. Given this context, the Scriptures Swift chose for this date, or, rather, the date Swift chose because of the Scriptures designated for September 26, 1701, in the *Queen Anne Book of Common Prayer*, is of ultimate relevance. The Scriptures for that date function as the most scathing commentary on the African slave trade, in that African slave traders and merchants are projected as Judases and the crucifiers of Christ, doing unto African slaves, "the least of these," what was done unto Christ. This will be brought to mind again in Part III, when Gulliver petitions the Emperor of Japan, that "his Majesty would condescend to excuse my performing the ceremony imposed on my countrymen of 'trampling upon the crucifix,'" for which he is to receive no accolades, having already been identified with the crucifiers of Christ.

It is significant, in the context of a protest of the African slave trade, that Judas betrayed Christ for the price of a slave, and that Christ was crucified in the garment of a slave, in that Christ is betrayed for money when black people are betrayed in being enslaved for money. So the second Scripture alluded to not only condemns Judas and the crucifying of Christ, but also the worship of money. The first Scripture would seem to prefigure Swift's condemnation of the priests who "take counsel against Jesus to put him to death." Malachi reproves the priests thusly:

> And now, O ye priests, this commandment is for you. If ye will not hear, and if ye will not lay it to heart, to give glory unto my name, saith the Lord of hosts, I will even send a curse upon you, and I will curse your blessings: yea, I have cursed them already, because ye do not lay it to heart.... I have made you contemptible and base before all the people, according as ye have not kept my ways, but have been partial in the law. Have we not all one father? hath not one God created us? why do we deal treacherously every man against his brother, by profaning the covenant of our fathers?

As if to give an example, Swift alludes to Matthew 27:

> When the morning was come, all the chief priests and elders of the people took counsel against Jesus to put him to death: And when they had bound him, they led him away, and delivered him to Pontius Pilate the governor. Then Judas, who had betrayed him, when he saw that Jesus was condemned, repented himself, and brought again the thirty pieces of silver to the chief priests and elders, saying, I have sinned in that I have betrayed the innocent blood. And they said, what is that to us? see thou to "that." And he cast down the pieces of silver in the temple, and departed, and went and hanged himself.

The chief priests took the "blood money" and bought the potter's field to bury strangers in, called "Aceldama," or "field of blood," located in Hinnonland, after which Houyhnhnmland (Part IV) is named. Gulliver, like Judas, commits the unforgivable sin of despair. Both are incapable of repentance.

> ... the chief priests and elders persuaded the multitude that they should ask for Barabbas and destroy Jesus.

Swift emphatically condemns the worship of money, not unmindful of Judas. For Judas, to whom money was of greater value than God, to find that money had no redeeming value was too devastating to bear. To Gulliver, also, money is of greater value than God, in that he does unto God what he does unto Africans in making them slaves, for money. As soon as he gets onboard the African slave ship that rescues him, he shows the captain the gold given him by the Emperor of Blefuscu, and gives the captain two purses of two hundred "sprugs" each. He says, "I shall not trouble the reader with a particular account of this voyage, which was very prosperous for the most part." His obsession with money continues as he goes on to say, after landing, "The short time I continued in England I made a considerable profit by showing my cattle to many persons of quality, and others: and before I began my second voyage, I sold them for six hundred pounds." Another indication of his love of money, rather his lust for money, is his saying, after having been away from home and family for three years on African slave trading voyages: "I stayed but two months with my wife and family for my insatiable desire of seeing foreign countries would suffer me to continue no longer." His "insatiable desire" (the will) was for money from the African slave trade, than which nothing was more lucrative. He obviously is not hurting for money, for he says:

> I left fifteen hundred pounds with my wife, and fixed her in a good house at Redriff. My remaining stock I carried with me, part in money, and part in goods, in hopes to improve my fortunes. My eldest uncle John had left me and estate in land, near Epping, of about thirty pounds a year; and I had a long lease of the Black Bull in Fetter Lane, which yielded me as much more so that I was not in any danger of leaving my family upon the parish....

Gulliver had arrived home on the 13th of April, 1702. The Scriptures for that date, following the foregoing protests of the African slave trade and white supremacy, are instituted in defense of "real" Christianity as correctives:

> Ye know how that it is an unlawful thing for a man that is a Jew to keep company, or come unto one of another nation; but God hath shewed me that I should not call any man common or unclean.... Of a truth I perceive that God is no respecter of persons: But in every nation he that feareth him, and worketh righteousness, is accepted with him [Acts 10: 28, 34–35].
>
> My brethren, show no partiality as you hold the faith of our Lord Jesus Christ, "the Lord" of Glory, with respect of persons. For if there come unto your assembly a man with a gold ring, in godly apparel, and there come in also a poor man in vile raiment; And ye have respect to him that weareth they gay clothing, and say unto him, Sit thou here in a good place; and say to the poor, Stand thou there, or sit here under my footstool: Are ye not then partial in yourselves, and are become judges of evil thoughts? Hearken, my beloved brethren, Hath not God chosen the poor of this world rich in faith, and heirs of the kingdom which he hath promised to them that love him? But ye have despised the poor. Do not rich men oppress you, and draw you before the judgment seats? Do not they blaspheme that worthy name by the which ye are called? If ye fulfill the royal law according to the scripture, Thou shalt love thy neighbour as thyself, ye do well: But if ye have respect to persons, ye commit sin, and are convicted by the law as transgressors [James 2:1–9].

Gulliver ends Part I by taking leave of his wife and children and going onboard the *Adventure*, a merchant ship of three hundred tons, the usual size of an African slave ship, saying, "...my account of this voyage must be referred to the second part of my *Travels*."

3

"Flagitious and Facinorous Acts"

Gulliver's "insatiable desire" for the African slave trade affords the perfect ironic transition from the end of Part I to the beginning of Part II: "Having been condemned by nature and fortune to an active and restless life," reflecting the contradiction between free will and necessity. The point Swift is making through Bernard's doctrine of the will, is that white-everyman-Gulliver "is not forced to be evil by some other cause, but simply chooses to be so at the behest of his own will."[1] "Insatiable desire" is of the free will. "Having been condemned by nature and fortune," implies "necessity," in other words, to be "forced" to be evil. "Voluntary consent," says Bernard, "is a self-determining habit of the soul. Its action is neither forced nor extorted. It stems from the will and not from necessity, denying or giving itself on no issue except by way of the will."[2]

> Where the will is absent, so is consent; for only what is voluntary may be called consent. Hence, where you have consent, there also is the will. But where the will is, there is freedom. and this is what I understand by the term "free choice."[3]

Gulliver's claiming necessity for his free-choice evil life in the African slave trade is an example of Excusing Sins, the Eighth Step of Pride. But the truth is:

> Among all living beings, to man alone was given the ability to sin, as part of his prerogative of free choice. But he was given it, not that he might, but rather that he might appear the more glorious did he not sin when he was capable of doing so.[4]

In Lilliput and Brobdingnag, Parts I and II, the focus is the Will of the Soul of white people, along with Curiosity, feeding the eyes and ears. Curiosity, the first step of pride, the first step of the path that leads away from God, incorporates external knowledge and sense perception, and thus is a more useful tool for satirizing Aristotle's approach to knowledge. Moreover, the use

3. "Flagitious and Facinorous Acts" 93

of Bonaventure's first light, the external light, as a frame for Lilliput, and his second light, sense perception, the lower light, as a frame for Brobdingnag, emphasize the fallibility of external knowledge, as we have seen, and sense perception. (Jesus "shall not judge after the sight of his eyes, neither reprove after the hearing of his ears" [Is 11:3]).

But chiefly, the African slave trade voyages afford the most efficacious transitions between the four parts of the *Travels*, Swift's emphasizing continuity by closing each part with the account of an African slave trade voyage, then mentioning the African slave trade voyage which opens the next part. The African slave trade is the organizing motif that gives meaning to the content, "fusing in one vital unity both structure and content"[5] (Read, 207). We were already told, for example, at the close of Part I, of Gulliver's voyage on the African slave ship, the *Adventure*, which opens Part II. Continuity is also achieved by the allusion to Bonaventure's first light, which framed Part I, the external light, which includes "navigation." Beginning with Gulliver's statement that the captain was "well experienced in the navigation of those seas," we are given a heavy, unintelligible dose of "navigation." But, of course, Bonaventure makes no mention of the use of navigation for the purpose of transporting slaves, which calls attention by contrast to the use Gulliver makes of navigation.

Gulliver sets sail on the *Adventure* on the 20th day of June, 1702. As commentary, one Scripture for that date is singularly definitive:

> And there was delivered unto Jesus the book of the prophet Isaiah. He opened the book, and found the place where it was written, "The Spirit of the Lord is upon me, Because he has anointed me to preach the gospel to the poor; he hath sent me to heal the brokenhearted, to set at liberty those who are oppressed; to proclaim release to the captives...."

To free the slaves, in other words, the proclaiming of which Swift has made his mission, as it was Christ's. What greater authorities can there be for protesting the African slave trade than Isaiah and Jesus Christ? What greater heresy than involvement in the trade notwithstanding? Neither Jews nor "nominal" Christians have any excuse. They are those whom Bernard speaks of as knowing the truth, yet living evil lives. Moreover, they had a role model in Peter Claver, a Catholic priest who took the words of Jesus seriously. Peter Claver in 1616 vowed to be "the slave of the blacks forever," and kept that vow until he died, exhausted in 1654.[6] The following is from a letter he wrote, dated 31 May 1627:

> Yesterday, May 30, 1627, on the feast of the Most Holy Trinity, numerous blacks, brought from the rivers of Africa, disembarked from a large ship. Carrying two baskets of oranges, lemons, sweet biscuits, and I know not what else, we hurried toward them. When we approached their quarters, we thought

we were entering another Guinea. We had to force our way through the crowd until we reached the sick. Large numbers of the sick were lying on the wet ground or rather in puddles of mud. To prevent excessive dampness, someone had thought of building up a mound with a mixture of tiles and broken pieces of bricks. This, then, was their couch, a very uncomfortable one not only for that reason, but especially because they were naked, without any clothing to protect them. We laid aside our cloaks, therefore and brought from a warehouse whatever was handy to build a platform. In that way we covered a space to which we at last transferred the sick, by forcing a passage through bands of slaves.... There were two blacks, nearer death than life, already cold, whose pulse could scarcely be detected. With the help of a tile we pulled some live coals together and placed them in the middle near the dying men. Into this fire we tossed aromatics. Of these we had two wallets full, and we used them all up on this occasion. Then, using our own cloaks ... we provided for them a smoke treatment, by which they seemed to recover their warmth and the breath of life. The joy in their eyes as they looked at us was something to see.

This was how we spoke to them, not with words but with our hands and our actions.... Then we sat, or rather knelt, beside them and bathed their faces and bodies with wine. We made every effort to encourage them with friendly gestures and displayed in their presence the emotions which somehow naturally tend to hearten the sick.[7]

Whether or not Swift read or knew of Peter Claver's letter, or of the Second Step of Truth, Brotherly Love, it describes, the intensity of Swift's protest of the African slave trade in defense of "real" Christianity calls for just such an archetypal manifestation of "real" Christianity in the context of the African slave trade, as that of Peter Claver.

Having wintered at the Cape of Good Hope, Gulliver sets sail again on the *Adventure*. Passing the Straits of Madagascar on the 19th of April, the winds began to blow with a great violence. One of the Scriptures alluded to for that date tells the story of David and Bathsheba. The allusion to this Scripture is not only to emphasize the crucial importance of Knowing Yourself, the First Step of Truth, but also the difficulty of knowing yourself, and that Aristotle's approach to knowledge, Curiosity, feeding the eyes and ears, is the chief cause of the difficulty of knowing oneself, if not the chief preventor. This emphasis is a key motive in Swift's creation of *Gulliver's Travels* as a mirror for white people to know themselves.

White people, Swift is saying, have in common with Hazael and David ignorance of themselves. In his sermon "On the Difficulty of Knowing One's Self," Swift uses Hazael as an example. When the prophet Elisha says to Hazael: "I know all the evil that thou wilt do unto the children of Israel ... their young men wilt thou slay with the sword, and wilt dash their children, and rip up their women with child."

But Hazael, not knowing himself so well as the other did, was startled and amazed at the relation, and would not believe it possible, that a man of his temper could ever run out into such enormous instances of cruelty and inhumanity. "What!" says he, "is thy servant a dog, that he should do this great thing?"

"And yet, for all this ... we find him, on the very next day after his return, in a very treacherous and disloyal manner, murdering his own master, and usurping his kingdom; which was but a prologue to the said tragedy, which he afterward acted upon the people of Israel."

Feeding his eyes (Curiosity), David lusted (the Will) after Bathsheba, took her to bed, and she conceived. When she then informed him of her state, David called her husband, Uriah, from the battlefield and tried to get him to lie with Bathsheba so it would be assumed the child she was carrying was Uriah's. But Uriah would not allow himself the luxury of lying with his wife while his men were encamped in the open fields (the Second Step of Truth). So David has Uriah sent to "the forefront of the hottest battle ... that he may be smitten, and die." After Uriah's death, and the mourning period was past, David took Bathsheba for his wife. "But the thing that David had done displeased the LORD." "And the LORD sent Nathan to David." Nathan tells David the following story:

> There were two men in one city; the one rich, and the other poor. The rich man had exceeding many flocks and herds: But the poor man had nothing, save one little ewe lamb, which he had bought and nourished up: and it grew up together with him, and with his children; it did eat of his own meat, and drink of his own cup, and lay in his bosom, and was unto him as a daughter. And there came a traveller unto the rich man, and he spared to take of his own flock and of his own herd, to dress for the wayfaring man that was come unto him; but took the poor man's lamb, and dressed it for the man that was come to him.

"And David's anger was greatly kindled against the man; and he said to Nathan, As the LORD liveth, the man that hath done this thing shall surely die: and he shall restore the lamb fourfold, because he did this thing, and because he had no pity."

And Nathan said to David, "Thou art the man."

The LORD then proceeds to remind David of all that he has done for David, which by comparison, makes the rich man in the story seem poor. The LORD anointed David King of Israel, and gave him all the wealth and possessions befitting a king, including several wives. Yet, David took all that Uriah had, one lamb, Bathsheba. So, "Wherefore" said the LORD, "hast thou despised the commandment of the LORD, to do evil in his sight? Thou hast killed Uriah ... and hast taken his wife to be thy wife."

And David said unto Nathan, "I have sinned against the LORD."

Swift takes the place of Elisha and Nathan to teach white people to know themselves by giving them a mirror image of themselves in the *Travels*, which proves they are neither superior nor supreme, and therefore, like Hazael, are not who they think they are; and the African slave trade, the context for the Scriptures alluded to, should remove all doubt. But when African slave trader Gulliver says in response to the request of the King of Lilliput, "I plainly protested, that I would never be an instrument of bringing a free and brave people into slavery," it's obvious he does not know himself, that, like Hazael, he is not the man he thinks he is.

The next date is also chosen to emphasize the importance of white people knowing themselves. On May 2, the captain of the African slave ship *Adventure* "bid us all prepare against a storm," says Gulliver. The Scriptures for that date identify white people with Jews. The first one is especially appropriate coming so soon after Gulliver tells us how well off he left his family, leaving his wife "fifteen hundred pounds" and "fixing her in a good house in Redriff." Moses tells the Jews:

> ... man doth not live by bread alone, but by every word that proceedeth out of the mouth of the Lord doth man live.... Beware that thou forget not the Lord thy God, in not keeping his commandments, and his judgments, and his statutes, which I command thee this day: Lest when thou hast eaten and are full, and hast built goodly houses, and dwelt therein; and when ... thy silver and thy gold is multiplied, and all that thou hast is multiplied; Then thy heart be lifted up, and thou forget the Lord thy God.... And thou say in thine heart, My power and the might of mine hand hath gotten me this wealth.... And it shall be, if thou do at all forget the Lord thy God, and walk after other gods, and serve them, and worship them, I testify against you this day that ye shall perish [Deut. 8].

In the companion Scripture, Paul's description of the Jews can be seen in Swift's depiction of white people, with the same exasperation because of the willful disbelief in Christ. Paul says to the Jews:

> Hearing ye shall hear, and shall not understand; seeing ye shall see, and not perceive: For the heart of this people is waxed gross, and their ears are dull of hearing, and their eyes have they closed; lest they should see with their eyes, and hear with their ears, and understand with their heart, and should be converted, and I should heal them [Acts 28:27].

In other words, like the Jews, white people do not desire to be converted. Even knowing the truth, they choose to live evil lives.

In the first Scripture for the evening, white people are again identified with the Jews. Moses tells them of "a people great and tall, the children of the Anakims," a race of giants such as the Brobdingnagians. He tells them that the Lord will destroy the giants, but not because of the righteousness

3. "Flagitious and Facinorous Acts" 97

of the Jews. On the contrary, Moses describes them in ways Swift makes white people identifiable:

> ... thou art a stiffnecked people ... ye have been rebellious against the Lord ... ye provoked the Lord to wrath ... ye sinned against the Lord and made a golden calf ... [money worship].

Paul's descriptions in the companion Scripture are to be applied to white people because "they did not like to retain God in their knowledge, [so] God gave them over to a reprobate mind," for example:

> Being filled with all unrighteousness, wickedness, covetousness, maliciousness; full of envy, murder, deceit, malignity, haters of God, despiteful, proud, boasters, inventors of evil things, without understanding, without natural affection, implacable, unmerciful: Who knowing the judgment of God, that they which commit such things are worthy of death, not only do the same, but have pleasure in them that do them.

In the latter, we are reminded of Gulliver's almost boastful, "Having been condemned," but, like Satan, sinning boldly (Curiosity). Also, from above, "inventors of evil things" will be significant again at the climax, when Swift has Gulliver say that white people "make no other use of reason than to improve and multiply the vices of nature." Gulliver is "without natural affection" when he "cannot endure [his] wife or children in his presence." Examples of all of the other evils mentioned by Paul above, which Swift projects as characteristic of white people, can most readily be found in politics and in the African slave trade.

The *Adventure* makes it through the storm intact. "But," Gulliver says, "we lay in the utmost distress for water." The reader is reminded of the opening statement of Part II, "Having been condemned," when Gulliver says:

> We thought it best to hold on the same course rather than turn more northerly, which might have brought us to the northwest parts of Great Tartary, and into the frozen sea.

"Northerly" is an allusion to Satan. In expounding on "Curiosity, the first step of pride," Bernard quotes Satan as saying: "I will establish my seat in the north." Bernard "interprets "north" to mean sinful men, and "seat," power over them.[8] In his description of "sinful men," we are forced to think of white-everyman-Gulliver:

> None of them was radiant with flashes of wisdom, none of them burned with spiritual love. As if finding an empty place, Satan didst assume dominion over those whom he couldst imbue with the brilliance of his cunning and inflame with the warmth of his malice....[9]

So Gulliver's "Having been condemned" means he is a "sinful man" over whom Satan has power. Bernard would be quick to add, "It is our own will that enslaves us to the devil, not his power."[10] And we are reminded: "Satan canst dwell only in the hearts of the proud."[11] "Great Tartary" and "the frozen sea" complete the prefigurative meaning of "Having been condemned":

> Tartarus, in Greek mythology, is that part of the underworld where the wicked suffer punishment for their misdeeds on earth, those such as Ixion and Tantalus, who have committed some direct outrage against the gods.[12]

White people's identification with Ixion, having already been made, is now underscored. "The frozen sea" is an allusion to Cocytus, "a lake which through frost had the semblance of glass and not of water," and in which Satan, "The emperor of the woeful realm stood forth from mid-breast out of the ice,"[13] in the pit of hell in Dante's *Inferno* (XXXIV, 28–29). Although scholars seem not to have discovered it, this is the first of many allusions to *Inferno*.

The African slave ship, the *Adventure*, comes into full view of "a great island or continent ... on the south side whereof was a small neck of land jutting out into the sea," fitting the description of Africa. The captain sends men in a longboat to search for water. Gulliver "*desires* to go with them, that [he] might *see* the country, and *make* what *discoveries* he can." The emphases call attention to three of the main focuses of Part II: Curiosity, the Will, and Sense Perception. Gulliver walks alone, makes observations, and says: "I now began to be weary, and seeing nothing to entertain my curiosity, I returned ... and the sea being full in my view, I saw our men already got into the boat, and rowing for life to the ship." He observes a huge creature, a monster, chasing them which was not able to overtake the boat. Swift alludes to Augustine for commentary on the subject of giants, commentary that provides the thrust of Swift's motives in the size differentials in Lilliput and Brobdingnag. Here in Brobdingnag, Gulliver is six inches, although a giant in Lilliput. "There is no doubt," says Augustine, "that,"

> according to the Hebrew and Christian canonical Scriptures, there were many giants before the deluge, and that these were citizens of the earthly society of men, and the sons of God, who were according to the flesh, sons of Seth ... they forsook righteousness ... and it pleased the Creator to produce them, that it might be demonstrated that neither beauty, not yet size and strength, are of much moment to the wise man, whose blessedness lies in spiritual and immortal blessings, in far better and more enduring gifts, in the good things that are the peculiar property of the good, and are not shared by good and bad alike.[14]

In other words, sense perception, by which beauty, strength, and size are discerned and shared by good and bad alike, is inferior and fallible.

3. "Flagitious and Facinorous Acts" 99

Keeping to the frame pattern, the first part, Lilliput, framed by Bonaventure's first light, the external light, the second part, Brobdingnag, is framed by Bonaventure's second light, sense perception, the lower light:

> The second light, which enables us to discern "natural forms," is the light of "sense perception." Rightly is it called the "lower" light because sense perception begins with a material object and takes place by the aid of corporeal light. It has five divisions corresponding to the five senses.[15]

Swift introduces his projection of the fallibility of the five senses, with a prefigurative identification of Gulliver, as "having been condemned," with Dante the pilgrim in hell, based on Bernard's doctrine of sense perception. Swift follows Dante in retracing his art to the theology of Bernard (Bonaventure's *De Reductione Artium Ad Theologiam*). He is also attacking Aristotle's philosophy of empiricism as Curiosity, "feeding the kids, the eyes and ears, which signify sin; for just as death enters into the world by sin, so by these windows it enters into the mind."[16] One of the reasons he identifies Gulliver with Dante the pilgrim is that, like Dante, Gulliver has "lost the straight way,"[17] so, like Dante, his perceptions are fallible: they see but do not perceive; they hear but do not understand. Their perceptions are indicative of their spiritual condition. But the pivotal difference between the two is that Dante makes spiritual progress, as we know from *Paradiso*. Gulliver makes no spiritual progress, and does nothing to aid spiritual progress.

Swift emphasizes the fallacy of sense perception by calling attention to the similarity between Gulliver's sense perceptions and pilgrim Dante's in the pit of hell, again prefiguratively identifying Gulliver's "having been condemned," with hell. Both Dante and Gulliver come upon giants unexpectedly. When Gulliver *sees* a giant like the one chasing his shipmates, he says: "He appeared as tall as an ordinary spire-steeple." When Dante *sees* giants, he says: "I seemed to see many lofty towers."[18] Virgil's response to Dante applies to both descriptions, a spire-steeple and lofty towers not being dissimilar:

> It is because you pierce the darkness from too far off that you stray in your imagining; and when you reach the place you will see plainly how much the sense is deceived by distance; therefore, spur yourself on somewhat more.... Before we go further forward, in order that the fact may seem less strange to you, know that these are not towers, but giants....[19]

Gulliver and Dante both react in fear. Gulliver says: "I was struck with the utmost fear and astonishment...." Dante says:

> As when a mist is vanishing, the sight little by little shapes out that which the vapor hides that fills the air; so, as I pierced the thick and murky atmosphere and came on nearer and nearer to the brink, error fled from me and fear grew upon me....[20]

The sense of hearing is next exposed. Speaking of the same giant, Gulliver says:

> I heard him call in a voice many degrees louder than a speaking-trumpet; but the noise was so high in the air, that at first I certainly thought it was thunder. Whereupon seven monsters like himself came towards him with reaping-hooks in their hands ... [69].

"Speaking-trumpet" and "high in the air" are allusions to Roland's trumpet; "thunder" is an allusion to Dante's description of it (the seven monsters refer to the seven giants Dante sees around the pit):

> I heard a blast from a horn so loud that it would have made a thunderclap seem faint, and it directed my eyes, following back on its course, wholly to one place. After the dolorous rout when Charlemagne lost the holy gest, Roland did not sound a blast so terrible.[21]

Dante is referring to the destruction of Charlemagne's rear-guard led by Roland. Roland put the horn to his lips; he gripped it firmly and blew with all his strength. The mountains are high and the horn's note carries far; a full thirty leagues away its prolonged note is heard.[22]

> ... he blew on his ivory horn with such force that it was split down the middle, and the veins and nerves of his neck were said to have burst.[23]

Swift also alludes to Roland to expose his pride and his anonymous author's racism, in projecting black people as "cursed" and "vile":

> And Ethiope, a land accursed and vile.
> In his command are all the Negro tribes;
> Thick are their noses, their ears are very wide;
> ... When Roland looks on these accursed tribesmen —
> As black as ink from head to foot their hides are,
> With nothing white about them but their grinders —[24]

The fallibility of the sense of hearing is emphasized by allusions to Nimrod, and to the mistaking of the voice of Nimrod for Roland's trumpet. Gulliver says of the giant farmer:

> He spoke often to me, but the sound of his voice pierced my ears like that of a watermill, yet his words were articulate enough. I answered as loud as I could, in several languages, and he often laid his ear within two yards of me, but all in vain, for we were wholly unintelligible to each other [72].

Upon approaching Nimrod, Virgil says to Dante:

> ... this is Nimrod, through whose ill thought one sole language is not used in the world. Let us leave him alone and not speak in vain, for every language is to him as his is to others, which is known to none.[25]

The allusion in both examples it to Scripture, to Nimrod's being responsible for the confusion of tongues at Babel, and to the Lord's punishment: "that they may not understand one another's speech. So the Lord scattered them abroad from thence upon the face of all the earth" (Gen. 11:7–9).

But, again, Swift has another reason for alluding to Nimrod, and that is his protest of white supremacy and the African slave trade, for Nimrod made men, not beasts, his prey. Swift says, for example:

> The Scripture mentioneth no particular acts of royalty in Adam over his posterity, who were contemporty with him, or of any monarch until after the flood; where the first was Nimrod, the mighty hunter, who, as Milton expresseth it, made men, and not beasts his prey. For men were easier caught by promises, and subdued by the folly or treachery of their own species. Whereas brutes prevailed only by their courage or strength, which among them are peculiar to certain kinds: Lions, bears, elephants and some other animals are strong or valiant, and their species never degenerate in their native soil, except they happen to be enslaved or destroyed by human fraud: But men degenerate every day, merely by the folly, the perverseness, the avarice, the tyranny, the pride, the treachery, or inhumanity of their own kind.[26]

Swift makes ironic uses of "some other animals," to attack white people's animalization of black people. Swift also uses Nimrod to further allude to Milton's depiction of Bernard's Second Ignorance, and to identify Nimrod with it. And he uses Milton's label, "execrable," for Nimrod, to identify white people with Nimrod, to characterize white people as execrable butchers and to define white supremacy and the African slave trade as the Second Ignorance. In Book XII of *Paradise Lost*, the Angel Michael explains to Adam what is to come after the First Fall, the Fall of Adam:

> Henceforth what is to come I will relate,
> Thou therefore give due audience, and attend.
> This second source of Men, while yet but few,
> And while the dread of judgment past remains
> Fresh in their minds, fearing the Deity,
> With some regard to what is just and right
> Shall lead their lives, and multiply apace,
> Laboring the soil, and reaping plenteous crop,
> Corn, wine and oil; and from the herd or flock,
> Oft sacrificing Bullock, Lamb, or Kid,
> With large Wine-offerings pour'd and sacred Feast,
> Shall spend thir days in joy unblam'd, and dwell
> Long time in peace by Families and Tribes
> Under paternal rule; till one shall rise
> Of proud ambitious heart, who not content
> With fair equality, fraternal state,
> Will arrogate Dominion undeserv'd
> Over his brethren, and quite dispossess

> Concord and law of Nature from the Earth;
> Hunting (and Men and not Beasts shall be his game)
> With war and hostile snare such as refuse
> Subjection to his Empire tyrannous:
> A mighty Hunter thence he shall be styl'd
> Before the Lord, as in despite of Heav'n.
> Or from Heav'n claiming second Sovranty;
> And from Rebellion shall derive his name,
> Though of Rebellion others he accuse.
>
> Whereto thus Adam fatherly displeas'd.
> O execrable Son so to aspire
> Above his Brethren, to himself assuming
> Authority usurpt, from God not giv'n:
> He gave us only over Beast, Fish, Fowl
> Dominion absolute; but man over men
> He made not Lord; such title to himself
> Reserving, human left from human free.²⁷

"Execrable" identifies white people with Nimrod, and characterizes white people as execrable butchers, in Swift's attack on colonialism:

> ... this execrable crew of butchers employed in so pious an expedition, is a modern colony sent to convert and civilize an idolatrous and barbarous people.

Dante's seven giants are alluded to by the seven monsters that came forth at the second of the monster farmer's voice through which Swift alludes to Nimrod, the first of Dante's giants. The next is "far more savage and bigger":

> Who had been the master to bind him I do not know, but he had his right arm shackled behind, and the other in front, by a chain which held clasped from the neck downward.... This proud one chose to try his strength against supreme Jove, said [Virgil], wherefore he has such requital. Ephialtes he is called, and he made the great endeavors when the giants put the gods in fear. The arms he plied he moves no more.... Never did mighty earthquake shake a tower so violently as Ephialtes forthwith shook himself. Then more than ever did I fear death, and nothing else was wanted for it but the fear, had I not seen his bonds.²⁸

Gulliver also has an earthshaking experience, caused by monster reapers (grim reaper?) that makes him wish for death:

> I heard reapers not above an hundred yards behind me. Being quite dispirited with toil, and wholly overcome by grief and despair, I ... heartily wished I might there end my days.

Gulliver's death wish absurdly turns to pride, and identifies him with a giant who is easily flattered by the prospect of fame on earth. Gulliver says, for example:

> In this terrible agitation of mind I could not forbear thinking of Lilliput, whose inhabitants looked upon me as the greatest prodigy that ever appeared in the world: where I was able to draw an imperial fleet in my hand, and perform those other actions which will be recorded for ever in the chronicles of that empire, while posterity shall hardly believe them, although attested by millions.

Virgil and Dante come to the giant Antaeus. Virgil asks him to "set us down below-and disdain not to do so," and then makes him an offer he can't refuse. Referring to Dante, he says: "this man can give of that which is longed for here.... He can yet restore your fame on earth...." Virgil first flatters him with the highest praise, saying: "...had you been at the high war of your brothers [against the gods], it seems that some still believe the sons of earth would have conquered." Antaeus "stretched out those hands of which Hercules once felt the mighty grip," and of Dante and Virgil "made one bundle." Dante says:

> I watched to see him stoop — and it was such a moment that I should have wished to go by another road: But he set us down gently on the bottom ... nor did he linger there thus bent, but raised himself like the mast of a ship.[29]

Gulliver similarly felt a mighty grip. Speaking of one of the reapers who spied him hiding in the corn, Gulliver says:

> At length he ventured to take me up behind by the middle between his forefinger and thumb ... he held me in the air above sixty foot from the ground ... he grievously pinched my sides, for fear I should slip through his fingers.... He then placed me softly on the ground [71].

Swift's allusion to Antaeus thusly through Dante is significant as indicative of his protest of the African slave trade. The birthplace of Antaeus being Africa, his parents being Earth and Neptune, and Dante's ship simile make Antaeus a giant-size symbol for Swift's protest, especially considering the historical fact that African slaves often "flung themselves on the beach, clutching handfuls of sand in a desperate effort to remain in contact with their native soil,"[30] their Mother Earth, Africa, where they never degenerate, except they happen to be enslaved or destroyed by the fraud of white people:

> Antaeus, the son of Neptune and Earth, was a mighty giant and wrestler of Libya, invincible as long as he remained in contact with his mother, Earth. Hercules discovered the source of his strength, lifted him from the ground, and crushed him while he held him so.[31]

Gulliver and Dante philosophize about the size of giants but come to different conclusions. Gulliver says, for example:

> ... as human creatures are observed to be more savage and cruel in proportion to their bulk, what could I expect but to be a morsel in the mouth of the first among these enormous barbarians who should happen to seize me? [70].

Dante's conclusion is one of the main points of the *Travels*, especially of the climax, and leading up to it:

> Nature assuredly, when she gave up the art of making creatures such as these, did right well to deprive Mars of such executors; and though she repents not of elephants and whales, he who looks subtly holds her therein more just and more discreet, for where the instrument of the mind is added to an evil will and to great power, men can make no defense against it.[32]

Or, as Swift had Gulliver say, with self-betraying irony: "Honesty hath no fence against superior cunning." Implicitly and demonstrably, Swift defines "white superiority" and "white supremacy," as "superior cunning," the combination of rationalism, an evil will, and great power. He emphatically states in one of his sermons: "Great abilities, without the fear of God, are most dangerous instruments, when they are trusted with power."[33]

In identifying Gulliver's monsters with Dante's giants in hell, Swift is identifying them with white supremacy via Bernard's Satan, who "turned toward the north in an unnatural course," aspiring to be equal to God, so that, "just as the most High, by his wisdom and goodness, was lord of all the children of obedience," Satan became "king over all the children of pride, ruling them by his cunning malice and malicious cunning, and in that way is like the most High."[34] Like Satan, all of the African slave ships took an "unnatural course." Regardless of difference in size, the monster Gulliver and the monster farmer are white supremacists, and thus most symbolic of Satan. The farmer treats Gulliver like white-everyman-Gulliver treats black people. And Swift, attacking Aristotle's philosophy of empiricism, demonstrates the great degree to which scientific sense perception, seeing others as scientific curiosities, is responsible for such treatment, and the insensitivity it produces.

The size differentials are designed to emphasize this fact. For example, the monster farmer takes Gulliver to show to his wife at home; "but she screamed and ran back as women in England do at the sight of a toad or a spider." However, "she was soon reconciled, and by degrees grew extremely tender of [Gulliver]." One of the best examples of insensitive scientific sense perception is Gulliver's description of her breast, as she nurses her baby:

> I must confess no object ever disgusted me so much as the sight of her monstrous breast, which I cannot tell what to compare with, so as to give the curious reader an idea of its bulk, shape and colour. It stood prominent six foot, and could not be less than sixteen in circumference. The nipple was about half the bigness of my head, and the hue both of that and the dug so varified with spots, pimples and freckles, that nothing could appear more nauseous: for I

3. "Flagitious and Facinorous Acts" 105

had a near sight of her, she sitting down the more conveniently to give suck and I standing on the table. This made me reflect upon the fair skin of our English ladies, who appear so beautiful to us, only because they are of our own size, and defects not to be seen but through a magnifying glass, where we find by experiment that the smoothest and whitest skins look rough and coarse, and ill coloured [74].

But that's just the point Swift is making; we're not supposed to look at another as if he or she were an experiment or specimen in a laboratory. As Bernard teaches: "sense-perception reveals corporeal objects not as they are in themselves but as they appear to our sensitivity."[35] That's why "we can know our neighbor only by love"[36] (Bernard). "If distortions and lack of correspondence in the speculum" of nature occur, it is not that there are distortions in creation, but rather in the attitude of the observer. Only the soul mirror which is able to subject itself to the will of Christ will be free of distortion,"[37] which, again, is why we can know our neighbors only by love.

In keeping with the dictates of Bonaventure's second light, the light of sense perception, the lower light, which illumines in regard to "natural form," Swift, by allusion to Bernard, creates a context for the multitude of natural forms he parades through Part II of *Gulliver's Travels*. They are, according to Bernard, "rays emanating from the Godhead, showing that he from whom they come truly is ... though not seeing him but what comes from him, you are made aware beyond all doubt that he exists, and that you must seek him."[38]

Swift depicts six inch Gulliver as seeing himself as one of "these countless creatures," but *not* seeing himself as a ray emanating from the Godhead, not being aware that God exists not that he must seek Him. For example, before being taken home by the farmer, and fearing being squashed to death under his foot, Gulliver compares himself to "a small dangerous animal such as a weasel in England," and says, "my good fortune" (not God) gave me so much presence of mind, that I resolved not to struggle in the least as he held me in the air above sixty foot from the ground....":

> All I ventured was to raise my eyes toward the sun, [not the Son] and place my hands together in a supplicating posture, and to speak some words in an humble melancholy tone, suitable to the condition I then was in [71].

"For," he says, "I apprehended every moment that he would dash me against the ground, as we usually do any little hateful animal which we have a mind to destroy."

> But my good star [not God] would have it, that he appeared pleased with my voice and gestures, and began to look upon me as a curiosity ... [not as a ray emanating from the Godhead] [71].

Every person and creature in Part II is looked upon as a "curiosity," not as a ray emanating from God, nor as a way of seeing God, which is the point of Swift's satiric emphasis in Part II. Perhaps the best, although the most repulsive example, exposing the close connection between curiosity and hatred, is Gulliver's attitude and reaction to the rats, which are behaving according to their nature, which ironically coincides with Gulliver's behaving according to "some natural necessities." He "ripped up the belly of one rat," and "with a strong slash across the neck he thoroughly dispatched" the other, and then "hid himself between two leaves of sorrel, and there discharged the necessities of nature." This too-candid gruesome description, in the unnecessary telling, calls attention to white people's unlimited thoughts, which should be limited thoughts, for the necessities of the body, indicating the thinking faculty of the soul, the Memory, is in the state of spiritual death. "In the state of spiritual life the memory is devoted to thoughts of God." The rats do not make Gulliver aware that God exists and that he should seek Him.[39]

The farmer, whom Gulliver calls "my master," fits Bernard's description of "carnal men," in being one who "investigates people as things to be used."[40] The farmer spread it about the neighbourhood that he "had found a strange animal in the field":

> but exactly shaped in every part like a human creature; which it likewise imitated in all its actions; seemed to speak in a little language of its own, had already learned several words of theirs, went erect upon two legs, was tame and gentle, would come when it was called, do whatever it was bid, had the finest limbs in the world, and a complexion fairer than a nobleman's daughter of three years old [77].

This is how Gulliver sees black people; as animals to be used by African slave traders. This way of seeing human beings, exposes the consequences of Aristotle's system of knowledge of starting with the external world and sense perception, which is why it is a foundation Swift is digging up. It is the reason for his emphasis upon Curiosity, the First Step of Pride, the first step of the path that leads away from truth (God).

Ironically prefiguring his own end, Gulliver commits Foolish Mirth, the Third Step of Pride, at the expense of one of his master's friends who is visiting. Gulliver, putting on a performance, says:

> This man, who was old and dim-sighted, put on his spectacles to behold me better, at which I could not forbear laughing ... for his eyes appeared like the full moon shining into a chamber at two windows. Our people, who discovered the cause of my *mirth*, bore me company in laughing, at which the old fellow was *fool* enough to be angry and out of countenance [77–78].

But it is Gulliver who is the fool. This old man gave Gulliver's master the idea of "showing Gulliver as a sight upon a market-day in the next town," so that "The heart of fools is in the house of mirth," ominously applies to Gulliver.

On Gulliver's first market-day trip, Swift has him obtusely identify himself with African slaves to expose his alarming insensitivity and lack of empathy. Gulliver travels to market lying in a box which "was close on every side, with a little door for him to go in and out, and a few gimlet-holes to let in air," suggestive of a slave's space in the hold of an African slave ship. He says:

> I was terribly shaken and discomposed in this journey ... for the horse went about forty foot at each step, and trotted so high, that the agitation was equal to the rising and falling of a ship in a great storm, but much more frequent.

He is shown again and again. The farmer, "finding how profitable Gulliver was like to be, resolved to carry him to all the towns and most considerable cities of the kingdom and all of the towns by the way, "and to step out of the road for fifty or an hundred miles, to any village or person of quality's house where he might expect custom." This goes on for ten weeks, and Gulliver is shown in eighteen large towns, besides many villages and to private families. He is shown "ten times a day." He tells the reader:

> The frequent labours I underwent every day made in a few weeks a very considerable change in my health.... I had quite lost my stomach, and was almost reduced to a skeleton. The farmer observed it, and concluding I soon must die, resolved to make as good a hand of me as he could.

He is commanded "to bring Gulliver immediately thither for the diversion of the Queen and her ladies." The Queen asks Gulliver whether he would be content to live at court. In response to the Queen, regardless of the very words he speaks, howbeit obtusely, he does not identify with African slaves. In not seeing himself in the farmer or in the African slave, he exposes his ignorance of the First Step of Truth, Knowing Yourself, and of the Second Step of Truth, Knowing Your Neighbor. He answers the Queen:

> I bowed down to the board of the table, and humbly answered that I was my master's slave, but if I were at my own disposal, I should be proud to devote my life to her Majesty's service.

Moreover, it should also have been déja vu to African slave trader Gulliver, when the Queen asks Gulliver's master "whether he were willing to sell Gulliver at a good price." And, as African slave traders like Gulliver were known to do, the farmer, "apprehending that Gulliver could not live a month, was ready enough to part with him, and demanded a thousand pieces of gold, which were ordered him on the spot." When the Queen observed Gulliver's coldness toward the farmer and asked the reason, Gulliver's answer could be understood as echoing the feelings of an African slave:

> I made bold to tell her Majesty that I owed no other obligation to my late master, than his not dashing out the brains of a poor harmless creature found by chance in his field; which obligation was amply recompensed by the gain he had made in showing me through half the kingdom, and the price he had now sold me for. That the life I had led was laborious enough to kill an animal of ten times my strength.

The Queen takes Gulliver to meet the King. From Gulliver's initial description of him, we are immediately made to know the cause of white people's ignorance of the Three Steps of Truth: knowledge of self, of others, of God; and the cause of white supremacy and the African slave trade, the oppression, dispossession, menticide and genocide of black people:

> The King, although he be as learned a person as any in his dominions, had been educated in the study of philosophy, and particularly mathematics.

His perceptions of Gulliver are those of a philosopher: "Philosophers, filled with vanity, investigate the arrangement and order of things, in order to gratify their scientific curiosity" (Bernard). Gulliver says, for example:

> ... when he observed my shape exactly, and saw me walk erect, before I began to speak, conceived I might be a piece of clock-work (which is in that country arrived to a very great perfection), contrived by some ingenious artist. But, when he heard my voice, and found what I delivered to be regular and rational, he could not conceal his astonishment.

Swift is here satirizing Deism, with its doctrine of God as divine Clockmaker, including the fact that a clock, once started, runs its own independent mechanical course (Boyle). In other words, God is inactive, and the world is a perfect machine, "autonomous and self-sufficient."

The King continues to satisfy his scientific curiosity:

> His Majesty sent for three great scholars who were then in their weekly waiting (according to the custom in that country). These gentlemen, after they had a while examined my shape with much nicety, were of different opinions concerning me. They all agreed that I could not be produced according to the regular laws of nature.... After much debate, they concluded unanimously that I was only "relplum scalcath," which is interpreted literally, "lusus naturae;" ["freak of nature"] [Landa].

Swift is also satirizing Plato's "philosopher-king":

> Until philosophers are kings, or the kings and princes of this world have the spirit and power of philosophy, and political greatness and wisdom meet in

one, and those commoner natures who pursue either to the exclusion of the other are compelled to stand aside, cities will never have rest from their evils, — no, nor the human race, as I believe, — and then only will this our state have a possibility of life and behold the light of day."[41]

According to Swift, however, "whoever could restore brotherly love in any degree among men, would be an instrument of more good to human society, than ever was, or will be done by all the statesmen and politicians [including philosophers] in the world."[42] He applies an obvious Scriptural protest to his protest of the African slave trade, and combines it with an indictment of governments which sponsor, encourage, and legalize the African slave trade, when they have the authority and power to abolish it. Clues come in the form of some of the variety of creatures that pester Gulliver, such as flies, wasps, lice, frogs, hailstones. Projecting African slaves as "God's people," he applies God's command to Pharoah to "Let my people go," to European and American governments, to let African slaves go free, to abolish the African slave trade. God sends plagues of flies, frogs, lice, hail, locusts, to punish Pharoah for not letting God's people go. With each plague, Pharoah promises to let God's people go if God will stop the plague, but Pharoah refuses once each plague is stopped. The analogy is lost on Christian governments, as Gulliver demonstrates.

Swift's fierce condemnation of scientific curiosity as a way of Knowing Your Neighbor is emphasized by his projection of the profound depth of arrogant insensitivity scientific curiosity affords and inspires, the size differentials being no exaggeration. On a day Gulliver is out to see the town, for example, the coachman is ordered to stop at several shops, "where the beggars, watching their opportunity, crowded to the sides of the coach, and," said Gulliver, "gave me the most horrible spectacles that ever a European eye beheld." "Spectacles" is the first arrogant insensitive insult:

> There was a woman with a cancer in her breast, swelled to a monstrous size, full of holes, in two or three of which I could have easily crept, and covered my whole body. There was a fellow with a wen in his neck, larger than five woolpacks, and another with a couple of wooden legs, each about twenty foot high. But the most hateful sight of all was the lice crawling on their clothes. I could see distinctly the limbs of those vermin with my naked eye, much better than those of an European louse through a microscope, and their snouts with which they rooted like swine.

His analogies are outrageously insensitive. His nurse is prevailed upon to see an execution, which, he says, was "very much against her inclination, for she was naturally tender-hearted: and as for myself, although I abhorred such kind of spectacles, yet my curiosity tempted me to see something that I thought must be extraordinary":

> The malefactor was fixed in a chair upon a scaffold erected for the purpose, and his head cut off at one blow with a sword of about forty foot long. The veins and arteries spouted up such a prodigious quantity of blood, and so high in the air, that the great "jet d'eau" at Versailles was not equal for the time it lasted; and the head, when it fell on the scaffold floor, gave such a bounce as made me start, although I was at least an English mile distant.

In another comparison, Swift exposes Gulliver's lack of religious sensibility. Gulliver says:

> I was very desirous to see the chief temple, and particularly the tower belonging to it, which is reckoned the highest in the kingdom. Accordingly one day my nurse carried me thither, but I may truly say I came back disappointed; for the height ... is no great matter for admiration, nor at all equal in proportion ... to Salisbury steeple ... it must be allowed that whatever this famous tower wants in height is amply made up in beauty and strength.

This is a direct allusion to Augustine's statement quoted earlier:

> ... neither beauty, nor yet size and strength, are of much moment to the wise man, whose blessedness lies in spiritual and immortal blessings, in far better and more enduring gifts, in the good things that are the peculiar property of the good, and are not shared by good and bad alike.[43]

Obviously, "beauty, size, and strength" *are* of much moment to Gulliver, and he is oblivious to "the good things that are the peculiar property of the good," such as "Sarum," the order of divine service used in Salisbury Cathedral from the eleventh century to the Reformation, for which it is famous, and which is not shared by good and bad alike.

Swift depicts an example that is a perversion of Augustine's statement in being characteristic of seeing others as slaves. It reflects Bernard's statement that "Carnal men filled with sensuality, investigate things themselves, in order to use them."[44] Aspects of sense perception are dealt with that haven't been dealt with before, but are not unlike scientific curiosity, in that "Knowing Your Neighbor" becomes using him/her "like a creature who had no sort of consequence." In both kinds of perceptions, love has nothing to do with it. Humanness has nothing to do with it!

The maids of honor often invited Gulliver's nurse to their apartments, and desired she would bring Gulliver along with her, "on purpose to have the pleasure of *seeing* and *touching* [him]." Gulliver relates his experience to the reader:

> They would often strip me naked from top to toe, and lay me at full length in their bosoms; wherewith I was much disgusted; because to say the truth, a very offensive smell came from their skins; which I do not mention or intend to the disadvantage of those excellent ladies, for whom I have all manner of respect; but I conceive that my sense was more acute in proportion to my littleness, and

3. "Flagitious and Facinorous Acts" 111

that those illustrious perons were no more disagreeable to their lovers, or to each other, than people of the same quality are with us in England.

In the latter comparison regarding "quality," skin odor, like skin color, Swift is saying, is shared by good and bad alike, and that by which "quality" is determined is shared by good and bad alike (obviously, since the "maids of honor" are not honorable), as is beauty, size, and strength." In other words, what is distinguishable by sense perception is of no moment to the wise man. As a white supremacist, Gulliver is not a wise man, to say the least. But Swift is also, through "my sense was more accute in proportion to my littleness," alluding to Bonaventure's definition of "proportion":

> The senses take delight in an object perceived through an abstracted likeness either because of its beauty, as in sight, or because of its sweetness, as in smell and hearing, or because of its wholesomeness, as in taste or touch, if we speak by way of appropriation. Now, all enjoyment is based on proportion.... When we ask the reason why a thing is beautiful or pleasant or wholesome, we find that the reason lies in the proportion of harmony. The basis of harmony is the same in large and small objects; neither is it increased by size nor does it change or pass away as things pass away, nor is it altered by motion. It abstracts, therefore, from place, time and motion, and consequently is unchangeable, unlimited, endless and is completely spiritual ... the whole world can enter into the human soul through the doors of the senses.... All these are vestiges in which we can see our God.... If all things that can be known generate a likeness of themselves, they manifestly proclaim that in them as in mirrors we can see the eternal generation of the Word, the Image and Son, eternally emanating from God the Father.
> In this way the species which delights as beautiful, pleasant and wholesome suggests that there is primordial beauty, pleasure and wholesomeness in that first Species, in which there is supreme proportion and equality with the generating Source.... If, therefore, "pleasure is the union of the harmonious with the harmonious," and if the Likeness of God alone contains in the highest degree the notion of beauty, delight and wholesomeness and if it is united in truth and intimacy and in a fulness that fulfills every capacity, it is obvious that in God alone there is primordial and true delight and that in all of our delights we are led to seek this delight.[45]

With this allusion to Bonaventure, and with the depiction of the "countless species of creatures," Swift is saying: "though not seeing God himself but what comes from him, you are made aware beyond all doubt that he exists, and that you must seek him."[46]

This is not possible to those who see other human beings as "things" of no consequence, to be used. Gulliver complains of this, although it is the way he sees black people:

> That which gave me most uneasiness among these maids of honour, when my nurse carried me to visit them, was to see them use me without any manner of ceremony, like a creature who had no sort of consequence. For they would

strip themselves to the skin, and put on their smocks in my presence, while I was place on their toilet directly before their naked bodies, which, I am sure, to me was very far from being a tempting sight, or from giving me any other emotions than those of horror and disgust. Their skins appeared so coarse and uneven, so variously coloured, when I saw them near, with a mole here and there as broad as a trencher, and hairs hanging from it thicker than packthreads; to say nothing further concerning the rest of their persons. Neither did they at all scruple while I was by to discharge what they had drunk, to the quantity of at least two hogsheads, in a vessel that held above three tuns. The handsomest among these maids of honour, a pleasant frolicsome girl of sixteen, would sometimes set me astride upon one of her nipples, with many other tricks, wherein the reader will excuse me for not being overly particular.

Swift is adamant there is nothing spiritual here, no way of seeing God. He alludes to Scripture: "For to be carnally minded is death; but to be spiritually minded is life and peace":

Because the carnal mind is enmity against God for it is not subject to the law of God, neither indeed can it be. So then they that are in the flesh cannot please God ... if ye live after the flesh, ye shall die: but if ye through the Spirit do mortify the deeds of the body, ye shall live [Rom. 8].

Gulliver goes on to tell the reader of his encounter with at least two of the countless species of creatures depicted to make white people "aware beyond all doubt that God exists, and that they must seek him." As a reminder of the plague of frogs the Lord visited upon the Egyptians because Pharoah would not let God's people go, Gulliver is pestered by a huge frog who "daubed Gulliver's face and clothes with its odious slime." Gulliver's next encounter is with a monkey, which he says caused the greatest danger he ever underwent in that kingdom. There's irony embedded in this encounter because the monkey takes Gulliver to be of its species, and in Part IV, racist Gulliver sees black people as monkeys to demonstrate that black people are not of the same species as white people. When Gulliver finally recovers after being rescued, he presumes to be boastful (the Fourth Step of Pride), bragging to the King about what he would have done to the monkey if he'd had his hanger. This he delivers in a "firm tone, like a person who was jealous lest his courage should be called in question." Loud laughter ensues. In presumptuous response he says:

This made me reflect how vain an attempt it is for a man to endeavour doing himself honour among those who are out of all degree of equality or comparison with him. And yet I have seen the moral of my own behaviour very frequent in England since my return, where a little contemptible varlet, without the least title to birth, person, wit, or common sense, shall presume to look with importance, and put himself upon a foot with the greatest persons of the kingdom [99–100].

To put this in proper perspective, Swift alludes to Bernard, who warns:

> Beware of comparing yourself with your betters or your inferiors, with a particular few or with even one. For how do you know but that this one person, whom you perhaps regard as the vilest and most wretched of all, whose life you recoil from and spurn as more befouled and wicked, not merely than yours, for you trust you are a sober-living man and just and religious, but even than all other wicked men; how do you know, I say, but that in time to come, with the aid of the right hand of the Most High, he will not surpass both you and them if he has not done so already in God's sight?[46]

And, to warn that "Pride [implicitly white supremacy] goeth before a fall," he has Gulliver relate the following:

> I went out ... to walk. There was a cow-dung in the path, and I must needs try my activity by attempting to leap over it. I took a run, but unfortunately jumped short, and found my self just in the middle up to my knees. I waded through with some difficulty, and one of the footmen wiped me as clean as he could with his handkerchief; for I was filthily bemired [100].

The King of Brobdingnag desires an account of the government of England.

The overarching arrogance of white supremacy is rendered absurdly ridiculous by Swift in his depiction of it in a six inch white man. Gulliver's outrageous beginning sets the tone. His choice of orators to emulate makes a mockery of his arrogance. Demosthenes, although the most famous of Greek orators, spoke in opposition to rather than in praise of his country; and Cicero, the greatest Roman orator, died for his loyalty to his ideal of liberty, hardly the ideal of an African slave trader. He begins:

> Imagine with thy self, courteous reader, how often I then wished for the tongue of Demosthenes or Cicero, that might have enabled me to celebrate the praise of my own dear native country in a style equal to its merits and felicity [102].

One of the first specifics of which he boasts is "our plantations in America." Expounding on parliament, religion, law, etc., he finishes with "a brief historical account of affairs and events in England for about an hundred years past," not, of course, mentioning the African slave trade, although during those hundred years past, 2,750,000 African slaves were shipped from all parts of Guinea to the New World, which included "our plantations in America." The King listens intently and asks numerous seriously pertinent questions. His conclusion Gulliver relates to the reader:

> He was perfectly astonished with the historical account I gave him of our affairs during the last century, protesting it was only an heap of conspiracies, rebellions, murders, massacres, revolutions, banishments, the very worst effects that avarice, faction, hypocrisy, perfidiousness, cruelty, rage, madness, hatred, envy, lust, malice, and ambition could produce [106].

All of that could be included in the African slave trade. So the appraisal Swift has the King make of the character of white people, is not a surprise:

> I cannot but conclude the bulk of your natives to be the most pernicious race of little odious vermin that nature ever suffered to crawl upon the surface of the earth.

Gulliver's responses confirm the accuracy of the King's conclusions, and demonstrate the pride taken in the history the King condemns. Moreover, he takes pride in that which is even worse than the King condemns. He says, disingenuously, being a liar, a hypocrite and a fraud:

> I artfully eluded many of his questions, and gave to every point a more favourable turn by many degrees than the strictness of truth would allow. For I have always borne that laudable partiality to my own country, which Dionysius Halicarnassensis with so much justice recommends to an historian. I would hide the frailties and deformities of my political mother, and place her virtues and beauties in the most advantageous light [107].

If I'm not mistaken, Dionysius of Halicarnassus was a Greek who wrote a history of Rome, and the observation he is famous for is that "the style is the man," which, ironically, is here proven true of Gulliver.

In his white supremacist pride, Gulliver is unwilling to admit that anything in his white supremacist culture is not superior, so he makes excused for the King, which is his way of excusing his own sins (the Eighth Step of Pride, Excusing Sins). He says, for example:

> But great allowances should be given to a king who lives wholly secluded from the rest of the world, and must therefore be altogether unacquainted with the manners and customs that most prevail in other nations: the want of which knowledge will ever produce many prejudices, and a certain narrowness of thinking, from which we and the politer countries of Europe are wholly exempted. And it would be hard indeed, if so remote a prince's notions of virtue and vice were to be offered as a standard for all mankind [107–108].

He speaks of the manners and customs of white supremacy in Europe, England, and America. It is the possession of which knowledge — scientific curiosity and carnal curiosity (sense perception), rationalism, law, and politics — upon which white supremacy is based, "that will ever produce many prejudices, and a certain narrowness of thinking," of which white people are most representative and symbolic. This is how Swift would have the reader interpret Gulliver's response to the King. The notion of vice and virtue that Swift is offering as a standard for all mankind is brotherly love. He agrees with Bernard, that, "A soul which does not possess love is without sensitivity."[47] And without sensitivity, you have "the very worst effects that avarice, faction, hypocrisy, perfidiousness, cruelty, rage, madness, hatred, envy, lust, malice, and ambition could produce," the African slave

3. *"Flagitious and Facinorous Acts"* 115

trade. If the African slave trade is not sufficient evidence of insensitivity, Swift offers further proof, which must be read in its entirety to have the intended effect of a preponderance of evidence, with which white people will find it easier to identify than with African slaves. Gulliver continues:

> To confirm what I have now said, and further to show the miserable effects of a confined education, I shall here insert a passage which will hardly obtain belief. In hopes to ingratiate my self farther into his Majesty's favour, I told him of an invention discovered between three and four hundred years ago, to make a certain powder, into an heap of which the smallest spark of fire falling, would kindle the whole in a moment, although it were as big as a mountain, and make it all fly up in the air together, with a noise and agitation greater than thunder. That a proper quantity of this powder rammed into a hollow tube of brass or iron, according to its bigness, would drive a ball of iron or lead with such violence and speed as nothing was able to sustain its force. That the largest balls, thus discharged, would not only destroy whole ranks of an army at once, but batter the strongest wall to the ground, sink down ships, with a thousand men in each, to the bottom of the sea; and when linked together by a chain, would cut through masts and rigging, divide hundreds of bodies in the middle, and lay all waste before them. That we often put this powder into large hollow balls of iron, and discharge them by an engine into some city we were besieging, which would rip up the pavement, tear the houses to pieces, burst and throw splinters on every side, dashing out the brains of all who came near. That I knew the ingredients very well, which were cheap, and common; I understood the manner of compounding them, and could direct his workmen how to make those tubes of a size proportionable to all other things in his Majesty's kingdom, and the largest need not be above two hundred foot long; twenty or thirty of which tubes, charged with the proper quantity of powder and balls, would batter down the walls of the strongest town in his dominions in a few hours, or destroy the whole metropolis, if ever it should pretend to dispute his absolute commands. This I humbly offered to his Majesty as a small tribute of acknowledgment in return of so many marks that I had received of his royal favour and protection [108].

The King's reaction articulates Swift's own reaction to the character of white people as epitomized by the African slave trade:

> The King was struck with horror at the description I had given of those terrible engines, and the proposal I had made. He was amazed how so impotent and groveling an insect as I (these were his expressions) could entertain such inhuman ideas, and in so familiar a manner as to appear wholly unmoved at all the scenes of blood and desolation, which I had painted as the common effects of those destructive machines, whereof he said, some evil genius, enemy to mankind, must have been the first contriver [108–109].

There is no doubt that Swift projects white people as the enemy to mankind, inhuman, wholly unmoved by blood, desolation, and destruction, and identifies them with Milton's Satan, the "Enemy of Mankind," whose "hollow Engines long and round/Thick ramm'd ... with touch of fire/Dilated and infuriate shall send forth/From far with thund'ring noise among our foes/Such implements of mischief as shall dash/To pieces, and o'erwhelm whatever stands/Adverse, that they shall fear we have disarm'd/The Thunderer of his only dreaded bolt."[48] Gulliver reaction to the King's reaction speaks volumes about Aristotle and white supremacy, and about the character of white people, and how sense perception can lead to insensitivity.

With self-betraying irony, Gulliver reveals the truth of the King's conclusions in his reaction (rooted in Aristotle), to them:

> A strange effect of narrow principles and short views! that a prince possessed of every quality which procures veneration, love, and esteem; of strong parts, great wisdom and profound learning, endued with admirable talents for government, and almost adored by his subjects, should from a nice unnecessary scruple, whereof in Europe we can have no conception, let slip an opportunity put into his hands, that would have made him absolute master of the lives, the liberties, and the fortunes of his people. Neither do I say this with the least intention to detract from the many virtues of that excellent king, whose character I an sensible will on this account be very much lessened in the opinion of the English reader: but I take this defect among them to have risen from their ignorance, by not having hitherto reduced politics into a science, as the more acute wits of Europe have done [109].

It is attributable to their wisdom, not reducing politics into a science, Swift is saying. The implication is that, since "politics is nothing but corruptions," (Swift) science made it so, and that the ideal of being absolute master of the lives, the liberties, and the fortunes of a people, as exemplified by the African slave trade, is a defect, which rose from the ignorance of Aristotle, as did politics and science. When Dante had lost the straight way, his perception from hell was that Aristotle was master of those who know. It was a hellish perspective.

Gulliver's insensitivity becomes obvious as he speaks of "a strong impulse that [he] should sometime recover [his] liberty," without ever giving a thought as to how many and how often African slaves have the same impulse. He sees no similarity between the King's proposal for him, and the breeding of African slaves, or that being an African slave "ill becomes the dignity of human kind":

> The King was strongly bent to get me a woman of my own size, by whom I might propagate the breed: but I think I should rather have died than undergone the disgrace of leaving a posterity to be kept in cages like tame canary birds, and perhaps in time sold about the kingdom to persons of quality for curiosities. I was indeed treated with much kindness; I was the favourite of a great king and queen, and the delight of the whole court, but it was upon such a foot as ill become the dignity of human kind [112].

The King looks at Gulliver with the same carnal and scientific curiosity that Gulliver (white people) looks at African slaves.

But Gulliver says, "My deliverance came sooner than I expected, and in a manner not very common." He attends the King and Queen to the south coast of the kingdom in his travelling-box. He longs to see the ocean, which, he says, "must be the only scene of my escape, if ever it should happen." A page takes Gulliver down to the shore in his box, where Gulliver lifts up one of his sashes, and "casts many a wistful melancholy look toward the sea." Not feeling very well, he decides to take a nap. He shuts the window "close down" and falls asleep, assuming his guard, the page, has gone among the rocks looking for birds' eggs, having found one or two "in the clefts." What happens next is the not very common manner of Gulliver's deliverance. He says:

> I found my self suddenly awaked with a violent pull upon the ring which was fastened at the top of my box for the conveniency of carriage. I felt the box raised very high in the air, and then borne forward with prodigious speed. I called out several times as loud as I could raise my voice, but all to no purpose. I looked towards my windows, and could see nothing but the clouds and sky. I heard a noise just over my head like the clapping of wings, and then began to perceive the woeful condition I was in; that some eagle had got the ring of my box in his beak, with an intent to let it fall on a rock like a tortoise in a shell, and then pick out my body and devour it. For the sagacity and smell of this bird enable him to discover his quarry at a great distance, although better concealed than I could be within a two-inch board [114].

With the five senses mentioned: *seeing* the clouds and sky; *hearing* the clapping of wings; *tasting*, devouring, Gulliver's body; the eagle's *sense of smell*; and *touching*, picking out Gulliver's body; and Gulliver's "woeful condition"; Swift defiantly proclaims the poverty of the senses compared to faith, simultaneous with alluding to the Second Coming of Christ:

> Wheresoever the body is, thither will the eagles be gathered together [Luke 17:37].

The superiority of faith, as Swift projects it, is articulated by Bernard:

> Faith cannot be deceived. With the power to understand invisible truths, faith does not know the poverty of the senses; it transcends even the limits of human reason, the capacity of nature, the bounds of experience. Why do you ask the eye to do what it's not equipped to do? And why does the hand endeavour to examine things beyond its reach? What you may learn from these senses is of limited value. But faith will tell you of me without detracting from my greatness [Christ].... And yet he could be touched, but by the heart, not by the hand; by desire, not by the eye; by faith, not by the senses.[49]

He concludes by quoting the Apostle Paul:

> What eye has not seen, nor ear heard, nor the heart of man conceived, is borne within itself by faith, as if wrapped in a covering and kept under seal.

Gulliver has no faith, he has only the poverty of the senses, which is why his woeful condition is ominous. He goes on, for example:

> In a little time I observed the noise and flutter of wings to increase very fast, and my box was tossed up and down like a signpost in a windy day. I heard several bangs or buffets, as I thought, given to the eagle (for such I am certain it must have been that held the ring of my box in his beak) and then all on a sudden I felt my self falling perpendicularly down for above a minute, but with such incredible swiftness that I almost lost my breath. My fall was stopped by a terrible squash, that sounded louder to my ears than the cataract of Niagara; after which I was quite in the dark for another minute, and then my box began to rise so high that I could see light from the tops of my windows. I now perceived that I was fallen into the sea. My box, by the weight of my body, the goods that were in it, and the broad plates of iron fixed for strength at the four corners of the top and bottom, floated about five foot deep in water. I did then, and do now suppose that the eagle which flew away with my box was pursued by two or three others, forced to let me drop while he was defending himself against the rest, who hoped to share in the prey [114].

"Prey" reminds us of Nimrod, who made men and not beasts his prey, which reminds us of white supremacy and the African slave trade, while the three eagles remind us of European powers fighting each other for control of the African slave trade, each not wishing to share in the prey of African slaves; and we are reminded of Scripture prefigurative of white-everyman-Gulliver's "woeful condition":

> The pride of thine heart hath deceived thee ... that saith in his heart, Who shall bring me down to the ground? Though thou exalt thyself as the eagle, and though thou set thy nest among the stars, thence will I bring thee down saith the Lord [Obadiah 1:3–4].

Using the irony of self-betrayal, Swift has Gulliver continue to obtusely identify his woeful condition with the woeful condition of the African slaves, which he has witnessed and caused. He thus possesses an alarming lack of feeling, an alarming insensitivity, which Swift holds up as a mirror to white people. Gulliver, for example, ventures to draw back the slip-board on the roof "to let in air, for want of which I found myself almost stifled," he says. What about how often the tightly packed African slaves were almost stifled "in the hold," where "the air becomes too thick and poisonous to breathe."[50] Swift is depicting the Second Step of Truth by exposing its opposite in Gulliver's gross insensitivity. For example, Swift puts Gulliver in a position to learn the African slaves' wants and needs from his own wants and needs, to know from his own miseries how to commiserate with African slaves who are miserable. But we see just the opposite in Gulliver's shocking obtuseness, in his saying:

3. "Flagitious and Facinorous Acts" 119

Perhaps many travellers have not been under greater difficulties and distress that I was at this juncture.

Millions of African slaves were under far greater difficulties and distress,

> expecting every moment to see my box dashed in pieces, or at least overset by the first violent blast, or a rising wave. A breach of one single pane of glass would have been immediate death.... I was not able to lift up the roof of my closet, which otherwise I certainly should have done, and sat on top of it, where I might at least preserve my self from being shut up, as I may call it, "in the hold."

Moreover, he has the death wish, than which there was no greater demonstration than the death wish of African slaves. He says, "I was four hours under these circumstances, expecting and indeed wishing every moment to be my last." What's four hours compared to four months in the hold of a slave ship? What more demonstratively determined death wish than to leap out of a boat or ship into the sea and stay under water till drowned or eaten by sharks; or to refuse all sustenance and wilfully starve to death?

Gulliver has a change of pace, as his box is pulled or towed along in the sea. He feels a tugging which made the waves rise near the tops of his windows, leaving him almost in the dark. In what Gulliver further relates, Swift alludes to Milton to identify white people with Satan, and with the downfall prefigured by the eagles, and symbolized by Satan and the eagles. Swift's eagles' "flutter of wings," and Milton's Satan's "Flutt'ring his pennons," call attention to that double symbol, and to the foreboding pronounced by Christ in the above quoted Scripture. Gulliver says:

> I ventured to unscrew one of my chairs, which were always fastened to the floor; and having made a hard shift to screw it down again directly under the slipping-board that I had lately opened, I mounted on the chair, and putting my mouth as near as I could to the hole, I called for help in a loud voice, and in all the languages I understood.... I found no effect from all I could do ... and in the space of an hour ... the box ... struck against something that was hard. I apprehended it to be a rock, and found my self tossed more than ever.

"Chair" is the key to the allusive identifying of white people with Satan in Milton's following description of Satan:

> As in a cloudy Chair ascending rides
> Audacious, but that seat soon failing, meets
> A vast vacuity: all unawares
> Flutt'ring his pennons vain plumb down he drops
> Ten thousand fadom deep, and to this hour
> Down had been falling, had not by ill chance
> The strong rebuff of some tumultuous cloud
> Instinct with Fire and Nitre hurried him
> As many miles aloft.[51]

As Gulliver continues, Swift makes a powerful indictment of white supremacy and the African slave trade by projecting the African slave ship as Milton's "Throne of Chaos." The thousand questions the sailors ask Gulliver are the "thousand various mouths" of Discord. Gulliver approaches an unknown like Satan approaches an unknown. Gulliver relates his anxiety:

> I plainly heard a noise upon the corner of my closet like that of a cable, and the grating of it as it passed through the ring. I then found myself hoisted up by degrees at least three foot higher than I was before.... I called for help till I was almost hoarse. In return to which, I heard a great shout repeated three times.... I heard a trampling over my head, and somebody calling through the hole with a loud voice in the English tongue. I answered, I was an Englishman ... and begged to be delivered out of the dungeon I was in.... Some of them upon hearing me talk so wildly, thought I was mad; others laughed; for indeed it never came into my head that I was now got among people of my own stature and strength. The sailors ... asked me a thousand questions.

Obviously, there is chaos, tumult, and confusion here, Gulliver's talking "wildly" no accident. Milton's is a good description of the scene:

> At length a universal hubbub wild
> Of stunning sounds and voices all confus'd
> Borne through the hollow dark assaults his ear
> With loudest vehemence: thither he plies
> Undaunted to meet there whatever power
> Or Spirit of the nethermost Abyss
> Might in that noise reside, of whom to ask
> Which way the nearest coast of darkness lies
> Bordering on light; when straight behold the Throne
> Of "Chaos," and his dark Pavilion spread
> Wide on the wasteful Deep; with him Enthron'd
> Sat Sable-vested "Night," eldest of things,
> The Consort of his Reign; and by them stood
> "Orcus" and "Ades," and the dreaded name
> Of "Demogorgon"; "Rumor" next and "Chance,"
> And "Tumult" and "Confusion" all imbroil'd,
> And "Discord" with a thousand various mouths.[52]

In Gulliver's begging to be delivered out of the dungeon he is in, "dungeon" as an allusion to Hell, Satan's dungeon identifies Gulliver's dungeon with the Hell symbolic of the dungeons at Fort St. George at Elmina, West Africa, which held for shipment one thousand African slaves begging to be delivered from the dungeons they are in. Gulliver stayed there three weeks. Satan asks directions of Chaos, who charts his course: "first Hell/Your dungeon stretching far and wide beneath."[53]

Gulliver's statement, "I was equally confounded at the sight of so many pigmies, for such I took them to be, after having so long accustomed my eyes to the monstrous objects I had left (Of course, they were "people" not objects), refers to the crew of the African slave ship, but also to the Lilliputians and the Brobdingnagians, to identify white people and politics with Satan and his peers at Pandaemonium, the high capital of Satan and his peers, where a solemn council was to be held:

> Behold a wonder! they but now who seem'd
> In bigness to surpass Earth's Giant Sons
> Now less than smallest Dwarf's, in narrow room
> Throng numberless, like that Pigmean Race
> Beyond the Indian Mount.[54]

The African slave ship is also identified with the Throne of Chaos in the last thing Chaos tells Satan: "Havoc and spoil and ruin are my gain."[55] Swift has Gulliver use "havoc" in a context that exposes an alarming obtuseness. Nothing is more symbolic of havoc and spoil and ruin for gain than the African slave trade. Gulliver insensitively relates havoc, spoil and ruin to some objects (spoils) he brought from Brobdingnag, upon which the seamen wreak havoc and ruin by greatly damaging them. Completely out of character, Gulliver says:

> I was glad not to have been a spectator of the havoc they made; because I am confident it would have sensibly touched me.

Inasmuch as he is obviously not sensibly touched by the spoils of the trade, the African slaves, he hasn't the capacity to be sensibly touched. Identifying himself as a "spectator" gives him away.

Swift's most profoundly powerful symbol of "the gigantic international operation of supplying, shipping, and disposing of this vast number of human chattels," the African slave trade, is Milton's "Universe of death," to which he alludes. For example, he has the African slave ship captain mention a "monstrous wooden chest" (suggestive of a coffin), which he also refers to as a "cavity" (suggestive of a grave), as in "some unhappy man must be shut up in the cavity." Gulliver asks the captain "whether he of the crew had seen any prodigious birds in the air about the time he was discovered;" Milton uses the words "prodigious" and "monstrous" which Gulliver uses. One of the sailors "said he had observed three eagles flying towards the north...." The "north" is the seat of Satan. Bernard "interprets the "north" to mean sinful men, and "seat," power over them." "Eagles" suggest rocks, caves, and shades of death. ("Wheresoever the body is, thither will the eagles be gathered together.") These are all clues to Swift's allusion to Milton's "Universe of death" as symbolic of the gigantic international African slave trade:

> Rocks, Caves, Lakes, Fens, Bogs, Dens, and shades of death,
> A Universe of death, which God by curse
> Created evil, for evil only good,
> Where all life dies, death lives, and Nature breeds,
> Perverse, all monstrous, all prodigious things,
> Abominable, inutterable, and worse
> Than Fables yet have feign'd, or fear conceiv'd,
> "Gorgons" and "Hydras," and "Chimeras" dire.[56]

To vivify his projection of the African slave trade as a Universe of death, Swift depicts white people as "Perverse, all monstrous, all prodigious things, Abominable, unutterable, and worse than the monsters: Gorgons, Hydras, and Chimeras," as we have seen, and will continue to see, especially in Part IV. And to emphatically identify African slave traders with Satan, Swift alludes to Satan's travels to call attention to white-everyman-Gulliver's travels:

> Meanwhile the Adversary of God and Man,
> "Satan" with thoughts inflam'd of highest design,
> Puts on swift wings, and towards the Gates of Hell
> Explores his solitary flight; sometimes
> He scours the right hand coast, sometimes the left,
> Now shaves with level wing the Deep, then soars
> Up to the fiery conclave tow'ring high.
> As when far off at Sea a Fleet descri'd
> Hangs in the Clouds, by "Equinoctial" Winds
> Close sailing from "Bengala," or the Isles
> Of "Ternare" and "Tidore," whence Merchants bring
> Thir spicy Drugs: they on the Trading Flood
> Through the wide Ethiopian to the Cape
> Ply stemming nightly toward the Pole. So seem'd
> Far off the flying Fiend.[57]

Gulliver says they doubled the Cape of Good Hope, and that "Our voyage was very prosperous, but I shall not trouble the reader with a journal of it." They come into the Downs on the "3rd day of June, 1706, about nine months after [his] escape." In other words, he's been African slave trading for nine months, on top of the four years of African slave trading since he "took shipping in the Downs on the 20th day of June, 1702." In the first Scripture for that date, Esther 9, there is no mention of God. Swift identifies the Jews with white people as being "unmoved at all the scenes of blood and desolation," insensitive, in other words. According to Biblical scholars:

> ... the heathen, paralyzed with fear, did not make an attack and yet were destroyed despite their nonresistance.... Although from a technical standpoint the Jews did not engage in unprovoked aggression, their action was hardly

confined to mere self-defense.... Evidently the Gentile rout turned into a veritable massacre.... Esther requested a second day of slaughter, even though the Jews had already won an overwhelming victory.

One is reminded the ruthlessness of Christopher Columbus and his slaughter of the Indians.

The second Scripture for the June 3rd date describes the punishment of white people for the African slave trade, a punishment we have already seen, but will see in an even more alarming manner in the end. In the Scripture, Mark 4, Jesus tells his disciples the meaning of the parable of the sower, introducing it with the following:

> And he said unto them, Unto you it is given to know the mystery of the kingdom of God. But unto them that are without, all these things are done in parables: That seeing they may see, and not perceive; and hearing they may hear, and not understand; lest at any time they should be converted, and their sins should be forgiven them.

The next Scripture alluded to sums up Part II's theme of the fallibility of sense perception (fleshly wisdom):

> For our rejoicing is this, the testimony of our conscience, that in simplicity and godly sincerity, not with fleshly wisdom, but by the grace of God, we have had our conversation in the world [I Cor. 1].

As Gulliver arrives home, the fallibility of sense perception is related to the great power of habit and prejudice, racism, in other words. He refers to "having been so long uses to stand with my head and eyes erect to above sixty foot,"

> I looked down upon the servants ... as if they had been pigmies, and I a giant.... This I mention as an instance of the great power of habit and prejudice.

The great power of habit and prejudice or habitual prejudice is based on the fact that "visible things are investigated by sense perception, which reveals corporeal objects not as they are in themselves but as they appear to our sensitivity."[58]

Gulliver ends this second part as he began it: claiming necessity instead of his free will. He opens with "insatiable desire" and "condemned by nature and fortune," and closes with: "my evil destiny," not realizing that "Voluntary consent is a self-determining habit of the soul." Gulliver, as white people, does not know himself (which is why Swift holds up the *Travels* as a mirror for white people). Gulliver's blaming necessity proves he does not know himself, and is an ironic contradiction which is an allusion to Satan. In blaming necessity, the implication is that his "evil destiny" is caused by the power of Satan. But, according to Bernard: "It is our own will that enslaves us to the devil, not his power,"⁵⁹ which is Swift's point. Gulliver is just as defiant (the Tenth Step of Pride, Defiance, contempt of Christ) as Satan. Swift alludes to Milton's Satan as a model of self-examination for Gulliver to know himself through Bernard's doctrine. Satan says to himself:

> Hadst thou the same free Will and Power to stand?
> Thou hadst: whom hast thou then or what to accuse,
> But Heav'n's free Love dealt equally to all?
> Be then his Love accurst, since love or hate,
> To me alike, it deals eternal woe.
> Nay curs'd be thou; since against his thy will
> Chose freely what it now so justly rues.
> Me miserable! which way shall I fly
> Infinite wrath, and infinite despair?
> Which way I fly is Hell; myself am Hell.⁶⁰

Gulliver, as white people, can accurately say these lines to himself. To say "my evil destiny" is to say "myself am Hell." But the point is, white-everyman-Gulliver had a free will choice of alternative, which he rejected for the Second Ignorance. Swift alludes to that point as a further explanation and as a message justifying his focus on the Will of the soul of white people, in Parts I and II. That message is the advice of the angel Raphael to Adam, who was guilty of the First Ignorance:

> Attend: That thou art happy, owe to God;
> That thou continu'st such, owe to thyself,
> That is, to thy obedience; therein stand.
> This was that caution giv'n thee; be advis'd.
> God made thee perfect, not immutable;
> And good he made thee, but to persevere
> He left it in thy power, ordain'd thy will
> By nature free, not over-rul'd by Fate
> Inextricable, or strict necessity;
> Our voluntary service he requires,
> Not our necessitated, such with him
> Finds not acceptance, nor can find, for how
> Can hearts, not free, be tri'd whether they serve
> Willing or no, who will but what they must
> By Destiny, and can no other choose?
> Myself and all th' Angelic Host that stand
> In sight of God enthron'd, our happy state
> Hold, as you yours, while our obedience holds;
> On other surety none; freely we serve,
> Because we freely love, as in our will
> To love or not; in this we stand or fall:
> And some are fall'n, to disobedience fall'n,
> And so from Heav'n to deepest Hell; O fall
> From what high estate of bliss into what woe!⁶¹

3. "Flagitious and Facinorous Acts" 125

This certainly puts Gulliver's "Having been condemned by nature and fortune" and "my evil destiny" in proper perspective as to consent, "a spontaneous inclination of the will."[62] The inclination of the will of white people toward Greek and Roman philosophy constitutes the self-determining habit of their soul. They make it their business *not* to hear God speaking within them, but rather to hear philosophers speaking without them. Due to "the great power of habit and prejudice," they hold forth in the style of the philosophers they have learned from. Or, to put it another way:

> The mind of man is at first (if you will pardon the expression) like a "tabula rasa," or like wax, which, while it is soft, is capable of any impression, till time has hardened it.[63]

4

Repository of Abominations

"Dungeon" affords a dramatic transition from the end of Part II, where it is twice used, to the beginning of Part III, where it is twice used. We remember Gulliver "begging to be delivered out of the dungeon [he] is in," and Chaos directing Satan to his dungeon, Hell, from which there is no deliverance for him. At the beginning of Part III, Gulliver travels to Fort St. George, at Elmina in West Africa, whose dungeon holds over one thousand African slaves poised for shipment. On the date Gulliver sets out for Fort St. George, Swift alludes to the dungeon of the prophet Jeremiah, whose deliverance from the dungeon he was in came by way of an African slave:

> Then took they Jeremiah, and cast him into the dungeon.... And in the dungeon there was no water, but mire: so Jeremiah sunk in the mire. Now when Ebedmelech the Ethiopian, one of the eunuchs which was in the king's house, heard that they had put Jeremiah in the dungeon; the king then sitting in the gate of Benjamin; Ebedmelech went forth out of the king's house, and spoke to the king, saying, "My lord the king, these men have done evil in all that they have done to Jeremiah the prophet, whom they have cast into the dungeon; and he is like to die for hunger in the place where he is: for there is no more bread in the city." Then the king commanded Ebedmelech the Ethiopian, saying, "Take from hence thirty men with thee, and take up Jeremiah the prophet out of the dungeon, before he die. So Ebedmelech took the men with him, and went into the house of the king under the treasury, and took thence old cast clouts and old rotten rags, and let them down by cords into the dungeon to Jeremiah. And Ebedmelech the Ethiopian said unto Jeremiah, "Put now these old cast clouts and rotten rags, under thine armholes under the cords." And Jeremiah did so. So they drew up Jeremiah with cords, and took him up out of the dungeon [Jer. 38:6–13].

Just as "these men have done evil in all that they have done to Jeremiah," we are reminded by the dungeons of Fort St. George, that white people have done evil in all that they have done to black people. Ironically, Swift alludes to a black slave's deliverance of the white captive, Jeremiah, from his dungeon,

4. Repository of Abominations 127

while white Gulliver delivers black captives from their dungeon into slavery. We are also reminded of Christ's mission: "To set at liberty those who are oppressed" and "To proclaim release to the captives." Accordingly, white people involved in the African slave trade are the Antichrist. Swift projects the heathen African slave, Ebedmelech, as superior to the white nominal Christian, Gulliver, according to Swift's definition of "superior": "No creature is more worthy in the sight of God than according to the goodness or holiness of their life."[1] The heathen African slave Ebedmelech is also notably superior in that he demonstrates "the Second Step of Truth, Knowing Your Neighbor [brotherly love]," of which Gulliver is ignorant. In this, Swift calls attention to the contrast between Gulliver's boast that his fellow African slave trader captain "treated me more like a brother than an inferior officer" and the "inferior," heathen, African slave Ebedmelech's act of brotherly love. White people are thus "inferior" because of the wickedness and *un*holiness of their lives, as demonstrated by the African slave trade and their treatment of black people. "There is no duty more incumbent upon those who profess the Gospel, than that of brotherly love ... in proportion as brotherly love declines, Christianity will do so too."[2] The heathen African slave, Ebedmelech, is, in other words, more of a "real" Christian than white-everyman-Gulliver who professes the Gospel nominally. By projecting a black man, Ebedmelech, as superior, Swift begins to prepare us for the quintessential irony of the *Travels* as a whole: that, notwithstanding traditional, historical, mythical, legendary, stereotypical, racist, biological, anthropological, political, sociological, and cultural claims to the contrary, white people are inferior to black people. Gulliver's coming to that realization is the climax of *Gulliver's Travels*. It is the irony of ironies.

Gulliver arrives at Fort St. George in West Africa on Good Friday, the 11th of April, 1707. Swift chose the day commemorating the crucifixion of Christ for the arrival of an African slave ship at a dungeon holding a thousand African slaves to identify the African slave trade with the crucifying of Christ, and the traders, like Gulliver, with the crucifiers, and also to identify the suffering African slave with the suffering Jesus, as being, like Jesus, "despised and rejected of men; a man of sorrows and acquainted with grief ... oppressed and afflicted ... brought as a lamb to the slaughter ... cut off out of the land of the living." Swift's allusion to the blackness of Christ crucified in the garment of a slave, is to identify black people with Christ as mankind, as a fierce refutation of the animalization of black people by white people as depicted in Part IV.

In identifying black mankind with Christ, to establish them as mankind, Swift alludes to Bernard, who says:

> ... that the splendor and image of the substance of God should be shrouded in the form of a slave, in order that a slave might live.... He even brought this blackness on himself by assuming the condition of a slave, and becoming as men are, he was seen as a man.[3]

According to Swift's allusion to the above, black people, as mankind, are guilty of the First Ignorance, the cause of the blackness Christ brought on himself by assuming the condition of mankind.

Gulliver stays at the slave dungeons of Fort St. George for three weeks, and then goes to Tonquin, where he is given power to "traffic" in a sloop the captain buys. Gulliver is out ten days when he is chased by pirates and overtaken. They commandeer his sloop and pinion him with strong cords. One of the pirates is a Dutchman who swears that Gulliver and his crew should be tied back to back and thrown overboard. With Gulliver's response, Swift again attacks "nominal" Christianity, which, as Swift demonstrates, fosters the African slave trade. Gulliver says:

> I spoke Dutch tolerably well; I begged him in consideration of our being Christians and Protestant ... that he would move the captains to take some pity on us.... The largest of the pirate ships was commanded by a Japanese captain [who] said we should not die. I made the captain a very low bow, and then turning to the Dutchman, said, I was sorry to find more mercy in a heathen, than in a brother Christian.

Of course, being African slave traders, neither one of them is a "real" Christian, being obviously unacquainted with mercy and brotherly love. Being "nominal" Christians, they are "malicious reprobates," a label Gulliver hurls at the Dutchman. It has, however, a boomerang effect, applying equally to the hurler.

Gulliver is set adrift in a small canoe. With his pocket-glass he sees several islands in the distance. He sails to five of them. The ones he describes are reflections of Milton's description of the "Universe of death," being still in the African slave trade environment. Of the last island, he says:

> I found the island to be all rocky, only a little intermingled with tufts of grass.... I took out my small provisions, and after having refreshed myself, secured the remainder in a cave, whereof there were great numbers.... I lay all night in the cave where I had lodged my provisions. My bed was the same dry grass and seaweed which I intended for fuel. I slept very little, for the disquiets of my mind prevailed over my weariness, and kept me awake. I considered how impossible it was to preserve my life in so desolate a place, and how miserable my end must be. Yet I found my self so listless and desponding, that I had not the heart to rise, and before I could get spirits enough to creep out of my cave, the day was far advanced. I walked a while among the rocks; the sky was perfectly clear, and the sun so hot, that I was forced to turn my face from it [125–126].

And that's because, "The eye, when troubled, cannot approach the light, because it has lost that likeness to that light in the heavens."[4] Gulliver has troubled eyes because of his unlikeness to the Son. In his so-called Age of Enlightenment, which it is not, Gulliver is not enlightened, for as Bernard states: "when you are enlightened you can see even now the Sun of Justice that "enlightens every man who come into this world."[5] The Psalmist says: "Come to him and be enlightened." The point is well made also by comparing Gulliver the pilgrim to Dante the pilgrim by the difference in their similar dark night of the soul. Dante says:

> Midway in the journey of our life I found myself in a dark wood, for the straight way was lost. Ah, how hard it is to tell what that wood was, wild, rugged, harsh; the very thought of it renews the fear! It is so bitter that death is hardly more so.... I cannot rightly say how I entered it, I was so full of sleep at the moment I left the true way; but when I had reached the foot of a hill, there at the end of the valley that had pierced my heart with fear, I looked up and saw its shoulders already clad in the rays of the planet that leads men aright by every path. Then the fear was somewhat quieted that had continued in the lake of my heart through the night I had passed so piteously.... It was the beginning of the morning, and the sun was mounting with the stars that were with it when Divine Love first set those beautiful things in motion, so that the hour of the day and the sweet season gave me cause for good hope.[6]

The significant difference is between Gulliver's "troubled eye," which "cannot gaze on the peaceful sun because of its unlikeness," and Dante's "peaceful eye," which "can behold it with some efficacy because of a certain likeness."[7] Consequently, Dante sees the sun (Son) as "leading men aright by every path," and as "set in motion by Divine Love," and as "cause for good hope,"[8] but Gulliver does not. Instead of "Christ in you, the hope of glory," (Col. 1:27) Gulliver hopes in philosophy, but philosophers don't leave hope at the bottom.[9]

For example, after he says he was forced to turn his face from the sun (the Son becomes obscured by philosophy), Gulliver says:

> ... when all on a sudden it became obscured, as I thought, in a manner very different from what happens by the interposition of a cloud. I turned back, and perceived a vast opaque body between me and the sun, moving forwards towards the island: it seemed to be about two miles high, and hid the sun six or seven minutes, but I did not observe the air to be much colder, or the sky more darkened, than if I had stood under the shade of a mountain. As it approached nearer over the place where I was, it appeared to be a firm substance, the bottom flat, smooth, and shining very bright from the reflection of the sea below. I stood upon a height about two hundred yards from the shore, and saw this vast body descending almost to a parallel with me, at less than an English mile distance. I took out my pocket-perspective, and could plainly discover numbers of people moving up and down the sides of it, which appeared to be sloping, but what those people were doing I was not able to distinguish.

This is the beginning of Swift's identifying the above "vast opaque body" with the "firm opacous Globe" of Milton's "Limbo of Vanity," the "Paradise of Fools,"[10] and Gulliver with Milton's Satan. Gulliver describes the bottom as "shining very bright from the reflection of the sea below," which is similar to Milton's description: "and underneath a bright Sea flow'd/Of Jasper, or of liquid Pearl..."[11] (PL III, 18–19). Gulliver speaks of "numbers of people moving up and down the sides of it"; Milton speaks of "mysteriously meant" Stairs:

> The Stairs were such as whereon "Jacob" saw Angels ascending and descending.[12]

Alluding to the Limbos of Dante and Milton, Swift creates a limbo (the Flying Island) full of the philosophers in Dante's Limbo, to project Milton's "Limbo of Vanity," the Paradise of Fools," using Milton's characterization of its inhabitants, and Dante's description of the kind of hope they lack.

For example, as Gulliver continues to relate his experience, he says:

> The natural love of life gave me some inward motions of joy, and I was ready to entertain a hope, that this adventure might some way or other help to deliver me from the desolate place and condition I was in. But at the same time the reader can hardly conceive my astonishment, to behold an island in the air, inhabited by men, who were able (as is should) seem to raise or sink, or put it into a progressive motion, as they pleased. But not being at that time in a disposition to philosophize upon this phenomenon, I rather chose to observe what course the island would take, because it seemed for a while to stand still [126].

The hope that Gulliver is ready to entertain, that philosophy will deliver him from the desolate place and condition he is in, is futile because, unlike Pandora, "philosophers do not leave hope at the bottom."[13] "Philosophy is illuminated by the radiance of human reason, which "is the highest state man can achieve without God, but is nothing compared to the glory of God."[14]

In addition, the wisdom of this world, philosophy, as projected in one of Swift's sermons, is foolishness with God. Moreover, in its depiction as the "Flying Island," philosophy incurs the wrath of God. In Revelation, when the seventh angel poured out his vial of the wrath of God, "every island fled"—one of the ways Swift condemns philosophy as truth.

In seeming to stand still in the air, the Flying Island not only suggests "limbo" but also Bernard's description of Satan, which might have influenced Milton. Bernard speaks of Satan as "Expelled from heaven, not able to remain on earth, and must therefore take a place in the air":

> ... vacillating between heaven and earth ... suspended in the air thou seest the angels descending and ascending by thee, but what they hear in the heavens or announce to the lands thou knowest not at all.

Further, Satan "canst dwell only in the hearts of the proud"[15] provides a good example of such in those who inhabit his Limbo of Vanity, the Paradise of Fools. Swift characterizes philosophers in much the same manner in "A Tale of a Tub," as well as in *Gulliver's Travels*. Milton says:

> None yet, but store hereafter from the earth
> Up hither like Aereal vapors flew
> Of all things transitory and vain, when Sin
> With vanity had filled the works of men:
> Both all things vain, and all who in vain things
> Build thir fond hopes of Glory or lasting fame,
> Or happiness in this or th' other life;
> All who have thir reward on Earth, the fruits
> Of painful Superstition and blind Zeal,
> Naught seeking but the praise of men, here find
> Fit retribution, empty as their deeds;
> All th' unaccomplisht works of Nature's hand,
> Abortive, monstrous, or unkindly mixt,
> Dissolv'd on Earth, flee thither, and in vain,
> Till final dissolution, wander here,
> Not in the neighboring Moon, as some have dream'd.[16]

Milton mentions again the "Stairs," through which Swift again identifies Gulliver with Satan:

> The Stairs were then let down, whether to dare
> The Fiend by easy ascent, or aggravate
> His sad exclusion from the doors of Bliss....
> "Satan" from hence now on the lower stair
> That scal'd by steps of Gold to Heaven Gate
> Looks down with wonder at the sudden view
> Of all this World at once.[17]

Gulliver calls and shouts with the utmost strength of his voice, trying to be noticed by the people of the Flying Island. He is finally discovered, and they see the distress he is in. He says:

> They made signs for me to come down from the rock, and go towards the shore, which I accordingly did; and the flying island being raised to a convenient height, the verge directly over me, a chain was let down from the lowest gallery, with a seat fastened to the bottom, to which I fixed my self, and was drawn up by pulleys [127].

As Satan's "Stairs were then let down," "a chain was let down" for Gulliver "from the lowest gallery," to suggest "the lower stair" Milton's Satan was "now on." Gulliver's being drawn up by pulleys is a satiric allusion to the philosopher Archimedes, who invented the pulley; and to Swift's sermon "On the Wisdom of This World," which explains the satire, and echoes the character of those in the "Limbo of Vanity." Speaking of philosophers, Swift says:

> It was the want of assigning some happiness proportioned to the soul of man, that caused many of them, either on the one hand, to be sour and morose, supercilious and untreatable; or, on the other, to fall into the vulgar pursuits of common men, to hunt after greatness and riches, to make their court, and to serve occasions; as Plato did to the younger Dionysius, and Aristotle to Alexander the great. So impossible it is for a man, who looks no farther than the present world, to fix himself long in a contemplation where the present world has no part: he has no sure hold, no firm footing; he can never expect to remove the earth he rests upon, while he had no support besides for his feet, but wants, like Archimedes, some other place whereon to stand.[18]

Archimedes is reputed to have said: "Give me a place to stand, and I will move the earth." He and other philosophers that people the flying island are those whom Dante refers to as "people of great worth suspended in that Limbo," and who, because "they were before Christianity, did not worship God aright," and thus are "without hope."[19] But to Swift, they are without hope because of their philosophies preventing such worship, and their vanity, both of which he ridicules in Part III. In not honoring them, his limbo has more in common with Milton's Limbo of Vanity than with Dante's Limbo, but then, Dante's is an unevolved hellish perspective. Swift associates philosophy with the Antichrist.

Once Gulliver is drawn up by pulleys and he says, "At my alighting I was surrounded by a crowd of people, but those who stood nearest seemed to be of *better quality*," we are reminded of the master he has learned from: Plato, in whose style Gulliver holds forth ("Each of us holds forth in the style of the master he has learned from" (Bernard). As we have seen, Gulliver is very much concerned with class, as well as with race, but this does not take us away from one of the main frames of reference here in Part III: Bonaventure's third light, the light of philosophical knowledge, class being an integral aspect of Plato's philosophy. Part III also represents the Memory of the soul of white people, which is projected as the "Repository of Abominations," also a major frame of reference. In addition, and not unrelated as a frame, is "Laputa," which means "Whore," as in "Whore of Babylon," in which the Second Ignorance is indicated. At his "alighting," Gulliver is in Laputa. Bernard uses the Psalmist to stress that the second ignorance is worse than the first:

> We must avoid ignorance at any cost, or if we are found to be still without understanding even after chastisement, more serious evils than the former will multiply upon us and it will be said of us: "We tried to cure Babylon; she has gotten no better" (Ps 48). "The 2nd ignorance was more to be feared, to be ashamed of, than the first, for the first brought man to a level with the beasts, the latter made him lower."[20]

As previously mentioned, Swift identifies white supremacy and the African slave trade with the Second Ignorance, so that Babylon becomes a significant symbol of the major centers of the African slave trade, such as London, Bristol, Liverpool, Lisbon, Amsterdam, New York, Charleston, Newport, etc, cities of the Antichrist (like Babylon) whose Antichrist merchants, laden with riches from the African slave trade, made these cities important centers:

> I saw a woman sit upon a scarlet colored beast, full of names of blasphemy, having seven heads, and ten horns. And the woman was arrayed in purple and scarlet colour, and decked with gold and precious stones and pearls, having a golden cup in her hand full of abominations and filthiness of her fornication: And upon her forehead was a name written, MYSTERY, BABYLON THE GREAT, THE MOTHER OF HARLOTS AND ABOMINATIONS OF THE EARTH.... And the woman which thou sawest is that great city, which reigneth over the kings of the earth.... Babylon the great is fallen, and is become the habitation of devils, and the hold of every foul spirit, and a cage of every unclean and hateful bird. For ... the merchants of the earth are waxed rich through the abundance of her delicacies.... And the merchants of the earth shall weep and mourn over her; for no man buyeth their merchandise any more: The merchandise of gold, and silver ... and slaves, and souls of men.... And every shipmaster, and all the company in ships, and sailors, and as many as trade by sea, stood afar off, and cried, weeping and wailing, saying, Alas, alas, that great city, wherein were made rich all that had ships in the sea by reason of her costliness.... And a mighty angel took up a stone like a great millstone, and cast it into the sea, saying, Thus with violence shall that great city Babylon be thrown down ... and the voice of the bridegroom and of the bride shall be heard no more at all in thee: for thy merchants were the great men of the earth [Rev. 17–19].

Swift further condemns the merchants when he has Gulliver travel to Barbados and the Leeward Islands, the Middle Passage, "by the direction of the merchants who employed [him]."

Using "Laputa" as a symbol of the ABOMINATIONS of the African slave trade, combined with Bernard's insights for the Memory of the soul of white people, Swift calls attention to the part Memory plays in the above prophecy from Revelation:

> ... all that itch of unlawful delight (Gulliver's "insatiable desire" for the African slave trade) and all the enticing pleasure ... imprinted certain bitter marks in the memory, it left behind it foul footsteps. For into that Repository, as into a Sink, all the abomination ran, all the filth flowed. A large Volume, in which all things are written, and that with the Pen of truth.[21]

Because "Sins exist in the memory even when past; and the memory of past sins is what constitutes the torment of hell, which is everlasting because the sins cannot be eradicated from the memory."[22]

Swift depicts the Laputans according to Bonaventure's third light, and makes satiric commentary according to Bernard's definition of the Memory.

The third light is the "inner" light, or the light of philosophical knowledge, which illumines in regard to "intellectual truth." "It is called "inner" because it inquires into inner and hidden causes through principles of knowledge and natural truth, which are inherent in man."[23] The memory is, therefore, a fitting focus. The memory being the thinking faculty the soul is responsible for thinking up philosophies, and is the repository for them, a repository of abomination, according to Swift, which proves it is not devoted to thoughts of God, and so is dead. The memory of the Laputans is in the state of spiritual death because its thoughts are not thoughts of truth, being devoted to philosophy and *not* to thoughts of God. In other words, philosophy is not truth. For example, Swift has Gulliver mention "having never till then seen a race of mortals so singular in their shapes, habits, and countenances":

> Their heads were all reclined either to the right, or the left; one of their eyes turned inward, and the other directly up to the zenith. Their outward garments were adorned with the figures of suns, moons, and stars, interwoven with those of fiddles, flutes, harps, trumpets, guitars, harpsichords, and many more instruments of music, unknown to us in Europe.

In the above, in one fell swoop, Swift ridicules Plotinus, Plato, Socrates, and Pythagoras. The Neoplatonists believed the soul looks in two directions, that it is turned both toward the spirit and toward matter. In Plato's *Republic*, Socrates says: "Just as our eyes were made for astronomy, so our ears were made for harmony movements, and these two are sister sciences."[24] Pythagoras discovered "the numerical relation between the length of strings and the musical notes which they produce when vibrating," and he greatly advanced the science of harmony.[25]

Swift projects the intense speculations "of philosophers and their followers as proof of the weakness of all human wisdom." Swift says, for example:

> I observed here and there many in the habits of servants, with a blown bladder fastened like a flail to the end of a short stick, which they carried in their hands. In each bladder was a small quantity of dried pease or little pebbles.... With these bladders they now and then flapped the mouths and ears of those who stood near them ... it seems, the minds of these people are so taken up with intense speculations, that they neither can speak, nor attend to the discourses of others, without being roused by some external taction upon the organs of speech and hearing.

"As if they had something more excellent and sublime to reveal, than that God who created the heaven and the earth, and all things that are therein" (Irenaeus).[26]

As he did the Will in Parts I and II, here in Part III, Swift is depicting the Memory of the soul of white people, not only in the state of spiritual death, but as unnatural as well:

> This flapper is likewise employed diligently to attend his master in his walks, and upon occasion to give him a soft flap on his eyes, because he is always so wrapped up on cogitation, that he is in manifest danger of falling down every precipice, and bouncing his head against every post, and in the streets, of jostling others or being jostled himself into the kennel.

This reminds us of Swift's satire of philosophers in "A Tritical Essay": "Archimedes, the famous mathematician, was so intent upon his problems, that he never minded the soldiers who came to kill him."[27]

Tongue in cheek, Swift has Gulliver follow the above with:

> It was necessary to give the reader this information, without which he would be at the same loss with me, to understand the proceedings of these people, as they conducted me up the stairs to the top of the island, and from thence to the royal palace. While we were ascending, they forgot several times what they were about, and left me to my self, till their memories were again roused by their flappers; for they appeared altogether unmoved by the sight of my foreign habit and countenance, and by the shouts of the vulgar, whose thoughts and minds were more disengaged.

The "vulgar" are your normal, everyday, natural, garden-variety people. We are also made aware that the King is attended by persons of "prime quality."

Before his throne was a large table filled with globes and spheres, and mathematical instruments of all kinds. He has dinner brought to Gulliver in two courses, of three dishes each: "a shoulder of mutton, cut into an equilateral triangle, a piece of beef into a rhomboides, and a pudding into a cycloid ... two ducks trussed up into the form of fiddles ... his servants cut our bread into cones, cylinders, parallelograms, and several other mathematical figures." In ridicule of Socrates in Plato's *Republic*, Swift presents the above focus on mathematics as another way of saying: "In the state of spiritual death the memory is devoted to thoughts which are not thoughts of truth."[28] In other words, mathematics is not truth, nor the way to truth, contrary to the thoughts of Socrates: "Numbers both lead toward the truth and compel the soul to use pure reason to find out the truth" and:

> The best natures must be trained in numbers, and secondly in geometry, for geometical knowledge is knowledge of that which is ... plane geometry will attract the soul towards truth.[29]

(Jesus said: "I am the way, the *truth*, and the life"—Swift's point.)

Gulliver comes to a conclusion that emerges as Swift's direct, straightforward, sans tongue-in-cheek description of white people, literally fulfilling his intention "to write a character of the present set of wits in our nation; their persons I shall describe particularly and at length, their genius and understanding in miniature"[30]:

> Although they are dextrous enough upon a piece of paper in the management of the rule, the pencil, and the divider, yet in the common actions and behaviour of life I have not seen a more clumsy, awkward, and unhandy people, nor so slow and perplexed in their conceptions upon all other subjects, except those of mathematics and music. They are very bad reasoners, and vehemently given to opposition, unless when they happen to be of the right opinion, which is seldom their case. Imagination, fancy, and invention, they are wholly strangers to....
> Most of them, and especially those who deal in the astronomical part, have great faith in judicial astrology, although they are ashamed to own it publicly. But what I chiefly admired, and thought altogether unaccountable, was the strong disposition I observed in them towards news and politics, perpetually enquiring into public affairs, giving their judgments in matters of state, and passionately disputing every inch of a party opinion. I have indeed observed the same disposition among most of the mathematicians I have known in Europe, although I could never discover the least analogy between the two sciences.... These people are under continual disquietudes, never enjoying a minutes peace of mind; and their disturbances proceed from causes which very little affect the rest of mortals. Their apprehensions arise from several changes they dread in the celestial bodies. For instance, that the earth, by the continual approaches of the sun towards it, must in course of time be absorbed or swallowed up....
> They are so perpetually alarmed with the apprehensions of these and the like impending dangers, that they can neither sleep quietly in their beds, nor have any relish for the common pleasures or amusements of life. When they meet an acquaintance in the morning, the first question is about the sun's health, how he looked at his setting and rising, and what hopes they have to avoid the stroke of the approaching comet.

By the help of "a very faithful memory," Gulliver learns the language of the Laputans, but feels himself "too much neglected, not without some degree of contempt," and receiving "so little countenance," the people "so abstracted and involved in speculation," he says he never met with such "disagreeable companions," and resolves to leave the island at the first opportunity. But first, he gives a philosophical account of the island to the reader. This account is obscure, pretentious, and full of unreadable technical jargon. Swift is ridiculing "the manner of the scientific papers contributed to the Royal Society,"[31] which Swift is about to ridicule as the Grand Academy of Lagado. The Royal Society of London for Improving Natural Knowledge is an English scientific academy founded in 1660 for the purpose of studying the whole field of knowledge. In "A Tale of a Tub," it is called the "Academy of Modern Bedlam." In general, the projects are attacked as positivism,

4. Repository of Abominations   137

"the only study of which Bernard disapproves, the study of the phenomenal world without reference to the source or function of things. This is curiosity, the first step of the path which leads away from truth."[32] It is the study of things and creatures for their own sake. Allusively, Swift is saying: "Spiritual men, filled with truth, investigate the function of things, in order to seek God" (which is the basis of Swift's satire). "The being of things reveals God's power, the arrangement of things reveals God's wisdom, and the utility of things reveals God's goodness."[33]

With a letter of recommendation to a great lord in Lagado, Gulliver leaves the flying island, being "let down from the lowest gallery, in the same manner as [he] had been taken up." The great lord tells Gulliver about how the "schemes of putting all arts, sciences, languages, and mechanics upon a new foot" led to the erecting of an "academy of PROJECTORS in Lagado." His lordship gives Gulliver a personal example of these projectors, which exemplifies the point of Swift's satire of positivism, that such projects are more of an exercise in curiosity than good effects and naturalness:

> He had a very convenient mill within half a mile of his house, turned by a current from a large river, and sufficient for his own family as well as a great number of his tenants. That about seven years ago a club of those projectors came to him with proposals to destroy this mill, and build another on the side of the mountain, on the long ridge whereof a long canal must be cut for a repository of water, to be conveyed up by pipes and engines to supply the mill: because the wind and air upon a height agitated the water, and thereby made it fitter for motion and because the water descending down a declivity would turn the mill with half the current of a river whose course is more upon a level ... after employing an hundred men for two years, the work miscarried, the projectors went off, laying the blame entirely upon His Lordship.

That example sets the tone for the projects in the Grand Academy. Gulliver is taken to the Academy, where he is represented as "a great admirer of projects, and a person of much curiosity and easy belief," which describes him exactly. In describing the Academy physically, Gulliver says: "This academy is not an entire single building, but a continuation of several houses on both sides of a street.... I was received very kindly by the Warden, and went for many days to the Academy. Every room hath in it one or more projectors, and I believe I could not be in fewer than five hundred rooms," which, along with the "Warden," are preludes to Swift's ridicule of the projectors and their projects. For example, he has Gulliver say:

> The first man I saw was of a meagre aspect, with sooty hands and face, he hair and beard long, ragged and singed in several places. His clothes, shirt, and skin were all of the same colour. He had been eight years upon a project for extracting sunbeams out of cucumbers, which were to be put into vials hermetically sealed, and let out to warm the air in raw inclement summers.

> I went into another chamber, but was ready to hasten back, being almost overcome with a horrible stink.... The projector of this cell was the most ancient student of the Academy. His face and beard were of a pale yellow; his hands and clothes daubed over with filth.... His employment from his first coming into the Academy was an operation to reduce human excrement to its original food, by separating the several parts, removing the tincture which it receives from the gall, making the odour exhale, and skimming off the saliva. He had a weekly allowance from the society of a vessel filled with human ordure, about the bigness of a Bristol barrel.
>
> There was a man born blind, who had several apprentices in his own condition: their employment was to mix colours for painters, which their master taught them to distinguish by feeling and smelling. It was indeed my misfortune to find them at that time not very perfect in their lessons, and the professor himself happened to be generally mistaken; this artist is much encouraged and esteemed by the whole fraternity.

To take this seriously, one would have to say with Bernard that only the eye bears some degree of likeness to that light in the heavens, the sun. "Since all other members of the body lack this likeness, they are incapable of seeing the light," and therefore color. "Even the eye itself, when troubled, cannot approach the light, because it has lost that likeness," as in the case of blindness.[34] But, in ridicule of the project and of such a thing as an Academy of projectors, Swift takes the tone he uses against critics:

> I must be so bold to tell my critics and witlings, that they can no more judge of this, than a man that is born blind, can have any true idea of colours.[35]

"The word 'projector' in the period meant one addicted to impractical or speculative activities."[36] Another such project is performed by an illustrious projector called "the universal artist":

> He told us he had been thirty years employing his thoughts for the improvement of human life. He had two large rooms full of wonderful curiosities, and fifty men at work. Some were softening marble for pillows and pincushions; others were petrifying the hoofs of a living horse to preserve them from foundering. The artist himself was at that time busy upon two great designs; the first, to sow land with chaff, wherein he affirmed the true seminal virtue to be contained.... The other was, by a certain composition of gums, minerals, and vegetables outwardly applied to prevent the growth of wool upon two young lambs; and he hoped in a reasonable time to propagate the breed of naked sheep all over the kingdom.

One of the most telling attacks on positivism is the project for "improving speculative knowledge by practical and mechanical operations," which is an attack on atomism as well. This professor "flattered himself that a more noble, exalted thought never sprang in any other man's head," which was that "by his contrivance the most ignorant person at a reasonable charge, and with a little bodily labour, may write books in philosophy, poetry, politics, law,

4. Repository of Abominations

mathematics and theology, without the least assistance from genius or study." He leads Gulliver to a twenty-foot-square frame placed in the middle of the room, his students standing "in ranks" around it:

> The superfices was composed of several bits of wood, about the bigness of a die, but some larger than others. They were all linked together by slender wires. These bits of wood were covered on every square with papers pasted on them, and on these papers were written all the words of their language in their several moods, tenses, and declensions, but without any order. The professor then desired me to observe, for he was going to set his engine at work. The pupils at his command took each of them hold of an iron handle, whereof there were forty fixed round the edges of the frame, and giving them a sudden turn, the whole disposition of the words was entirely changed. He then commanded six and thirty of the lads to read the several lines softly as they appeared upon the frame; and where they found three or four words together that might make part of a sentence, they dictated to the four remaining boys who were scribes. This work was repeated three or four times, and at every turn the engine was so contrived, that the words shifted into new places, as the square bits of wood moved upside down.
>
> Six hours a day the young students were employed in this labour, and the professor showed me several volumes in large folio already collected, of broken sentences, which he intended to piece together, and out of those rich materials to give the world a complete body of all arts and sciences.... He assured me ... that he had emptied the whole vocabulary into his frame, and made the strictest computation of the general proportion there is in books between the numbers of particles, nouns, and verbs, and other parts of speech.

Swift has Gulliver tell of one outrageous project after another, attacking not only positivism, but other philosophies fashionable in the seventeenth and eighteenth centuries, especially the mathematization and mechanization of the world and nature. Some are outrageous on the positive side, being so far contrary to the evil hypocritically practiced. For example, the professors in the school of political projectors, "were proposing schemes for persuading monarchs to choose favourites upon the score of their wisdom, capacity and virtue":

> ... of teaching ministers to consult the public good; of rewarding merit, great abilities and eminent service; of instucting princes to know their true interest by placing it on the same foundation with that of their people: of choosing for employments persons qualified to exercise them; with many other wild impossible chimeras, that never entered before into the heart of man to conceive, and confirmed in me the old observation, that there is nothing so extravagant and irrational which some philosophers have not maintained for truth.

The irony, of course, is that the above last statement applies to the projects that have gone before, not to the one immediately preceding it. In Gulliver's next description, Swift ridicules the philosophy (Plato's) that man is by nature a political animal. Gulliver goes on to describe other political projects, emphasizing Swift's direct affirmation: "Politics is nothing but corruptions." Finally, after a few more descriptions, and seeing nothing that can invite him to a longer continuance, Gulliver leaves Lagado.

While waiting for a ship bound for Luggnagg, he is persuaded to visit the island of Glubbdubdrib, which is Hell, in the sense that "the memory of past sins is what constitutes the torment of hell, which is everlasting because the sins cannot be eradicated from the memory." (A reminder: Part III exposes the Memory of the soul of white people.) Our first clue Glubbdubdrib is Hell, or prefigurative of Hell, is Gulliver's initial description, which includes an allusion to Dante's *Inferno*:

> Glubbdubdrib, as nearly as I can interpret the word, signifies The Island of "Sorcerers" or "Magicians." It is about one third as large as the Isle of Wight, and extremely fruitful: it is governed by the head of a certain tribe, who are all magicians. This tribe marries only among each other, and the eldest in succession is prince or governor.... The Governor and his family are served and attended by domestics of a kind somewhat unusual. By his skill in necromancy, he hath power of calling whom he pleaseth from the dead, and commanding their service for twenty-four hours....

Scripture is unequivocal in condemning such to Hell, as Swift was well aware:

> I will be a swift witness against the sorcerers ... saith the Lord of hosts [Mal. 3:15].
> The fearful, and unbelieving, and the abominable, and murderers, and whoremongers, and sorcerers, and idolaters, and all liars, shall have their part in the lake which burneth with fire and brimstone: which is the second death [Rev. 21:7].
> Blessed are they that do his commandments, that they may have the right to the tree of life, and may enter in through the gates into the city. For without are dogs, and sorcerers....

Gulliver further describes Glubbdubdrib in a manner suggestive of Dante's Hell: The Governor "hath a noble palace and a park of about three thousand acres, surrounded by a wall of hewn stone twenty foot high. In this park are several smaller inclosures for cattle, corn and gardening." In Hell, Dante "came to the foot of a noble castle ... encircled by lofty walls," and says: "There before me, on the enameled green, the great spirits were shown to me...."[37] Gulliver comes upon spirits suggestive of the ghost of Hamlet's father:

> ... we entered the gate of the palace between two rows of guards, armed and dressed after a very antic manner, and something in their countenances that made my flesh creep with a horror I cannot express.

The ghost of Hamlet's father appears wearing "the very armor he had on/When he the ambitious Norway combated."[38] In other words, he was "armed and dressed after a very antic manner." What he is forbidden to tell Hamlet would, in Gulliver's words, make his flesh creep with a horror he could not express:

> I could a tale unfold whose lightest word
> Would harrow up thy soul, freeze thy young blood,
> Make thy two eyes, like stars, start from their spheres,
> Thy knotted and combined locks to part
> And each particular hair to stand on end
> Like quills upon the fretful porpentine.[39]

Similarly relevant, also, is the fact that Gulliver, like Hamlet, listens to the wrong ghost. But Hamlet at least questions his father's ghost:

> Angels and ministers of grace defend us!
> Be thou a spirit of health or goblin damned,
> Bring with thee airs from Heaven or blasts from Hell,
> Be thy intents wicked or charitable,
> Thou comest in such a questionable shape
> That I will speak to thee.[40]

In keeping with Scripture:

> Beloved, believe not every spirit, but try the spirits whether they are of God because many false prophets are gone out into the world. Hereby know ye the Spirit of God: Every spirit that confesseth that Jesus Christ is come in the flesh is of God: And every spirit that confesseth not that Jesus Christ is come in the flesh is not of God: and this is that "spirit" of antichrist, whereof ye have heard that it should come; and even now already is in the world [I John 4:1–3].

But Gulliver, unlike Hamlet, asks no questions of the spirits appearing before him. However, inasmuch as Hamlet is determined to speak to the ghost regardless of whether he's from heaven or hell, he and Gulliver are on the same Step of Pride, the Tenth Step, Defiance, which is to "contemn Christ in open disobedience."[41] Another example of Hamlet's open disobedience: "Vengeance is mine," saith the Lord, "I will repay." But Hamlet listens to his father's ghost, who says to him: "If thou didst ever thy dear father love — Revenge his foul and most unnatural murder."[42] In "open disobedience," Gulliver listens to the ghostly Governor and his ghostly entourage.

After Gulliver's flesh creeps with a horror he cannot express, at the sight of those who caused such a reaction, he passed through several apartments between servants of the same sort. He comes to the "chamber of presence," where he is permitted to sit on a stool near his Highness's throne. Gulliver says:

> To let me see that I should be treated without ceremony, he dismissed all his attendants with a turn of his finger, at which to my great astonishment they vanished in an instant, like visions in a dream, when we awake on a sudden.

Swift here provides three clues to the meaning of what Gulliver is about to relate: "visions in a dream," "chamber of presence," and later, "illustrious persons." Beginning with the initial allusion, through Gulliver's mention of "a noble palace" to Dante's "noble castle," which "is best understood as "the Castle of Fame" (special dwelling of those whose "honored name" has won them a privileged place in Dante's "Limbo").⁴³ Swift alludes to the "Chamber of Fame" in his own essays in "The Tatler," and to Boccaccio's *The Fates of Illustrious Men* (*De Casibus Vicorum Illustrious*), about which is said:

> Boccaccio transformed the manner in which history and biography had been written in the great collections before his time. The Fates is the only collection that makes use of the vision technique to organize the continuity of the stories. As Boccaccio sits in his study, a cavalcade of all the great names of history pass before him. Many of them still bear the physical signs of their earthly end.... It is a fundamental idea of *The Fates* that all rulers, conqueror and conquered, meet the same end, and the vision framework made this novel point of view seem natural.⁴⁴

Similarly, Swift uses the vision framework in "The Tatler," in his "Chamber of Fame." Regarding his "catalogues of illustrious persons," he says:

> I yesterday employed the whole afternoon in comparing them with each other; which made so strong an impression upon my imagination, that they broke my sleep for the first part of the following night, and at length threw me into a very agreeable vision.... I dreamed that....⁴⁵

Swift uses the vision framework or technique in having Gulliver, as he says, "like visions in a dream," call up "vast numbers of illustrious persons." The "lower world," from the vantage point of Glubbdubdrib, symbolizes the Chamber and Castle of Fame as signifying the fates of illustrious men named in that world and in Dante's Castle of Fame and Swift's Chamber of Fame, most, if not all of whom, are the same.

Gulliver "had the honour to dine with the Governor, where a new set of ghosts served up the meat, and waited at table," and he observes himself to be less terrified than he had been in the morning." He says he "grew so familiarized to the sight of spirits, that after the third or fourth time they gave me no emotion at all." Recalling that "The beginning of sin is pride, the beginning of pride is the turning away from God"⁴⁶ and that, the First Step of Pride is Curiosity; and that, positivism is curiosity (Bernard), Swift has Gulliver add: "If I had any apprehensions left, my curiosity prevailed over them." He goes on to say:

4. Repository of Abominations 143

> For his Highness the Governor ordered me to call up whatever persons I would choose to name, and in whatever numbers among the dead from the beginning of the world to the present time, and command them to answer any questions I should think fit to ask; with this condition, that my questions must be confined within the compass of the times they lived in. And one thing I might depend upon, that they would certainly tell me the truth, for lying was a talent of no use in the lower world.

Swift's first attack via Gulliver's calling up illustrious persons is directed at white people's criteria for "greatness." Gulliver says, for example:

> I made my humble acknowledgements to his Highness for so great a favour. We were in a chamber, from whence there was a fair prospect into the park. And because my first inclination was to be entertained with scenes of pomp and magnificence, I desired to see Alexander the Great, at the head of his army just after the battle of Arbela, which upon a motion of the Governor's finger immediately appeared in a large field under the window, where we stood. Alexander was called up into the room.... He assured me upon his honour that he was not poisoned, but died of a fever by excessive drinking.

Dante places Alexander in "the river of blood ... in which boils everyone who by violence injures others":

> ... the boiled were uttering piercing shrieks. I saw people in it, down even to the eyebrows, and the great centaur said, "These are tyrants who took to blood and plunder. Here they lament their merciless crimes: here is Alexander, and cruel Dionysius...."[47]

Two of Dante's chief authorities on ancient history, Orosius and Lucan, describe Alexander as follows:

> ... a veritable whirlpool of evils and a hurricane that swept the whole East in its fury ... insatiable for human blood ... always thirsty for flesh slaughter. After oppressing the world for twelve years, he died at Babylon still thirsting for blood.[48]
>
> Driven by the impulse of destiny, he rushed through the peoples of Asia, mowing down mankind; he drove his sword home in the breast of every nation; he defiled distant rivers, the Euphrates and the Ganges, with Persian and Indian blood; he was a pestilence to earth, a thunderbolt that struck all peoples alike, a comet of disaster to mankind.[49]

But Gulliver not only includes Alexander in the "vast numbers of illustrious persons called up," but also in his hypocritical prevarication: "I chiefly fed my eyes with beholding the destroyers of tyrants and usurpers, and the restorers of liberty to oppressed and injured nations," his being, as an African slave trader, one of the destroyers of liberty to oppressed and injured nations, especially Africa.

As previously mentioned, Swift, in projecting the contrast between

Homer and Aristotle, makes a statement not only crucial to understanding the style of *Gulliver's Travels*, but also to the realization that rationalism is an inferior route to truth. A similar statement by a twentieth-century Classics scholar, makes Swift's point. Gulliver is desirous of seeing Homer and Aristotle. He says:

> I knew and could distinguish those two heroes at first sight, not only from the crowd, but from each other. Homer was the taller and comelier person of the two, walked very erect for one of his age, and his eyes were the most quick and piercing I ever beheld. Aristotle stooped much, and made use of a staff. His visage was meager, his hair lank and thin, and his voice hollow.

It is possible to see Swift's depiction as the personification of Charles Roland Beye's observations, in: *Ancient Greek Literature And Society*:

> The early Greeks did not depend upon logic and reason. The fifth century advanced upon rationalism but never became an age of enlightenment. Mythopoesis rather than reason was the chariot for the Greek mind. The literature reveals a genius that can encompass impossible contradictions, illogicalities and absurdities, can make them ring true in synthesis, reflecting reality in a way that rational discourse does not know.[50]

This is supported as well by Swift's further satire of philosophers as he has Gulliver call them up from the lower world. The words put into the mouth of Aristotle, are corroborated by a twentieth-century scientist. Gulliver says:

> I then desired the Governor to call up Descartes and Gassendi, with whom I prevailed to explain their systems to Aristotle. This great philosopher freely acknowledged his own mistakes in natural philosophy, because he proceeded in many thing upon conjecture, as all men must do; and he found that Gassendi, who had made the doctrine of Epicurus as palatable as he could, and the "vortices" of Descartes, were equally exploded. He predicted the same fate to "attraction," whereof the present learned are such zealous asserters. He said that new systems of nature were but new fashions, which would vary in every age; and even those who pretend to demonstrate them from mathematical principles would flourish but a short period of time, and be out of vogue when that was determined.

As a prelude to the twenty-first century, a prominent California scientist, in the last years of the twentieth century, said the following:

> ... we all thought that in science you create a solid layer of findings, through experiment and careful investigation, and then you add a second layer, like a second layer of bricks, all very carefully, and so on. Occasionally some adventurous scientist stacks the bricks up in towers, and these towers turn out to be insubstantial and they get torn down, and you proceed again with the careful layers. But we now realize that the very first layers aren't even resting on solid ground. They are balanced on bubbles, on concepts that are full of air, and those bubbles are being burst today, one after the other.[51]

"Having been always a great admirer of old illustrious families," Gulliver "desired the Governor would call up a dozen or two of kings with their ancestors in order for eight or nine generations. But my disappointment was grievous and unexpected." He finds himself able to trace the particular features by which certain families are distinguished, up to their originals:

> I could plainly discover from whence one family derives a long chin, why a second hath abounded with knaves for two generations, and fools for two more.... How cruelty, falsehood, and cowardice grew to be characteristics by which certain families are distinguished as much as by their coat of arms....

The trenchant irony against historians, notable in "The Tatler," is here echoed. Gulliver says:

> I was chiefly disgusted with modern history. For having strictly examined all the persons of greatest name in the courts of princes for an hundred years past, I found how the world had been misled by prostitute writers ... how low an opinion I had of human wisdom and integrity, when I was truly informed of the springs and motives of great enterprises and revolutions in the world, and of the contemptible accidents to which they owed their success.

This is all leading up to Swift's allusion, for conversionary purposes, to Boccaccio's purpose in *The Fates of Illustrious Men*, a purpose in keeping with Swift's projection of *Gulliver's Travels* as a mirror, a mirror that flatters not. Boccaccio says:

> I was wondering how the labor of my studies could benefit the state when I recalled the conduct of illustrious princes. These rulers are so attached to vice and debauchery, are so unrestrained ... I realize how they not only suppress others with their power but also, which is worse, with foolish temerity rise up against the Worker of all good Himself. I was astounded. I condemned their folly and admired the everlasting patience of our Father. Then I found what I had been looking for. What would be more charitable to them in their license, more useful for their eternal salvation, then to call them back to the straight road if possible? ... I believe it is my duty ... to penetrate their guard, then to shatter an illusion that may cause their death.... I shall relate examples of what God or (speaking their own language) Fortune can teach them about those she rises up. And, so that there can be no accusation against any specific time or sex, my idea has been to present succinctly — yet still with useful detail — those rulers and other famous persons, women as well as men, who have been overthrown from the beginning of the world until now ... from among the mighty I shall select the most famous, so that when our princes see these rulers, old and spent, prostrated by the judgment of God, they will recognize God's power, the shiftiness of Fortune, and their own insecurity. They will learn the bounds of their merrymaking, and the misfortunes of others, they can take council for their own profit.[52]

In the process of providing "impressive examples," he declares "What shameful wickedness! How dishonorable and disgraceful the depravity of these thieves and gluttons—I will not call them kings."[53] Swift's example chimes in, as he has Gulliver say:

> Three kings protested to me, that in their whole reigns they did never once prefer any person of merit, unless by mistake or treachery of some minister in whom they confided: neither would they do it if they were to live again; and they showed with great strength of reason, that the royal throne could not be supported without corruption, because that positive, confident, restive temper, which virtue infused into man, was a perpetual clog to public business.

Gulliver continues to call up people of "quality," of "high titles and prodigious estates," "persons of high rank, who ought to be treated with the utmost respect due to their sublime dignity by us their inferiors," and for whom Gulliver has had "profound veneration," going all the way back to the Roman empire. He concludes:

> As every person called up made exactly the same appearance he had done in the world, it gave me melancholy reflections to observe how much the race of human kind was degenerate among us, within these hundred years past.

In other words, the degeneracy "within these hundred years past" is worse than the degeneracy that went on before, of which Gulliver has given us a history starting with "Alexander the Great." "Within these hundred years past" highlights the first major acceleration, 1607–1707, of the traffic in African slaves. "By 1617, 28,000 slaves were being shipped annually from Angola and the Congo. From 1680 to 1700, 300,000 slaves were shipped in English vessels alone."[54] Gulliver arrived at Fort St. George in West Africa in 1707. The immensity of the traffic continued to accelerate. Degeneracy increased with the increase in shipments. One experienced British official on the Gold Coast, wrote regretfully:

> It may be safely affirmed that from our first settlement on the coast until the abolition of the slave trade in 1807, we did not confer one lasting benefit upon the people.[55]

Those whom Gulliver calls up from the lower world represent the foundations Swift is digging up, the collective race-memory of white people, of which Gulliver is characteristic, and to which his particular traits are traceable, although he doesn't identify with any of them, or recognize from whence he came. In other words, Swift not only shows us what has gone into the making of white-everyman-Gulliver and Gulliver's inability to recognize his degenerate roots, but Swift holds up this mirror to his white readers, that they may recognize their own self-denial in Gulliver's ironic self-betraying degeneracy in "I descended so low..." in considering it *low* to appreciate the following:

I descended so low as to desire that some English yeoman of the old stamp might be summoned to appear, once so famous for the simplicity of their manners, diet and dress, for justice in their dealings, for their true spirit of liberty, for their valour and love of their country. Neither could I be wholly unmoved after comparing the living with the dead, when I considered how all these pure native virtues were prostituted for a piece of money by their grandchildren, who in selling their votes, and managing at elections, have acquired every vice and corruption that can possibly be learned in a court.

Gulliver should know, inasmuch as he himself prostituted those same virtues for a piece of money via the lucrative African slave trade.

Gulliver takes leave of the Governor of Glubbdubdib, and sets sail for Luggnagg, arriving on Maundy Thursday, April 21, 1709, a date chosen to project the proper attitude of kings toward their subjects, in stark contrast to what Boccaccio terms the "presumptuous pride of kings," which is symbolized by the King of Luggnagg. The most relevant Scriptures alluded to for that date are John 13 and I Peter 5. Christ was crucified on Good Friday. Maundy Thursday was the day before, on which, traditionally, Christ gave his new commandment and washed the feet of his disciples. The latter act Swift uses as an example in his sermon "On Mutual Subjection":

> He riseth from supper, and laid aside his garments; and took a towel, and girded himself [like a slave]. After that he poureth water into a basin, and began to wash the disciples' feet, and to wipe them with the towel wherewith he was girded.... So after he had washed their feet, and had taken his garments, and was set down again, he said unto them, Know ye what I have done to you? Ye call me Master and Lord, and ye say well; for so I am. If I then, your Lord and Master, have washed your feet; ye also ought to wash one another's feet. For I have given you an example, that ye should do as I have done to you.
>
> A new commandment I give unto you, That ye love one another; as I have loved you, that ye also love one another. By this shall all men know that ye are my disciples, if ye have love one to another.

And Peter exhorts us "to be subject one to another, and be clothed with humility: for God resisteth the proud, and giveth grace to the humble." But there is a big difference between humility and humiliation, which the "court style" of the King of Luggnagg and the example and commandment of Christ distinguish. Gulliver, for example, "desires that His Majesty would please to appoint a day and hour when it would be his gracious pleasure that Gulliver might have the honour to 'lick the dust before His Majesty's footstool.'" Gulliver tells the reader:

> This is the court style, and I found it to be more than matter of form. For upon my admittance two days after my arrival, I was commanded to crawl upon my belly, and lick the floor as I advanced.

He echoes the expression of self-humiliation from a Persion poem: "When I shall have the good fortune to kiss the dust of thy feet, then I shall believe that fortune flatters me." It is neither self-humiliation nor Fortune that Swift is promoting. (Gulliver is Fortune's child; Dante is not; and Boccaccio proposes examples of "what Fortune can teach kings about those she raises up.")

Swift is projecting the advantages (to say the least) of believing in God, compared to believing in Fortune, and attacking the concept and practice of "the divine right of kings" and the presumptive pride of kings. Gulliver says that on account of his being a stranger, care was taken to have the floor so clean that the dust was not offensive. But he goes on to say:

> However, this was a peculiar grace, not allowed to any but persons of the highest rank, when they desire an admittance. Nay, sometimes the floor is strewed with dust on purpose, when the person to be admitted happens to have powerful enemies at court. And I have seen a great lord with his mouth so crammed, that when he had crept to the proper distance from the throne, he was not able to speak a word.... When the King hath a mind to put any of his nobles to death in a gentle indulgent manner, he commands to have the floor strowed with a certain brown powder, of a deadly composition, which being licked up infallibly kills him in twenty-four hours. But in justice to this prince's great clemency ... strict orders are given to have the infected parts of the floor well washed after every such execution.

But to those who wait upon the Lord, God's love is far more desirable than any earthly king's clemency:

> ... kings shall be thy nursing fathers, and their queens thy nursing mothers: they shall bow down to thee with their face toward the earth, and lick up the dust of thy feet; and thou shalt know that I am the lord: for they shall not be ashamed that wait for me.

Singularly relevant also, in exposing the absurdity of earthly kings having "divine right," is the Scripture:

> To whom will ye liken God? or what likeness will ye compare unto him?

The King of Luggnagg exemplifies the point of Swift's argument:

> Among other theological arguments made use of in those times in praise of monarchy, and justification of absolute obedience to a prince, there seemed to be one of a singular nature: it was urged, that Heaven was governed by a monarch, who had none to control his power, but was absolutely obeyed: then it followed, that earthly governments were the more perfect, the nearer they imitated the government in Heaven. All which I look upon as the strongest argument against despotic power, that ever was offered; since no reason can possibly be assigned, why it is best for the world, that God Almighty has such a power, which does not directly prove, that no mortal man should ever have the like.[56]

4. Repository of Abominations

Having been countenanced by the court, Gulliver, while in Luggnagg, makes many acquaintances among "persons of the best fashion." In a conversation with one of them he is told about the "struldbruggs" or "immortals." He is "struck with inexpressible delight" upon hearing about them. The irony of his wish to be a struldbrugg is poignant because he will get what he wishes for without realizing what he wishes for. He goes on and on in transports of joy, expounding on all that he would achieve if he were to live forever. ("Happiest beyond all comparison are those excellent "struldbruggs," who being born exempt from that universal calamity of human nature, have their minds free and disengaged, without the weight and depression of spirits caused by the continual apprehension of death.") The "struldbruggs" never die. Swift, in one of his essays, states, on the contrary, that:

> It is impossible that any thing so natural, so necessary, and so universal as death, should ever have been designed by Providence as an evil to mankind.[57]

Swift's statement in another essay, "Every man desires to live long, but no man would be old," is told to Gulliver in an effort to set him right in a few mistakes. Gulliver is told that "the system of living contrived by him was unreasonable and unjust,

> because it supposed a perpetuity of youth, health, and vigour, which no man could be so foolish to hope, however extravagant he might be in his wishes. That the question therefore was not whether a man would choose to be always in the prime of youth, attended with prosperity and health, but how he would pass a perpetual life under all the usual disadvantages which old age brings along with it. For although few men will avow their desires of being immortal upon such hard conditions ... yet every man desired to put off death for some time longer, let it approach ever so late, and he rarely heard of any man who died willingly, except he were incited by the extremity of grief or torture....
> Only in this island of Luggnagg the appetite for living was not so eager, from the continual example of the "struldbruggs" before their eyes.

The gentleman goes on to give Gulliver a particular account of the "struldbruggs":

> When they came to fourscore years, which is reckoned the extremity of living in this country, they had not only all the follies and infirmities of other old men, but many more which arose from the dreadful prospect of never dying.... Envy and impotent desires are their prevailing passions. But those objects against which their envy seems principally directed, are the vices of the younger sort, and the deaths of the old. By reflecting on the former, they find themselves cut off from all possibility of pleasure; and whenever they see a funeral, they lament and repine that others are gone to an harbour of rest, to which they themselves never can hope to arrive.

The descriptions of the horrifying "strudlebruggs" go on and on. Swift's allusions to Dante's *Inferno* give them deeper meaning. The "strudlebruggs" are described to be identified with those who:

> have no hope of death, and their blind life is so abject that they are envious of every other lot. The world does not suffer that report of them shall live. Mercy and justice disdain them.... They cursed God, their parents, the human race, the place, the time, the seed of their begetting and of their birth. Then, weeping loudly, all drew to the evil shore that awaits every man who fears not God.[58]

By an even deeper meaning, the deepest, we are again reminded that Part III of *Gulliver's Travels* projects the Memory of the soul of white people, particularly to say that:

> Sins exist in the memory even when past; and the memory of past sins is what constitutes the torment of hell, which is everlasting because the sins cannot be eradicated from the memory.[59]

That definition gives us insight into the "struldbruggs," their immortality, a living death. And further:

> This is the worm which does not die: the memory of things past. Once it is inserted, or rather is born in a person through sin, it clings there stubbornly, never after to be removed. It does not stop gnawing at the conscience; and feeding on this truly inexhaustible food, it perpetuates its life. I shudder at this gnawing worm and such a living death, this dying life.[60]

Guilty of the Second Ignorance, it can be said of Gulliver that "It would have been better for that man if he had not been born."[61]

Gulliver leaves Luggnagg and sails to Japan. At landing he shows the custom-house officers his letter from the King of Luggnagg to his Imperial Majesty. They knew the seal perfectly well. "It was as broad as the palm of my hand," says Gulliver. The impression was "a king lifting up a lame beggar from the earth," which is an allusion to a parable of Jesus that echoes his warning: "It would have been better for that man if he had not been born":

> There was a certain rich man, which was clothed in purple and fine linen, and fared sumptuously every day: And there was a certain beggar named Lazarus, which was laid at his gate, full of sores, and desiring to be fed with the crumbs which fell from the rich man's table: moreover the dogs came and licked his sores. And it came to pass, that the beggar died, and was carried by the angels into Abraham's bosom: the rich man also died and was buried; And in hell he lift up his eyes, being in torments, and seeth Abraham afar off, and Lazarus in his bosom. And he cried and said, Father Abraham, have mercy on me, and send Lazarus, that he may dip the tip of his finger in water, and cool my tongue; for I am tormented in this flame. But Abraham said, Son, remember that thou in thy lifetime receivedst thy good things, and likewise Lazarus evil things: but now he is comforted, and thou are tormented. And beside all this,

between us and you there is a great gulf fixed: so that they which would pass from hence to you cannot; neither can they pass to us, that would come from thence. Then he said, I pray thee therefore, father, that thou wouldest send him to my father's house: For I have five brethren; that he may testify unto them, lest they also come into this place of torment. Abraham saith unto him, They have Moses and the prophets; let them hear them. And he said, Nay, father Abraham: but if one went unto them from the dead, they will repent. And he said unto him, If they hear not Moses and the prophets, neither will they be persuaded, though one rose from the dead [Luke 16:19–31].

In conjuction with the above parable, Swift inserts another ominous foreboding prefigurative of the self-betraying irony of Gulliver's "Having been condemned," in the context of the African slave trade and white supremacy. Prefatory to this insert is the telling Scripture marking Gulliver's departure from Luggnagg, which exposes him as one who serves Mammon:

No man can serve two masters: for either he will hate the one, and love the other; or else he will hold to the one, and despise the other. Ye cannot serve God and mammon [Matt. 6:24].

The insert of Gulliver's petition reveals what condemns him, what has all along condemned him, reveals him as "Having been condemned." Gulliver petitions the Emperor of Japan, "that for the sake of my patron the King of Luggnagg, his Majesty would condescend to excuse my performing the ceremony imposed on my countrymen of 'trampling upon the crucifix.'" With this petition, Swift alludes to condemning Scripture:

... if we sin wilfully after that we have received the knowledge of the truth, there remaineth no more sacrifice for sins. But a certain fearful looking for of judgment and fiery indignation, which shall devour the adversaries. He that despised Moses' law died without mercy under two or three witnesses. Of how much sorer punishment, suppose ye, shall he be thought worthy, who hath trodden under foot the Son of God, and hath counted the blood of the covenant, wherewith he was sanctified, and unholy thing, and hath done despite unto the Spirit of grace? [Heb. 10:26–29].

White people trampled upon the crucifix, that is, "hath trodden under foot the Son of God, and hath counted the blood of the covenant an unholy thing, and hath done despite unto the Spirit of grace," with each and every African slave trade voyage, and with each and every animalization, oppression, subjection to discrimination, lynching, torture, and genocide of black people.

Gulliver is passing himself off as a Dutch merchant, so the Emperor is surprised at Gulliver's petition:

When this petition was interpreted to the Emperor, he seemed a little surprised, and said he believed I was the first of my countrymen who ever made any scruple in this point, and that he began to doubt whether I was a real Hollander or no; but rather suspected I must be a Christian.

Gulliver, of course, is neither a real Hollander nor a "real" Christian, and not performing the ceremony does not make him a "real" Christian. With respect to "real" Christianity, he is as nominal as the ceremony is nominal, the former in name only, the latter in form only. If Gulliver were a "real" Christian, he would not be an African slave trader. There is a historical aspect to the Emperor's surprise as well:

> The notion that the Dutch East India traders had renounced their religion as an expediency to carry on trade with the Japanese sprang up during the seventeenth century.... Although the Dutch never actually stamped upon the crucifix to satisfy the Japanese authorities, the merchants nevertheless were compelled to avoid all outward signs of religion as a condition of their remaining in Nagasaki. A letter from the Director-General carefully stipulates the conditions of the Dutch rights in Japan and warns the traders to guard themselves from the outward observances of religion, so that they may keep their Christianity secret and concealed.[62]

Gulliver arrives in Nagasaki on June 9, 1709, and falls into the company of "some Dutch sailors belonging to the *Amboyna* of Amsterdam, a stout ship of 450 tons," suggestive of an African slave ship. Historically, "Amboyna" is one of the spice islands in the East Indies, an African slave trade port of call. Swift is here calling attention to the Dutch brutality toward the English over control of the island. Ten Englishmen were tortured and executed, all slave traders fighting over control of the African slave trade, all in the same boat, "Having been condemned," as the Scriptures surrounding their African slave trade voyage reveal as commentary. Says Gulliver:

> We sailed with a fair wind to the Cape of Good Hope, where we stayed only to take in fresh water. On the 6th of April we arrived safely at Amsterdam, having lost only three men by sickness in the voyage, and a fourth who fell from the foremast into the sea, not far from the coast of Guinea.

To accompany his mention of three *major* African slave trade ports of call at once, Cape of Good Hope, Amsterdam, and Guinea, Swift chooses Scriptures that call attention to God's judgment on such as those who perpetrate the African slave trade in serving Mammon:

> And the earth opened her mouth, and swallowed them up, and their houses, and all the men ... and all their goods. They, and all that appertained to them, went down alive into the pit, and the earth closed upon them and they perished from among the congregation ... ye shall understand that these men have provoked the LORD [Num. 16:31–33].
>
> Go to now, ye rich men, weep and howl for your miseries that shall come upon you. Your riches are corrupted, and your garments are motheaten. Your gold and silver is cankered; and the rust of them shall be a witness against you, and shall eat your flesh as it were fire. Ye have heaped treasure together for the last days.

4. Repository of Abominations

From Amsterdam Gulliver soon after sets sail for England, arriving home on the 10th of April, 1710, "after an absence of five years and six months complete." For the April 10 date, Swift chooses three very appropriate Scriptures. In the first one, the Lord says: "How long refuse ye to keep my commandments and my laws?" The second one offers a far more meaningful motive for travel than the African slave trade, and a far greater worthiness in the sight of God, than white supremacy:

> Go ye therefore, and teach all nations, baptizing them in the name of the Father, and of the Son, and of the Holy Ghost, teaching them to observe all things whatsoever I have commanded you: and, lo, I am with you always, even unto the end of the world [Matt. 28:19–20].

The third Scripture serves as a transition from bad to worst, from the end of the third part to the beginning of the fourth part:

> Repent ye therefore, and be converted, that your sins may be blotted out....
> It shall come to pass, that every soul which will not hear Jesus Christ shall be destroyed from among the people.

5

Black Superiority

Much of Part IV is included in the first chapter, "The African Slave Trade," because most of Part IV is about the African slave trade. Gulliver, while reaching the pinnacle of his profession, "Captain" of an African slave ship, goes from bad in Part III to worst in Part IV. His going from bad to worst is depicted as the reason of the Soul consenting to his "insatiable desire" (64) for the African slave trade, causing the death of the whole Soul. The all-encompassing context in Part IV is the African slave trade. The other major frames of reference are the Reason of the soul of white people, Bonaventure's fourth light, and the last two Steps of Pride; and they must be seen in the context of the African slave trade. The setting for Part IV is Hinnom, which rhymes with Houyhnhnm, and Hinnomland with Houyhnhnmland. "Hinnom," a valley to the south and west of Jerusalem"

> ... appears to have become the common cesspool of the city, into which its sewage was conducted, to be carried off by the waters of the Kedron. From its ceremonial defilement, and from the detested and abominable fire of Molech, if not from the supposed ever-burning funeral piles, the later Jews applied the name of this valley ... to denote the place of eternal torment. In this sense the word is used in the Gospels.... South of the valley is a steep hillside, rocky and full of sepulchres, the traditional site of Aceldama, or "field of blood."[1]

The crux of the satire in Part IV is "pride in reason," which is shown to create white supremacist monsters, like the Houyhnhnms, and Gulliver, who holds forth in their style as representing the masters from whom he has learned, which is why Houyhnhnmland is also a parody of Plato's *Republic*.

We saw in Lilliput and Brobdingnag how the Will of the soul of white people dies. In Laputa, we saw how the Memory of the soul of white people dies. Now, in Houyhnhnmland, Swift shows us how the Reason of the soul of white people dies, causing the death of the whole soul:

... if a sin is suggested to the memory by thought, that is a blemish in the soul, although not a disease. But if the will is moved to the sin by an emotional desire for it, then the soul is diseased, although not fatally. But if the reason also is inclined to the sin by intention, so that the sin in consented to, then the soul dies.[2]

The "reason" is the choosing faculty. It distinguishes good and bad, true and false, expedient and inexpedient. It does so infallibly so long as it is illumined by the light which created it. But when it has lost that light it makes errors. Being thus fallible, it cannot restore itself by its own power, but must be aided by faith, which infallibly makes those distinctions which "corrupt reason is no longer able to make." The soul is "blind" by the corruption of the reason, and "the reason is obscured by pride."[3]

Part IV is illumined by Bonaventure's fourth light, the "higher" light, or the light of grace and of Sacred Scripture, which illumines in regard to "saving truth,"[4] vastly contrary to pride in reason as demonstrated. The fourth light provides crucial insight, as a clue to the understanding of *Gulliver's Travels*:

> Now the fourth light, which illumines the mind for the understanding of "saving truth," is the light of "Sacred Scripture." This light is called "higher" because it leads to things above by the manifestation of truths which are beyond reason and also because it is not acquired by human research, but comes down by inspiration from the "Father of lights." Although in its literal sense, it is "one," still, in its spiritual and mystical sense, it is "threefold," for in all the books of Sacred Scripture, in addition to the "literal" meaning which the words clearly express, there is implied a threefold "spiritual" meaning: namely, the "allegorical," by which we are taught what to believe concerning the Divinity and humanity; the "moral" by which we are taught how to live; and the "anagogical" by which we are taught how to keep close to God. Hence all of Sacred Scripture teaches these three truths: namely, the eternal generation and Incarnation of Christ, the pattern of human life, and the union of the soul with God. The first regards "faith"; the second, "morals"; the third, the "purpose of both."[5]

Like Sacred Scripture teaches, in *Gulliver's Travels*, in addition to the literal sense, Swift teaches a threefold "spiritual" meaning: the "allegorical," the "moral," and the "anagogical," as defined by Bonaventure.

Certainly one timely example of how *not* to live, and how *not* to cleave to God, is provided in Gulliver's having descended to Bernard's last two Steps of Pride: the Eleventh Step, Freedom to Sin, and the Twelfth Step, Habitual Sinning. In terms of the Eleventh Step, Gulliver now "enters upon the ways which seem good to men" but which will plunge him at last into the depths of hell, that is, into contempt of God. For, "when the wicked cometh, then cometh also contempt"[6]:

... he has not yet lost all fear of God. The rational faculty, still faintly whispering, opposes the will with this fear, and he commits the first offences with considerable hesitation; but, like a man trying to ford a stream, he is drawn into the whirlpool of vice, not all at once but little by little.[7]

Ultimately, Gulliver descends to the Twelfth Step of Pride, Habitual Sinning:

As lust awakens, reason is lulled to sleep, and the habit becomes binding. The wretch is drawn into the depths of sin, the captive is given over to the tyranny of vice, so that, swallowed up by a whirlpool of carnal desires and forgetting both his own reason and the fear of God, "the fool saith in his heart, There is no God."[8]

"The twelfth step, therefore, may be called the habitual sinning by which the fear of God is lost and contempt of God incurred."[9]

Gulliver accepts an advantageous offer to be captain of the *Adventure*, a stout merchantman of 350 tons. He sets sail on September 7, 1710. The Scriptures chosen for that date are ominous but appropriate for the relevant stage of Gulliver's African slave trade travels and the certainty of his desolation. For example:

I saw the Lord standing upon the altar: and he said, Smite the lintel of the door, that the posts may shake: and cut them in the head, all of them; and I will slay the last of them with the sword: he that fleeth of them shall not flee away, and he that escapeth of them shall not be delivered [Amos 9:1].

The second Scripture for the 7 September date speaks of those who "shall be cast out into outer darkness: there shall be weeping and gnashing of teeth." Bernard uses this Scripture in connection with the Second Ignorance, of which Gulliver is guilty. The third Scripture is equally fitting, especially as suggestive of white supremacy. From "For thy violence against thy brother" until the end of the Scripture is depicted from the climax to the end of the *Travels*.

Behold, I have made thee small among the heathen: thou art greatly despised. The pride of thine heart hath deceived thee ... that saith in his heart, Who shall bring me down to the ground? Though thou exalt thyself as the eagle, and though thou set thy nest among the stars, thence will I bring thee down, saith the Lord.... For thy violence against thy brother ... shame shall cover thee, and thou shalt be cut off for ever ... as thou hast done, it shall be done unto thee: thy reward shall return upon thy own head [Obadiah].

By the next Scripture we know that Gulliver *is* condemned, and that he walks *not* after the spirit, but after the flesh:

There is therefore now no condemnation to them which are in Christ Jesus, who walk not after the flesh, but after the Spirit [Rom. 8].

If Gulliver walked after the Spirit, he would know himself, which he does not: "The Spirit itself beareth witness with our spirit, that we are the children of God." That he does not know this is pivotally obvious at the climax.

On the 14th of September, Gulliver meets up with African slave-ship Captain Pocock of Bristol, at Tenerife, who was going to the bay of Campechy, all African slave trade ports of call. The first Scripture for that date is chosen to attack African slave ship ports of call, in the name of Nineveh:

> Woe to the bloody city! it is all full of lies and robbery; the prey departeth not.... Thou hast multiplied thy merchants above the stars of heaven ... thy captains are as the great grasshoppers, which camp in the hedges in the cold day, but when the sun ariseth they flee away, and their place is not known where they are [Nah. 3].

The above and following Scriptures remind us of Swift's debt to Shakespeare's protest of the African slave trade and "nominal" Christianity, not only in *Othello* but also in the *Merchant of Venice*, whose ships go to African slave trade ports of call, and whose "spitting" on Shylock is behavior anathematic to "real" Christianity.

On the 16th day of September, Gulliver says that Captain Pocock "was parted from us by a storm" and that "his ship foundered, and none escaped, but one cabin-boy." (179) The first Scripture for the 14th suggests the wicked "making men like fish of the sea":

> dragging them out with his net, gathering them in his seine ... for by them he lives in luxury, and his food is rich.... He keeps on emptying his net, and mercilessly slaying nations [Habakkuk 1].

In the context of "catching" black brethren, we are reminded of Shakespeare's thoughts regarding unnatural evil and degeneracy, in Albany's repudiation of Goneril:

> Most barbarous, most degenerate, have you madded!
> If that the Heavens do not their visible spirits
> Send quickly down to tame these vile offenses,
> It will come.
> Humanity must perforce prey on itself,
> Like monsters of the deep [King Lear, IV, ii, 43–49].[10]

The African slave trade is the consummate example of humanity preying on itself. Captain Pocock's catastrophe is marked by allusions to the severe judgment of God in the word of the Lord which came unto Zephaniah:

> I will utterly consume all things from off the land, saith the Lord. I will consume man and beast.... And them that are turned back from the Lord; and

those that have not sought the Lord, nor inquired for him ... the day of the Lord is at hand.... Howl, ye inhabitants of Maktesh, for *all the merchant people are cut down*; all they that bear silver are cut off ... the mighty man shall cry bitterly. That day is a day of wrath, a day of trouble and distress, a day of wasteness and desolation, a day of darkness and gloominess, a day of clouds and thick darkness.... And I will bring distress upon men, that they walk like blind men, because they have sinned against the Lord: and their blood shall be poured out as dust, and their flesh as the dung. Neither their silver nor their gold shall be able to deliver them in the day of the Lord's wrath.

Of Captain Pocock, Gulliver says, with self-betrying irony and lack of self-knowledge: "he was an honest man, and a good sailor, but a little too positive in his own opinions, which was the cause of his destruction, as it hath been of several others like [Gulliver]" (179).

For if he had followed my advise, he might at this time have been safe at home with his family as well as myself [179].

The cause of Captain Pocock's destruction is the African slave trade, as it is the cause of Gulliver's destruction, even as he criticizes Pocock, who, if he had followed Gulliver's advice, would have met with destruction. Gulliver is not "safe" in terms of salvation, which is what counts the most, so the Scriptures Swift chooses make fitting commentary on the situations he depicts and protests in defense of "real" Christianity.

Following the irony of Gulliver's criticism of Pocock, Swift, to emphasize the condemnatory message of the preceding Scriptures, emphasizes notorious aspects unmistakably identifiable with the African slave trade, and with Gulliver's travels via the triangular trade from England to Africa to the West Indies, and back to England: *Calentures*— an African fever, *Barbados, and the Leeward Islands*. "Barbadoes was the mother of the West Indian sugar islands.... Even before the intensive cultivation of sugar began to exhaust the soil of Barbadoes, the plantation system spread to ... the Leeward chain"[11] ("*where I touched by the direction of the merchants who employed me*") in 1711. "From 1698 to 1707, 34,583 slaves were shipped to Barbadoes."[12] Moreover, "It was widely admitted that slaves in the West Indies were treated more harshly than those in the English colonies in the mainland."[13] Gulliver's orders are also that he "should trade with the Indians in the South Sea" (129–180), another *major* African slave trade port of call. Why haven't other scholars connected these places and activities to the African slave trade? In his "Notes," Louis Landa mentions "the commercial rivalry between England and Holland,"[14] but he doesn't mention that "the commercial rivalry" had to do with the African slave trade, which in 1709 would have been the case, even to the point of war. Also puzzling for the same reason, is Landa's Note on Gulliver's racist animalization of black Africans:

Swift's description of the Yahoos may have been suggested, according to Professor R.W. Frantz, by the accounts of large apes or of the Hottentots to be found in contemporary voyage literature. The word "Yahoo" derives, possible, from two common expressions of disgust in the period, "yah" and "ugh."[15]

Considering the allusions to the African slave trade that precede Gulliver's racist animalization of black people, the suggestion of Hottentot should, it would seem, have called to mind the African slave trade. The question as to why other scholars fail to mention the African slave trade, given so many clues, remains unanswered. White-everyman-Gulliver doesn't mention it either. Perhaps Swift is projecting a conspiracy of silence in honor of "white supremacy," as indicative of the character of white people, for which he deemed a mirror such as *Gulliver's Travels* was needed. He certainly had a model at hand in Shakespeare's mirror. Swift's is a mirror held up to the nature of white people, to show "they imitate humanity so abominably."[16]

Proof of the latter, in one respect, is Gulliver's racist perception of black people as animals, which exposes his inhumanity, racism causing troubled vision and distortions, verifying Bernard's teaching:

> Visible things are investigated by means of sense perception, which reveals corporeal objects not as they are in themselves but as they appear to our sensitivity.[17]

and the teaching of Robert Grosseteste:

> ... the soul itself is a mirror, whose spiritual condition dictates the rectitude with which it records the figures of nature. Only the soul/mirror which is able to subject itself to the will of Christ will be free of distortion. If distortions and lack of correspondence in the "speculum" of nature occur, it is not that there are distortions in creation, but rather in the attitude of the observer.[18]

But then, Gulliver's entire related account of coming upon "several animals in a field" (181) is fraudulent and disingenuous. He's been trafficking in black Africans for most of his life, but to cover this up he pretends, in coming upon them in a field, that he is discovering them for the first time. Swift provides the first clue exposing Gulliver's racism, that those whom Gulliver animalized are human beings. He has Gulliver see "many tracks of human feet, and some of cows, but most of horses" (181). The black Africans, that is, the black Yahoos, are the human beings, and Gulliver knows this. They are human beings with skin of a "brown buff colour" (181). His white supremacist description of black people not only proves the inferiority of sense perception, but that his reason is obscured by pride; it makes errors, having "lost the light which created it; and the soul is "blind" by the corruption of the reason.[19] In other words, not only is the belief in white superiority and supremacy, proof of the reason's loss of the light which created it, such beliefs obscure and corrupt the reason, and trouble the vision so that distortions occur, not in creation, but in the white supremacist attitude of the observer.

What seems to have confused noted scholars such as Louis A. Landa and Victoria Glendinning in their interpretation of the yahoos is the failure to see Swift's projection of black and white yahoos, and his depiction of black yahoos according to the white supremacist perception of black people. In his exegesis, Landa describes the black yahoos as "figures and images of the flesh":

> The noisome putridity of these creatures, their envelopment in stench and dungy vileness, is, of course, emblematic of their moral natures.[20]

Actually, the black yahoos have better moral natures than the white yahoos, as the comparison later demonstrates. Glendinning gives the following rendition:

> The Houyhnhnms share their country with the Yahoos—hairy, smelly, filthy, aggressive, carrion-eating, tree-climbing, savage creatures with hooked claws ... "abominable" animals, but recognizably human in form. The horses classed Gulliver, because of his shape, with the Yahoos, and were surprised by his accomplishments. He was a "clean, civil, reasoning Yahoo."[21]

But, what exactly is an abominable animal recognizably human in form? A white supremacist would say "a nigger," which is what Gulliver says in words that reveal the feelings the epithet defines:

> Upon the whole, I never beheld in all my travels so disagreeable an animal, or one against which I naturally conceived so strong antipathy. So that thinking I had seen enough, full of contempt and aversion, I got up and pursued the beaten road [181].

Glendinning is also mistaken in saying "*Gulliver* is about morality, but it is not about Christianity."[22] In fact, Swift makes a crucial distinction between morality and a Christian religious conscience:

> ... it is found by experience, that those men who set up for morality without regard to religion, are generally virtuous but in part; they will be just in their dealings between man and man; but if they find themselves disposed to pride, lust, intemperance, or avarice, they do not think their morality concerned to check them in any of these vices; because it is the great rule of such men, that they may lawfully follow the dictates of nature, wherever their safety, health, and fortune are not injured. So that upon the whole there is hardly one vice, which a mere moral man may not, upon some occasion, allow himself to practice.[23]

The African slave trade is a perfect example of men disposed to pride (white supremacy), lust, and avarice who do not think their morality concerned to check them in any of these vices because, regarding fortune, the African slave trade "was so enormously profitable that nothing else could compete with it."[24]

Glendinning asks the question: "Did Swift believe in God? Many of his ecclesiastical superiors suspected he did not, because of his light way of writing about religious divisions and his conspicuous lack of professed piety."[25] Perhaps those "ecclesiastical superiors," like Bishop Berkeley, were "nominal" Christians, or worse, and did not understand "real" Christianity. Bishop Berkeley's "philosophical language" in the above quote certainly demonstrates such ignorance.

Glendinning also states that Swift "endorsed nominal Christianity."[26] Nothing could be farther from the truth. In his essay on the subject, "The Abolishing of Christianity," a masterpiece of irony, Swift attacks "nominal" Christianity while pretending to support it. Swift's ultimate concern in *Gulliver's Travels* is "real" Christianity. In his "A Sermon On Brotherly Love," Swift states:

> ... our want of brotherly love hath almost driven out all sense of religion from among us, which cannot well be otherwise: for, since our Saviour laid so much weight upon his disciples loving one another, that he gave it among his last instructions; and since the primitive Christians are allowed to have chiefly propagated the faith by their strict observance of that instruction; it must follow, that in proportion as brotherly love declineth, Christianity will do so, too.[27]

Nothing better demonstrates the disappearance of brotherly love than the African slave trade and white supremacy, which explains the absence of "real" Christianity in *Gulliver's Travels*, except by corrective allusion, and which absence explains Swift's protest of white supremacy and the African slave trade.

A famous eighteenth-century actor puts in proper perspective the difference between morality, with its propensity for hypocrisy, and "real" Christianity:

> The famous actor George Frederick Cooke appeared drunk on the stage of the theater Royal in Liverpool and was booed by the audience. Reeling to the footlights, he shouted, "I have not come here to be insulted by a set of wretches, every brick in whose infernal town is cemented with an African's blood."[28]

Gulliver's disingenuous "discovery" of "several animals in a field," as if seeing black people for the first time, is part of Gulliver's cover-up, part of Swift's emphasis upon hypocrisy and fraud as character traits. Instead of having Gulliver come right out and tell the reader he's an African slave trader, he has him show his true colors by impersonating a discoverer or explorer/traveler like Amerigo Vespucci, who makes real discoveries (and whose letters were rediscovered in the eighteenth century).

> They had beards like goats, and thick hair, some frizzed.... Their shape was very singular, and deformed.... Their bodies were bare, so that I might see their skins, which were of a brown buff colour. They had no tails ... and often stood on their hind feet. They climbed high trees, as nimbly as a squirrel, for they had strong extended claws.... They would often spring, and bound, and leap with prodigious agility.... Upon the whole, I never beheld in all my travels so disagreeable an animal, or one against which I naturally conceived so strong antipathy. So that thinking I had seen enough, full of contempt and aversion, I got up and pursued the beaten roads [181],

Except for the animalization of black people, Gulliver's descriptions here and elsewhere have the fake aura of an explorer's observations. For example, Vespucci's discovery, except for Gulliver's conspicuous racism, is suggested. It's from a letter from Vespucci to Lorenzo di Pierfrancesco dé Medici, written in the year 1502 from Lisbon concerning Vespucci's return from the new lands he was sent to explore by His Majesty the King of Portugal:

> We found the entire land inhibited by people completely naked, men as well as women, without at all covering their shame. They were sturdy and well-proportioned in body, white in complexion, with long black hair and little or no beard. I strove hard to understand their life and customs, since I ate and slept among them for twenty-seven days; and what I learned of them is the following. They ate sitting upon the ground; their food includes many roots and herbs and very good fruits, endless fish, a great abundance of shellfish.... The meat they most commonly eat is human flesh, as we shall tell.... They are a warlike people and very cruel to one another; and all their arms and sallies are, as Petrarch says, "entrusted to the wind," for they are bows, arrows, spears and stones; and they use no protective armor for their bodies, since they go about naked as the day they were born. Nor do they maintain any order when they make war, except that they do what their elders advise. And when they fight, they kill one another most cruelly, and the side that emerges victorious on the field buries all of their own dead, but they dismember and eat their dead enemies; and those they capture they imprison and keep as slaves in their houses: if females they sleep with them; if males, they marry them to their daughters. And at certain times when a diabolical fury comes over them, they invite their relatives and the people to dinner, and they set them out before them — that is, the mother and all the children they have got from her — and performing certain ceremonies kill them with arrows and eat them; and they do the same to the aforesaid male slaves and the children that have come from them. And this is certain, for in their houses we found human flesh hung up for smoking, and a lot of it.... And what I most marvel at, given their wars and their cruelty, is that I could not learn from them why they make war upon one another: since they do not have private property, or command empires or kingdoms, and have no notion of greed either for things or for power, which seems to me to be the cause of wars and all acts of disorder. When we asked them to tell us the cause, the only reason they could give was that this curse had begun "in olden times," and that they wish to avenge the death of their

ancestors: in sum, a bestial thing.... Since we journeyed there in the name of discovery, and with that commission departed from Lisbon, and not to seek after profit, we did not make obstacles to our exploration of the land nor seek after profit ... it is my hope that, now that his Most Serene Highness is sending voyages there, not many years will pass before the land brings vast profit and revenue to the kingdom of Portugal.... For the present I remain here in Lisbon, waiting for the king to decide what to do with me: may it please God that it be whatever most befits His holy service and the salvation of my soul.[29]

Except for the white cannibals, Vespucci's descriptions are reflected more in Gulliver's description of white yahoos than of black yahoos. One of the most significant likenesses is the love of war, killing, and cruelty. One of the most glaring differences is Vespucci's claimed desire to please God with holy service (but he picks up a few slaves) and his concern for the salvation of his soul, desires and concerns totally lacking in Gulliver. Nevertheless, Swift has Gulliver pass himself off as a Vespucci-type explorer/discoverer to hide the fact he's an African slave trader whose travels are only to African slave trade ports of call, striving not to *be* but to *appear* superior (Fifth Step of Pride). In this way Swift calls attention to the hypocrisy and fraud in the character of white people which he is projecting.

One of the black human beings Gulliver animalizes goes directly up to Gulliver and receives "a good blow" from Gulliver's hanger. Gulliver says, referring to "the ugly monster" (Gulliver is the ugly monster, as we shall see):

> When the beast felt the smart, he drew back, and roared so loud, that a herd of at least forty came flocking about me from the next field, howling and making odious faces; but I ran to the body of a tree, and leaning my back against it, kept them off, by waving my hanger. Several of this cursed brood getting hold of the branches behind leaped up into the tree, from whence they began to discharge their excrements on my head: however, I escaped pretty well ... but was almost stifled with the filth, which fell about me on every side [181–182].

Landa is mistaken in claiming this indicates the moral corruption of the black Yahoos, saying: "Swift has employed an old device abundant in Christian literature (though not only there) — there metaphorical association of physical corruption with moral corruption."[30] Swift is alluding to the warning of Bernard in one of Bernard's conversionary sermons previously mentioned, and the warning is meant to address white-everyman-Gulliver and is ingeniously used by Swift as prefigurative of the *Travels*' climax:

> My brethren, who of us, when he takes notice that the garment which he wears, is all over bedawbed with foul spattle, and defiled with filthy ordure, does not vehemently abhor it, does not presently put it off, does not with indignation cast it away from him? wherefore he that discovers not his Gar-

ment, but himself within, under his garment, to be in such an manner defiled, ought so much more to grieve, and be in consternation, by how much neerer he carries about him what he abhors. For the defiled Soul cannot so cast away itself, as it can its bespotted Coat. In fine, who is there amongst us of so great patience and vertue, that if perhaps (as we read concerning "Mary the Sister of Moses") he should see his flesh by a certain leprosy on the sudden white with an ill whiteness, should be able to bear it with an equal mind, and give his Creator thanks? Now what is this flesh of ours but a certain rotten Coat which we are clothed? ... But there, there is vehement tribulation, and a most just cause of grief, when a Sinner awaked out of sleep of his miserable pleasure, shall begin to deprehend and see that internal leprosy which he has got to himself with much study and labour. For no body hates his own flesh, much less can the Soul hate itself.[31]

Swift would have found the racism of Mary, the sister of Moses, especially amenable to the equating of white supremacy with inner leprosy reflected by the whiteness of her skin:

And Miriam and Aaron spake against Moses because of the Ethiopian woman whom he had married: for he had married an Ethiopian woman.... And the anger of the Lord was kindled against them.... And behold, Miriam became leprous, "white" as snow: and Aaron looked upon Miriam, and, behold she was leprous. And Aaron said unto Moses, "Alas, my lord, I beseech thee, lay not the sin upon us, wherein we have done foolishly, and wherein we have sinned. Let her not be as one dead, of whom the flesh is half consumed when he cometh out of his mother's womb [Num. 12].

Swift has the black yahoos discharge their excrement on Gulliver as a way of signifying Gulliver's moral corruption, *not* that of the yahoos, who have been deprived, by slavery, of the freedom to be corrupt. As Bernard states, "On what basis, in fact, can one impute anything to a man, whether good or bad, if he is not known to have the free disposal of himself? ... where there is no freedom, neither is there merit, nor consequently judgment...."[32] In other words, Gulliver is not defiled by the excrement of the African slaves, but by his animalization of them. "Those things which proceed out of the mouth, [like "ugly monsters," "cursed brood," "herd," "deformed," "beast," etc.] come forth from the heart; and they defile the man. For out of the heart proceed evil thoughts; [like contempt, aversion, and strong antipathy] these are the things which defile a man" (Matt. 15), not to mention the desire to exterminate black people from the face of the earth.

The African slaves are put to flight by the approach of their slave master, a Greek monster, the Centaur, emblematic of white supremacy, the African slave trade, pride in reason, and the origins of these emblems in Plato and Aristotle, all at the same time and in the same image. Swift depicts the master-slave-plantation system (Aristotle's praedial slavery) beginning with over forty animalized African slaves put to flight by the approach of a single arrogant horse presented as the perfection of nature, demonstrably superior to humans, as idealized by Socrates in Plato's *Republic*, for the imitation of mankind. Swift is satirizing Socrates by depicting white mankind as following this teaching of Socrates, and thinking of itself as Socrates thought of horses. For, to imitate Socrates' conception of a horse is to think of oneself as superior and supreme, as in white supremacy. (The medieval symbol of pride is a man on a horse.) In Houyhnhnmland, Socrates' classism conception of the horse is metamorphosed into white supremacist Greek monsters, Centaurs, called Houyhnhnms, the racist, discriminatory, African slavery context reflecting the discriminatory classism context of the Socrates conception. Swift could also draw on Dante and Shakespeare for this depiction of the Houyhnhnms. Dante puts the Centaurs in the "River of Blood," the punishment for "the Violent Against Their Neighbors." The Houyhnhnms are violent against their neighbors the black yahoos, to the extent of debating whether or not to "exterminate them from the face of the earth." Drawing on Shakespeare, Swift combines Albany's castigation of Goneril, and Lear's castigation of Goneril and Regan, to equate the African slave trade, and its perpetrators, with unnatural, monstrous evil. And like Shakespeare, Swift identifies unnatural evil with contempt of Christ. Albany's outrage against Goneril is a fitting example in Shakespeare's *King Lear*:

> O Goneril!
> You are not worth the dust which the rude wind
> Blows in your face. I fear your disposition.
> That nature which contemns its origin
> Cannot be bordered certain in itself.
> She that herself will sliver and disbranch
> From her material sap, perforce must wither
> And come to deadly use.[33]

By "its origin" Shakespeare means not only her earthly father, King Lear, but also her heavenly Father, for the same reason Swift alludes to Gulliver's heavenly Father when he opens the *Travels* with Gulliver saying, "My father." Neither Gulliver nor Goneril know "Our Father," God, and both come to "deadly use." Goneril's response to Albany, "the text is foolish,"[34] refers to the Bible text Shakespeare alludes to with Albany's castigation:

> I am the true vine, and my Father is the husbandman.... Abide in me, and I in you.... I am the vine, ye are the branches: He that abideth in me, and I in him, the same bringeth forth much fruit.... If a man abide not in me, he is cast forth as a branch, and is withered; and men gather them, and cast them into the fire, and they are burned [John 15:1–6].

Albany ends with a timely assessment of Goneril's unnatural evil, of a kind that manifests as Gulliver's unnatural evil:

> If that the Heavens do not their visible spirits
> Send quickly down to tame these vile offenses
> It will come.
> Humanity must perforce prey on itself,
> Like monsters of the deep.[35]

Humanity was already preying on itself like monsters of the deep, in the African slave trade, when Shakespeare wrote *King Lear*, or at least when it was first performed in 1606. (By 1617, 28,000 slaves were being shipped annually from Angola and the Congo).

Combine humanity preying upon itself like monsters of the deep, with Lear's castigation of his daughters

> Down from the waist they are Centaurs,
> Though women all above [IV, vi, 126–127].[36]

and the image of the Houyhnhnms emerges.

Landa is mistaken when he says the Houyhnhnms constitute "moral perfection"[37]; and Glendinning is mistaken when she calls Houyhnhnmland "Eden."[38] And when the "cursed brood" discharge their excrements on Gulliver's head, it is not Swift's "excremental vision," as it is called by Norman O. Brown, of which there is no such thing. Swift is just identifying moral corruption with physical corruption, not as in the medieval play, *Mankind*, in which moral corruption is identified with the dischargers of excrement, but as in "whited sepulchres," identifying inner filth with white skin, the moral with the physical, as in Miriam's racism identified with leprosy. Gulliver's racism is also identified with excrement, the filth that almost stifles him.

"In the midst of this distress," he says:

> I observed them all to run away on a sudden as fast as they could, at which I ventured to leave the tree, and pursue the road, wondering what it was that could put them in this fright. But looking on my left hand, I saw a horse walking softly in the field, which my persecutors having sooner discovered, was the cause of their flight. The horse started a little when he came near me, but soon recovering himself, looked full in my face with manifest tokens of wonder: he viewed my hands and feet, walking round me several times. I would have pursued my journey, but he placed himself directly in the way, yet looking with a very mild aspect, never offering the least violence. We stood gazing at each other for some time; at last I took the boldness to reach my hand towards his neck, with a design to stroke it, using the common style and whistle of jockeys when they are going to handle a strange horse. But this animal, seeming to receive my civilities with disdain, shook his head, and bent his brows, softly raising up his left forefoot to remove my hand. Then he neighed three or four

times, but in so different a cadence, that I almost began to think he was speaking to himself in some language of his own.

Right away, Swift exposes the inner filth and leprosy indicative of racism, in the egregious distinction Gulliver makes between black human beings, even as animalized, and horses, relegating black human beings to a level lower than brute beasts. But the irony is that it is white people, because of their racism and violence against black people, who are on the lowest level, lower than black people, lower than animals, and lower than the animals they perceive black people to be, as Swift is soon to demonstrate. Gulliver continues to be in awe of this Greek monster, the Centaur, in much the same way that Humanists stand in awe of the philosophers the Houyhnhnms symbolize:

> While he and I were thus employed, another horse came up; who applying himself to the first in a very formal manner, they gently struck each other's right hoof before, neighing several times by turns.... They went some paces off, as if it were to confer together, walking side by side, backward and forward, like persons deliberating upon some affair of weight, but often turning their eyes towards me, as it were to watch that I might not escape. I was amazed to see such actions and behaviour in brute beasts, and concluded with myself, that if the inhabitants of this country were endued with a proportionable degree of reason, they must needs be the wisest people upon earth.

The Houyhnhnms, always spelled with a capital *H*, have never before seen a white human being, so naturally they are "curious" about Gulliver, and view him or try to know him by means of scientific curiosity, as Gulliver, in imitation of the philosophers they symbolize, deceitfully viewed the African slaves as if for the first time. But it is important to be mindful of the racial distinctions being made, based on color and stereotypes, as clues that Swift is talking about white human beings and black human beings and racism. Also, since the Houyhnhnms view all human beings, black or white, as "yahoos" (lower case *y*), we can take that as a clue that the black yahoos the Houyhnhnms enslave are black human beings and not animals as described by Gulliver. He tells of being closely examined:

> The two horses came up close to me, looking with great earnestness upon my face and hands.... [They] felt the lappet of my coat, and finding it to hang loose about me, they both looked with new signs of wonder. They stroked my right hand, seeming to admire the softness and *colour*.... They were under great perplexity about my shoes and stockings, which they felt very often, neighing to each other, and using various gestures, not unlike those of a philosopher, when he would attempt to solve some new and different phenomenon.

Bernard says: "Philosophers, filled with vanity, investigate the arrangement and order of things, in order to gratify their scientific curiosity,"[39] which seems to be the case above. But, in the main he says, which is the point here, "We can know our neighbors only by love, and this purifies the minds eye so as to make it able to contemplate Truth in itself."[40] Swift stresses this over and over with every such contrariety as Aristotle's way of knowing by vain scientific curiosity.

Another clue that Gulliver is a white yahoo, and all of the other yahoos, the only other humans presented, are black, is Gulliver's impression that the common Houyhnhnms "perhaps were really amazed at the sight of a man so very different in habit, *feature, and complexion* [white, in other words] from those who might probably live in so remote a climate." He goes on with praise of the Houyhnhnms:

> Upon the whole, the behaviour of these animals was so orderly and rational, so acute and judicious, that I at last concluded, they must needs be magicians, who had thus metamorphosed themselves upon some design, and seeing a stranger in the way, were resolved to divert themselves with him.

Swift here alludes to Ovid's *Metamorphoses* to identify the Houyhnhnms as Centaurs, a Greek monster having the head of man and the body of a horse. Another clue is the irony of Gulliver's observation: "I plainly observed, that their language expressed the passions very well," since they lack passion itself. This seems also an allusion to the violence their language hides, and their treatment of their yahoos suggest: "When their neighbours and Lapithae were holding a feast for the wedding of their king, Pirithous, with Hippodamia, the Centaurs, whom they had invited, tried to carry off Hippodamia and other women. A battle resulted, in which the Centaurs were defeated, and were driven from their haunts about Mt. Pelion."[41] The most famous of the Centaurs was Chiron. Chiron was wounded in the knee by a poisoned arrow. According to Greek mythology, "Chiron was wise and just, and learned in music and medicine."[42]

> He educated some of the most famous Greek heroes, such as Asclepius, Jason, and Achilles.[43]

In his "A Tritical Essay," Swift mentions Ixion, who is the father of the Centaurs. There is enough, in other words, to suggest that these talking Houyhnhnms, considered by Gulliver "wise and just" like Chiron, are Centaurs. Their enslaving of the black yahoos makes them monsters (Greek) via the philosophy of slavery by Aristotle.

Speaking of the two horses he had thus far mentioned, Gulliver says: "I could frequently distinguish the word 'yahoo,' which was repeated by each of them several times." Foolishly, he adds:

5. Black Superiority 169

... although it was impossible for me to conjecture what it meant, yet while the two horses were busy in conversation, I endeavoured to practice this word upon my tongue; and as soon as they were silent, I boldly pronounced yahoo in a loud voice, imitating, at the same time, as near as I could, the neighing of a horse.

He thus unwittingly identifies himself as a "yahoo," which he is soon to bitterly regret. "Yahoo" is what the Houyhnhnms call their black African slaves, so obviously it's a derogatory term, a charged word or epithet like "nigger." So when Gulliver comes along, looking just like a black man except for the color of his skin and clothes, it stands to reason the Houyhnhnms would consider him a "yahoo," to Gulliver's "everlasting mortification," when he sees whom else the Houyhnhnms call "yahoo." Swift's intent is to bring white people face to face, as in a mirror, with their vile racist inhumanness, partly for the reason James Baldwin states: "Not everything that is faced can be changed, but nothing can be changed until it is faced," and change is what Swift is after before it is too late, as it will soon be shown to be for Gulliver. But Swift is hoping for "miraculous changes" (metamorphoses) in his white readers.

Speaking of the two horses, Gulliver says, "the two friends took their leave," ironically giving animals human attributes. He never gives the black human beings human attributes, however. One of the horses, the grey, makes signs that Gulliver should walk before him. Gulliver thinks it "prudent to comply," and he is conducted to the grey's house. Meanwhile, he is still expecting to be greeted by human beings. Amazed by the behavior of the horses, he is confirmed "that a people who could so far civilize brute animals must needs excel in wisdom all the nations of the world." That sounds like something Aristotle told Alexander, that the Greeks were the wisest people in the world and could control the world, and sent out Alexander to massacre and conquer the world, turning him into a "civilized" monster, as the Houyhnhnms are "civilized" monsters, holding forth in the style of Aristotle and Plato.

As Gulliver is escorted through the grey horse's house, he waits to hear a human voice. Hearing none, he says:

> I began to think that this house must belong to some person of great note among them, because there appeared so much ceremony before I could gain admittance. But that a man of quality should be served all by horses was beyond my comprehension. I feared my brain was disturbed by my sufferings and misfortunes: I roused myself, and looked about me in the room where I was left alone.... I rubbed my eyes often, but the same objects still occurred. I pinched my arms and sides, to awake myself, hoping I might be in a dream. I then absolutely concluded that all these appearances could be nothing else but necromancy and magic.

We are again reminded of *Metamorphoses*, and for good reason: The allusion to "a sudden transformation," which is prefaced by a kind of manger scene. The grey horse comes to the door and makes Gulliver follow him into a third room, where he sees "a very comely mare, together with a colt and foal, sitting on their haunches, upon mats of straw, not unartfully made, and perfectly neat and clean." Gulliver is next led out into a kind of court, where was another building at some distance from the house" (slave quarters). He says:

> Here we entered, and I saw three of those detestable creatures, which I first met after my landing.... They were all tied by the neck with strong withes, fastened to a beam.

With this scene, Swift alludes to "a sudden transformation" which identifies these "detestable creatures" as black human beings of the First Ignorance, and therefore on a higher level than Gulliver, who is guilty of the Second Ignorance. "The first ignorance brought man to a level with the beasts, the second made him lower." But mainly, Swift is calling attention to and establishing the fact that these creatures "tied by the neck" are black human beings, not animals. They are of the first fall, Adam's fall, the fall of man, and thus, fittingly chastised by Bernard in the following:

> Alas! a sad and pitiable change, that man, a native of Paradise, lord of the earth, citizen of heaven, member of the household of the Lord of hosts, a brother of the blessed spirits and co-heir of the heavenly powers, finds himself lying in a stable by a sudden transformation due to this own weakness ... and tied to the manger because of his untamed roughness.[44]

("And the brutes, if they could speak, would surely say: "See, Adam has become like one of us.")

Another distinction is made, identifying them as slaves, presumably, of course, African slaves, distinguishing them from servants, presumably indentured servants:

> The master horse ordered a sorrel nag, one of his servants, to untie the largest of these animals, and take him into the yard.

Swift also establishes them as black human beings by distinguishing them by color and feature, in having them compared to white Gulliver:

> The beast and I were brought close together, and our countenances diligently compared, both by master and servant, who thereupon repeated several times the word "yahoo." My horror and astonishment are not to be described, when I observed, in this abominable animal, a perfect human figure; the face of it indeed was flat and broad, *the nose depressed, the lips large,* and *the mouth wide....* The forefeet of the yahoo differed from my hands in nothing else but the length of the nails, the coarseness and *brownness of the palms,* and the

hairiness on the backs ... *the same* in every part of our bodies, *except* as to *hairiness and colour*. (Emphasis added, showing historically typical, well caricatured Negroid features.)

Even though Gulliver admits to seeing in the black man "a perfect human figure," Gulliver still speaks of him in animal terms, which means Gulliver can't hide his racist distortions. And by these racist distortions we know the one described is black, and a human being. Gulliver is horrified because that means that this "yahoo" is of the same species as he, white Gulliver, is. We also know that this "yahoo" is black by the use of the word "kennel," as in "the yahoo's kennel," and the yahoo was "sent back to his kennel." "Kennel" was used onboard African slave ships to designate the slave quarters. Most of all, we know the yahoos spoken of are black people because of white people's hatred of them. With the use of the irony of self-betrayal, Swift has Gulliver betray his hatred with a hypocritical confession:

> ... as to those filthy yahoos, although there were few greater lovers of mankind, at that time, than myself, yet I confess I never saw any sensitive being so detestable on all counts; and the more I came near them, the more hateful they grew, while I stayed in that country.

And, of course, to remove all doubt, there is segregation, so we know these yahoos are black. Gulliver says, for example:

> When it grew towards evening, the master horse ordered a place for me to lodge in; it was but six yards from the house, and separated from the stable of the yahoos.

Swift's aim is to vividly expose white-everyman-Gulliver's racism, and the heresies of white supremacy. As previously mentioned, this book is a mirror held up to white people, to inspire a change of heart in them, a miraculous change (a metamorphoses).

Using Aristotle's philosophy of slavery to stigmatize and stereotype black people as inferior, and justify the African slave trade, Gulliver concentrates on those qualities that, according to Aristotle, stereotype white people as superior, and justify the African slave trade and white supremacy. Gulliver says, for example:

> My principal endeavour was to learn the language, which my master ... and his children, and every servant of his house were desirous to teach me. For they looked upon it as a prodigy that a brute animal should discover such marks of a rational creature.... The curiosity and impatience of my master were so great, that he spent many hours of his leisure to instruct me. He was convinced that I must be a yahoo, but my teachableness, civility and cleanliness astonished him; which were qualities altogether so opposite to those animals [black people].... He was extremely curious to know from what part of the country I came, and how I was taught to imitate a rational creature,

because the yahoos (whom he saw I exactly resembled in my head, hands and face, that were only visible), with some appearance of cunning, and the strongest disposition of mischief, were observed to be the most unteachable of all brutes.

Of course, we never see anyone trying to teach them anything. They are presumed unteachable by their race and enslavement.

Gulliver also tries to distinguish himself from the black yahoos, who go naked, by his clothes. He says: "The Houyhnhnms who came to visit my master, out of a design of seeing and talking with me, could hardly believe me to be a right yahoo, because my body had a different covering from others of my kind." Early one morning, Gulliver is caught virtually naked while asleep by one of his master's servants. Upon the servant's report, Gulliver is sent for. He tells the reader:

> I had hitherto concealed the secret of my dress, in order to distinguish myself as much as possible from that cursed race of yahoos, but now I found it in vain to do so any longer.

By "that *cursed* race of yahoos," we know he means black people, "cursed" being one of the oldest racist labels white people put on black people, dating at least as far back as the tenth century, in *Le Chanson de Roland*.

Gulliver is asked to strip in front of his master, who walks around Gulliver several times, and Gulliver tells us the result:

> ... he said, it was plain I must be a perfect yahoo; but that I differed very much from the rest of my species, in the *whiteness* and smoothness *of my skin* (emphasis added).

If Gulliver differs in the whiteness of his skin from the rest of his species, meaning the yahoos of Houyhnhnmland, it means they are black human beings, and as such, are of the same species as Gulliver, much to his racist dismay, which he makes known to his master:

> I expressed my uneasiness at his giving me so often the appellation of yahoo, an odious animal, for which I had so utter an hatred and contempt; I begged he would forbear applying that word to me, and take the same order in his family, and among his friends whom he suffered to see me. I requested likewise, that the secret of my having a false covering to my body might be known to none but himself, at least as long as my present clothing should last; for as to what the sorrel nag his valet had observed, his Honour might command him to conceal it.

All this, Gulliver says his master consented to, and thus the secret was kept. Besides, his master is more astonished at Gulliver's capacity for speech and reason than at the figure of his body, and prefers that Gulliver give an account of himself. In this account, Swift has Gulliver make a statement of conspicuous irony that sheds light on Gulliver's degenerate and brutal nature, his being an African slave ship captain. He owns his resemblance to the yahoo in every part, but cannot account for "their degenerate and brutal nature." Who could have a more degenerate and brutal nature than an African slave ship captain?

The similarity between the African slave trade and the art of war can be traced to the barbarian, Aristotle, who said: "Humanity is divided into two: the masters and the slaves; or, if one prefers it, the Greeks and the barbarians, those who have the right to command; and those who are born to obey." As previously noted, Aristotle also said the following:

> ... anything which conquers does so because it excels in some good. It seems therefore that force is not without virtue. If then nature makes nothing without some end in view, nothing to no purpose, it must be that nature had made all of them for the sake of man. This means that it is according to nature that even the art of war, since hunting is a part of it, should in a sense be a way of acquiring property; and that it must be used both against such men as are by nature intended to be ruled over but refuse; for that is the kind of warfare that is by nature just.[45]

The unnatural, unfeeling, inhuman, arrogant, barbarism of this foundation of western civilization, which Swift is digging up, is emphasized, not only in Gulliver's perpetuation of the African slave trade, but also in his callous boasting of his knowledge of the "art of war." Gulliver's master desires Gulliver to "give him some particular account of that land which we call Europe, especially of my own country":

> In obedience therefore to his Honour's commands, I related to him the Revolution under the Prince of Orange; the long war with France entered into by the said prince, and renewed by his successor the present queen, wherein the greatest powers of Christendom were engaged, and which still continued: I computed, at his request, that about a million of yahoos might have been killed in the whole progress of it, and perhaps a hundred of more cities taken, and five times as many ships burnt or sunk.

Gulliver is then asked "what were the usual causes or motives that made one country go to war with another." Gulliver answered they were innumerable, but that he will only mention a few of the chief. The lengthiness of the narration is effective in emphasizing the intensity of Swift's fierce indignation at white people's making an art of war, and glorying in it, "wholly unmoved at all the scenes of blood and desolation," as Gulliver demonstrates. Expounding on the causes of war, Gulliver states:

> Sometimes the ambition of princes, who never think they have land or people enough to govern: sometimes the corruption of ministers, who engage their master in a war in order to stifle or divert the clamour of the subjects against their evil administration. Difference in opinion hath cost many millions of

lives: for instance, whether flesh be bread, or bread be flesh; whether the juice of a certain berry be blood or wine; whether whistling be a vice or a virtue; whether it be better to kiss a post, or throw it into the fire; what is the best colour for a coat, whether black, white, red, or grey; and whether it should be long or short, narrow or wide, dirty or clean, with many more. Neither are any wars so furious and bloody, or of so long continuance, as those occasioned by difference in opinion, especially if it be in things indifferent.

Sometimes the quarrel between two princes is to decide which of them shall dispossess a third of his dominions, where neither of them pretend to any right. Sometimes one prince quarrelleth with another, for fear the other should quarrel with him. Sometimes a war is entered upon, because the enemy is too strong, and sometimes because he is too weak. Sometimes our neighbours want the things which we have, or have the things which we want; and we both fight, till they take ours or give us theirs. It is a very justifiable cause of war to invade a country after the people have been wasted by famine, destroyed by pestilence, or embroiled by factions amongst themselves. It is justifiable to enter into a war against our nearest ally, when one of his towns lies convenient for us, or a territory of land, that would render our dominions round and compact. If a prince send forces into a nation where the people are poor and ignorant, he may lawfully put half of them to death, and make slaves of the rest, in order to civilize and reduce them from their barbarous way of living. [The African slave trade is a good example.] It is a very kingly, honourable, and frequent practice, when one prince desires the assistance of another to secure him against an invasion, that the assistant, when he hath driven out the invader, should seize on the dominions himself, and kill, imprison or banish the prince he came to relieve. Alliance by blood or marriage is a sufficient cause of war between princes, and the nearer the kindred is, the greater is their disposition to quarrel: poor nations are hungry, and rich nations are proud, and pride and hunger will ever be at variance. For these reasons, the trade of a soldier is held the most honourable of all others: because a soldier is a yahoo [white person] hired to kill in cold blood as many of his own species, who have never offended him, as possibly he can.

And being no stranger to the art of war, I gave him a description of cannons, culverins, muskets, carabines, pistols, bullets, powder, swords, bayonets, battles, seiges, retreats, attacks, undermines, countermines, bombardments, sea-fights; ships sunk with a thousand men, twenty thousand killed on each side; dying groans, limbs flying in the air, smoke, noise, confusion, trampling to death under horses' feet; flight, pursuit, victory; fields strewed with carcases left for food to dogs, and wolves, and birds of prey; plundering, stripping, ravishing, burning and destroying. And to set forth the valour of my own dear countrymen, I assured him, that I had seen them blow up a hundred enemies at once in a siege, and as many in a ship, and beheld the dead bodies drop down in pieces from the clouds, to the great diversion of all the spectators.

The art of war, then, like the African slave trade, is attributable to the philosophy of Aristotle as set forth in his *Politics*, which is one of the foundations of western civilization that Swift is digging up.

Gulliver was going on with more particulars on the art of war, when his master commanded him to silence, and begins to establish the basis of black superiority, which builds to the climax. He says that "whoever understood the nature of yahoos might easily believe it possible for so vile an animal to be capable of every action Gulliver had named, if their strength and cunning equalled their malice." He is here speaking of the whole human species, for which Gulliver's discourse of white people had increased his abhorrence. He goes on to distinguish between black and white, using the white supremacist perception of black people as animals, which is an allusion to Bernard that drops white people to a lower level even than animalized black people. Gulliver's master says, for example:

> That although he hated the yahoos [black people] of this country, yet he no more blames them for their odious qualities, than he did a "gnnayh" (a bird of prey) for its cruelty, or a sharp stone for cutting his hoof. But when a creature pretending to reason could be capable of such enormities, he dreaded lest the corruption of that faculty might be worse than brutality itself.

He should know, being the epitome. So this came straight from the horse's mouth. What he says is an allusion to Bernard's definition of the Second Ignorance, which relegates Gulliver, white — everyman — Gulliver and white people. Bernard says:

> Do you not think that man endowed with reason but failing to live reasonably is more of a beast than the beasts themselves? For if the beast does not control himself by reason he has an excuse based on his very nature, for that gift was totally denied to him; but man has no excuse, because reason is a special prerogative of his nature. A man then in this condition is rightly judged to go forth from the company of other living creatures and drop to a lower level, since he is the only creature who violates the laws of his nature by a degenerate way of life.... It is demonstrably clear, therefore, that man is inferior to the herds, in this life by the depravity of his nature, in the next by the severity of the punishment.[46]

Swift applies this to white people since they say that black people, being animals, lack reason. It is white people who violate the laws of human nature by a degenerate way of life, such as the African slave trade, white supremacy, and the love of war and violence, proving that the corruption of reason is worse than brutality itself.

Gulliver informs the reader of his master's significant conclusion:

> He seemed therefore confident, that instead of reason, we were only possessed of some quality fitted to increase our natural vices; as the reflection from a troubled stream returns the image of an ill-shaped body, not only larger, but more distorted.

This is an allusion to St. Francis and Francis Bacon, which makes Swift's point exactly; that "quality" is "pride in reason," and he puts it in the mouth of "pride in reason" while alluding to the source of the analogy from the horse's mouth. The quality fitted to increase white people's vices is defined by St. Francis of Assisi and Francis Bacon, as the "pride of intellect," and "pride of human reason," which St. Francis called "the sublest and meanest of all the forms of pride." Bacon says:

> Let men please themselves as they will in admiring and almost adoring the human mind, this is certain: that, as an uneven mirror distorts the rays of objects according to its own figure and section, so the mind ... cannot be trusted.[47]

The object of both St. Francis and Bacon was to humiliate and destroy the pride of human reason. Such enormities as the love of violence, conquering, war, the African slave trade, white supremacy, are caused by "pride in reason," which constitutes the corruption of reason.

Another example of the corruption of the reason is the law, which just as uncritically as Gulliver explained the causes of war, he explains law to his master. The same cannot be said of Swift, who defines law as "that insatiable gulf of injustice and oppression, the law."[48] The quintessential example of that definition, it goes without saying, is the legalization of: white supremacy, the African slave trade, apartheid, the dispossession, oppression, animalization, menticide, and genocide of black people, which is implicitly and explicitly projected, especially in Part IV. All to which the practice of law, as uncritically described by Gulliver, gives enabling encouragement.

The first fault Swift finds is exposed in his having Gulliver says: "I assured his Honour, that law was a science...." Swift is also criticizing "the are of proving by words multiplied for the purpose, that white is black, and black is white," an art lawyers practice "according as they are paid." "To this society all the rest of the people are slaves." Other faults Swift finds that prove the accuracy of his definition of the law are the following, with which Gulliver finds no fault, as reflecting the character of white people:

> ... it being against all rules of law that any man should be allowed to speak for himself.
> My lawyer, being practiced almost from his cradle in defending falsehood, is quite out of his element when he would be an advocate for justice, which as an office unnatural, he always attempts with great awkwardness, if not with ill will.
> ... judges ... are picked out from the most dextrous lawyers who are grown old or lazy, and having been biased all their lives against truth and equity, lie under such a fatal necessity of favoring fraud, perjury, and oppression that I have known several of them refuse a large bribe from the side where justice lay, rather than injure the faculty by doing any thing unbecoming their nature or their office.

5. Black Superiority 177

> It is a maxim among these lawyers, that whatever hath been done before may legally be done again: and therefore they take special care to record all the decisions formerly made against common justice and the general reason of mankind. These, under the name of "precedents," they produce as authorities, to justify the most iniquitous opinions; and the judges never fail of decreeing accordingly.
>
> In pleading, they studiously avoid entering into the merits of the cause, but are loud, violent, and tedious in dwelling upon all circumstances which are not to the purpose.
>
> ... this society hath a peculiar cant and jargon of their own, that no other mortal can understand, and wherein all their laws are written, which they take special care to multiply; whereby they have wholly confounded the very essence of truth and falsehood, of right and wrong.
>
> In the trial of persons accused for crimes against the state the method is much more short and commendable: the judge first sends to sound the disposition of those in power, after which he can easily hang or save the criminal, strictly preserving all due forms of law.

As he must do next, Gulliver is falsely hard put to explain to his master white people's love of money as a character trait, which, as an African slave trader is the most lucrative profession, he does with self-betraying irony. Like himself, white people, he says, "think they can never have enough of it to spend or to save, as they found themselves inclined from their natural bent either to profusion or avarice." He gives an example validating the African slave trade when he says: "I assured him, that this whole globe of earth must be at least three times gone round, before one of our better female yahoos could get her breakfast, or a cup to put it in." He also informs his master uncritically, that:

> The rich man enjoyed the fruit of the poor man's labour, and the latter were a thousand to one in proportion to the former. That the bulk of our people were forced to live miserably, by labouring every day for small wages to make a few live plentifully.

Another protest, not by Gulliver, but by Swift, more underlying, is suggestive of the African slave trade:

> In order to feed the luxury and intemperance of the males, and the vanity of the females, we send away the greatest part of our necessary things to other countries, from whence in return we brought the materials of diseases, folly, and vice, to spend among ourselves (rum, sugar, etc.).

Gulliver goes on to explain to his master what a doctor is, what diseases are, and what a minister of state is. He is then complimented by his master's thinking he is of noble birth, which leads into Swift's attack on color prejudice and the discrimination idealized in Plato's *Republic*, which becomes the racism Swift is protesting in *Gulliver's Travels* as idealized in Houyhnhnmland, a parody of *The Republic*. Gulliver says of his master:

> He made me observe, that among the Houyhnhnms, the white, the sorrel, and the iron-grey were not so exactly shaped as the bay, the dapple-grey, and the black; nor born with equal talents of the mind, or a capacity to improve them; and therefore continued always in the condition of servants, without ever aspiring to match out of their own race, which in that country would be reckoned monstrous and unnatural.

Swift is saying the same in true in Europe and America, with the skin color reversed; and a black person might get lynched for trying, at least in America. The prejudice against blacks is so great that, "a weak disease body, a meager countenance, and sallow complexion are the true marks of noble blood.... The imperfections of his mind run parallel with those of his body, being a composition of spleen, dulness, ignorance, caprice, sensuality and pride." And what is worse: "Without the consent of this illustrious body no law can be enacted, repealed, or altered, and these nobles have likewise the decision of all our possessions without appeal."

Swift's genius for irony is certainly well represented in Gulliver's feigned intimacy with the reader, in which he reveals in his own character what he conceals about the character of white people, which means it's even worse than he's described. This we know to be true because he never mentions the African slave trade. In attempting to justify fraud, he says:

> The reader may be disposed to wonder how I could prevail on myself to give so free a representation of my own species, among a race of mortals who were already too apt to conceive the vilest opinion of human kind from that entire congruity betwixt me and their yahoos [African slaves].

Since when in his thinking was there "an entire congruity" between black people and white people? That's what the reader may be disposed to wonder. It's a ploy to keep white people from looking so bad, especially since his master lumps them all together, black and white, as yahoos (human beings). If Gulliver admits to "an entire congruity," it means that the vices of white people are natural, just the vices of human nature. He makes a Hypocritical Confession, the Ninth Step of Pride:

> But I must freely confess, that the many virtues of those excellent quadrupeds, placed in opposite view to human corruptions, had so far opened my eyes and enlarged my understanding, that I began to view the actions and passions of man in a very different light, and to think the honour of my own kind not worth managing;

(We can suspect it's because he's had to admit that black people are "his own kind." In the midst of lying, he goes on to say, completing his statement above:)

which, besides, it was impossible for me to do before a person of so acute a judgment as my master, who daily convinced me of a thousand faults in myself, whereof I had not the least perception before, and which with us would never be numbered even among human infirmities: I had likewise learned from his example an utter detestation of all falsehood or disguise; and truth appeared so amiable to me, that I determined upon sacrificing every thing to it.

He continues his hypocritical confession:

Let me deal so candidly with the reader as to confess, that there was yet a much stronger motive for the freedom I took in my representation of things. I had not been a year in this country before I contracted such a love and veneration for the inhabitants, that I entered on a firm resolution never to return to human kind, but to pass the rest of my life among these admirable Houyhnhnms in the contemplation and practice of every virtue; where I could have no example or incitement to vice. But it was decreed by Fortune, my perpetual enemy, that so great a felicity should not fall to my share. However, it is now some comfort to reflect, that in what I said of my countrymen I extenuated their faults as much as I durst before such an examiner, and upon every article gave as favourable a turn as the matter would bear. For, indeed, who is there alive that will not be swayed by his bias and partiality to the place of his birth?

Here he admits to lying, and justifies lying. He could have learned that in Plato's *Republic*, where there is great incitement to vice, including genocide. Plato and Aristotle are Gulliver's foundation, his incitement to unnatural vices such as the African slave trade, white supremacy, conquering, colonialism. Swift is attacking utopia, Plato's *Republic*, of which Houyhnhnmland is a parody. Passing the rest of his life among the Houyhnhnms *would* be an incitement to vice, as we have seen. And he would *not* be "practicing every virtue," because "Virtue ... must be acquired from the Word in order that the soul, overcoming the devil, the world, and itself, may actually perform the good which it has come to will and to know,"[49] says Bernard. Needless to say, the light of the Word does not exist in Houyhnhnmland, nor is Gulliver's reason ever illumined by it.

His hypocritical confessions are a good example. In the first instance, if the honor of his own kind is not worth managing, why "extenuate their faults?" and "upon every article give as favourable a turn as the matter will bear," and even admit, upon later reflection, to deriving some comfort from having done so? In the second instance, his falseness is obvious because he admits to lying and disguise, after claiming an utter detestation for all falsehood and disguise. And since the reader is *not* "disposed to wonder how [Gulliver] could," since the reader knows he didn't, "prevail on himself to give so free a representation of his own species, among a race of mortals who were already too apt to conceive the vilest opinion of human kind from that entire congruity betwixt [Gulliver] and their yahoos," Swift lets the reader know by having Gulliver use it that the hypocritical confession is a cover-up for the fact there is no "entire congruity," because white people, whom Gulliver calls "my own species," and "human kind," are the "vilest" compared to the Houyhnhnms' yahoos, black people, and Gulliver's hypocritical confession is one of the proofs. And Swift is most concerned to expose what is said about those who choose it. According to Bernard, "A false and proud confession is more perilous than a willful and stubborn defense." Those who choose it "know they will not be believed if they excuse themselves," so they "contrive a more subtle method of defense by responding with a deceitful confession."

> "There is" indeed, as it is written, "one that humbleth himself wickedly, and his interior is full of deceit."[50]

Of such is white-everyman-Gulliver.

What Swift is attacking is that Gulliver chose the "expedient," when he could have chosen the "good" or the "true," in keeping with Bernard's teaching that the function of the reason of the soul is "intention," and intention is of three kinds: "the reason may be intent on the expedient, the good, or the true." He goes on to say: "Without love, we deliberately choose as expedient that which we correctly know to be wrong. Without wisdom, we ignorantly choose as expedient that which we incorrectly believe to be right."

> Intention on the good is called religion. Although all men seek the expedient, all men do not seek the good.... The fundamental requirements of true religion are good will and enlightened understanding. The understanding is enlightened by the Word of God, and the will is purified by the Spirit of God. But without love we do not will to perform the good which we know. And without understanding, the stronger our good will the more we err. Intention on the true is called "consideration," which is thought intent on research, or the intention of the mind when it is searching for the true.[51]

Bernard goes on to define the three kinds of consideration: the practical, when the senses are used in an orderly and unified manner to win God's favor; the scientific, when everything is prudently and diligently scrutinized and pondered to discover God; and the speculative, when it recollects itself and, insofar as it is aided by God, frees itself for the contemplation of God.[52]

Therefore, it is because the reason of the soul of white people is not intent on the good, is not intent on the true, that the criticisms by the Houyhnhnm master are valid, ironically. The first criticism prefigures the climax, and neither the good nor the true have any part in the development of what it describes. Gulliver says of his master that:

He looked upon us as a sort of animals to whose share, by what accident he could not conjecture, some small pittance of reason had fallen, whereof we made no other use than by its assistance to aggravated our natural corruptions, and to acquire new ones which Nature had not given us. That we disarmed ourselves of the few abilities she had bestowed, had been very successful in multiplying our original wants, and seemed to spend our whole lives in vain endeavours to supply them by our own inventions [209].

In other words, white people make no other use of reason than to improve and multiply the vices of nature. And this they do from pride in reason and belief in the teaching of the master Houyhnhnm that reason alone is sufficient. He says:

That our institutions of government and law were plainly owing to our gross defects in reason, and by consequence, in virtue; because reason alone is sufficient to govern a rational creature [209].

On the contrary, gross defects in reason occur when the reason has lost the light which created it. Gulliver's master's teaching on the connection between reason and virtue, that gross defects in virtue are caused by gross defects in reason, is a corrective allusion to Bernard:

Virtue, the moral strength which subjects all activity to reason, must be acquired from the Word of [God] in order that the soul ... may actually perform the good which it has come to will and to know.[53]

Based on Gulliver's story, the Houyhnhnm master continues to make comparisons between his enslaved blacks (yahoos), and white people as exposed by Swift in Gulliver's descriptions. In all instances the blacks come out on top. For example, when they have battles "there were terrible wounds made by their claws on both sides," but

they seldom were able to kill one another, for want of such convenient instruments of death as [white people] had invented.

When two yahoos are fighting over a stone they both saw at the same time, "a third would take the advantage, and carry it away from both." Gulliver's master finds in that "some resemblance to [white people's] suits at law." So Gulliver doesn't correct him, knowing the yahoo decision "was much more equitable than many degrees among us":

... because the plaintiff and defendant there lost nothing beside the stone they contended for, whereas our courts of equity would never have dismissed the cause while either of them had any thing left [211].

Swift also exposes the fact that, although, like white people, the black yahoos were said to be "fonder of what they could get by rapine or stealth at a greater distance, than much better food provided for them at home," they don't cross oceans to rape, steal, and enslave innocent people to get what they're fonder of.

Fraudulently, Gulliver persists in denying that his master's African slaves are of the same species as white people. He volunteers to make more discoveries but all he does is animalize them, and then speak of them in more white racist stereotypes. He asks to be allowed to "go among the *herds* of yahoos." His master says yes, "being perfectly convinced that the hatred Gulliver bore 'those brutes'" would never allow him to be corrupted by them. That's ironic, considering how much the African slaves in many ways had been corrupted by their slave masters. Gulliver speaks of them as "odious animals" who "have some imagination," says Gulliver, "that I was of their own species." He says he "catches" a three-year-old child, and refers to him as "it," "imp," "cub," "vermin," and says, "I observed the young animal's flesh to smell very rank, and the stink was somewhat between a weasel and a fox, but much more disagreeable."

What Gulliver claims to "discover" are traditional white racist stereotypes he'd embraced his whole white supremacist life:

> By what I could discover, the yahoos appear to be the most unteachable of all animals, their capacities never reaching higher than to draw or carry burthens. Yet I am of opinion this defect ariseth chiefly from a perverse restive disposition. For they are cunning, malicious, treacherous and revengeful. They are strong and hardy, but of a cowardly spirit, and by consequence insolent, abject, and cruel.

The first "discovery" gives proof of the master Gulliver has learned from, those whom the Houyhnhnms symbolize (Plato, et al.), singularly detectable by their style of discriminating among the Houyhnhnms:

> ... among the Houyhnhnms, the white, the sorrel, and the iron-grey were not so exactly shaped as the bay, the dapple-grey, and the black; nor born with equal talents of the mind, or a capacity to improve them; and therefore continued always in the condition of servants.

Given the enslavement of the black yahoos, and all that it symbolizes, the Houyhnhnms are more representative of other famous horses:

> ... behold a white horse: and he that sat on him had a bow; and a crown was given unto him: and he went forth conquering, and to conquer.
>
> And there went out another horse that was red: and *power* was given to him that sat thereon to take peace from the earth, and that they should kill one another: and there was given unto him a great sword.
>
> ... and lo a black horse; and he that sat on him had a pair of balances in his hand.... A measure of wheat for a penny, and three measures of barley for a penny; and see thou hurt not the oil and the wine.
>
> ... behold a pale horse: and his name that sat on him was Death, and Hell followed with him. And power was given unto them over the fourth part of the earth, to kill with sword, and with hunger, and with death, and with the

beasts of the earth [Rev. 6:2–8].

There is a suggestion of these Horses of the Apocalypse in the Houyhnhnms: the white in the white; the red in the sorrel and the bay; the black in the black; and the pale in the iron-grey and the dapple-grey.

Gulliver's second discovery, concerning the disposition of the black yahoos, is outrageously absurd. Who could be more perverse and restive than a white supremacist with an "insatiable desire" for the African slave trade in the perpetuation of which he spends most of his life? In his distortions of the black yahoos as cunning, malicious, treacherous, revengeful, cowardly, insolent, abject, and cruel, it's not that there are distortions in the black yahoos, but rather in the racist attitude of Gulliver. "Only the soul/mirror which is able to subject itself to the will of Christ will be free of distortion."[54] Also, the distortions indicate Gulliver is still in denial about black people being of the same species as white people, that subconsciously he knows they are, so he speaks with self-betraying irony, in that the distortions he tallies are not naturally attributable to animals, only to humans. He concludes his "discoveries" with a description of a slave-plantation-setup reflecting Aristotle's philosophy of praedial slavery:

> The Houyhnhnms keep the yahoos for present use not far from the house; but the rest are sent abroad to certain fields, where they dig up roots.... Nature hath taught them to dig deep holes with their nails on the side of a rising ground, wherein they lie by themselves, only kennels of the females are larger, sufficient to hold two or three cubs.

"Kennels" is the term used onboard African slave ships in reference to slave quarters. Captain Thomas Phillips, in his account of an African slave trade voyage made in 1693–1694, speaks of slaves having "gone down to their kennels between decks."[55] As an African slave ship captain himself, Gulliver would have been familiar with the term.

Even with his next episode, we still can't be certain he's convinced black people are of the same species as white people. "The weather exceeding hot," Gulliver "stripped himself stark naked" and took a swim, or as he puts it: "I went down softly into the stream." This is to distinguish the behavior of a quality white person from "animal" behavior. He goes on with his story:

> It happened that a young female yahoo, standing behind a bank, saw the whole proceeding, and inflamed by desire ... came running with all speed, and leaped into the water within five yards of the place where I bathed. I was never in my life so terribly frightened.... She embraced me after a most fulsome manner; I roared as loud as I could, and the nag [his protector the sorrel nag] came galloping towards me whereupon she quitted her grasp, with the utmost reluc-

tancy, and leaped upon the opposite bank, where she stood gazing and howling all the time I was putting on my clothes [215].

Gulliver says in conclusion: "This was matter of diversion to my master and his family, as well as of mortification to myself:

> For now I could no longer deny that I was a real yahoo in every limb and feature, since the females had a natural propensity to me as one of their own species ... she could not be above eleven years old.

First of all, Gulliver's racism boomerangs. Whatever he has said a yahoo is, he can no longer deny *he* is. Secondly, his animalizing of an eleven-year-old black girl because of the racist belief that black people were totally denied the gift of reason is an ironic allusion to a truth that confirms the little girl's humanness. The truth is, "Passion, one of the four natural emotions, is not subject to reason" (Bernard). To add to this, Swift says in one of his essays:

> Although reason were intended by Providence to govern our passions; yet it seems that in two points of the greatest moment to the being and continuance of the world, God has intended our passions to prevail over reason. The first is the propagation of our species.... The other is the love of life.[56]

After Gulliver's "mortifying" realization (for the sake of the reader) that he can no longer deny he's a yahoo, he abruptly changes the subject, and begins an account of the manners and customs of the Houyhnhnms. He thus proceeds from mortification over the natural and human to glorification of the unnatural and inhuman, still seeking to distinguish and distance himself from black people. Being a monster is one way.

Perhaps what is most repulsively unnatural about the Houyhnhnms is their lack of passion, the absence of love, since love is not subject to reason. Gulliver's first praise is therefore to be seen as a contradiction: "As these noble Houyhnhnms are endowed by nature with a general disposition to all virtues...." Not so, without love. As previously mentioned, Swift is satirizing the Humanistic worship of the Hellenistic philosophers the Houyhnhnms symbolize, the foundations of western civilization, which Swift is digging up. This is especially true here in Part IV, where Swift brings white-everyman-Gulliver face to fact with his adoration of the philosophers whose philosophies made him the racist African slave trader he is just by living in the structures of reason they created. One of these Aristotelian philosophers, Thomas Aquinas, erroneously stated:

> ... what is essential for man is his intellect, which means his ability to live in meanings and structures of reason. Not the will but the intellect makes him human. Man has the will in common with animals; the intellect, the rational structure of his mind, is peculiar to man.[57]

Swift's argument, as we have seen, is that what is essential for man, as Augustine and Bernard said, is his will. Not the intellect but the will makes him human. In Part IV, especially, Swift proves that the reason, the intellect, makes man not human but a monster, and also that man does not have the will in common with animals. As Bernard states:

> To consent is to be saved. That is why the animal spirit does not receive this salvation; it lacks the power of voluntary consent, by which it might tranquilly submit to a saving God, whether by acquiescing in his commands, or by believing his promises, or by giving thanks for his benefits.... It is voluntary consent that distinguishes man from natural appetite which man shares with the animals. For voluntary consent is a self-determining habit of the soul.... It stems from the will.[58]

Gulliver goes on to tell us the Houyhnhnms "have no conceptions or ideas of what is evil in a rational creature." But, obviously, since they have African slaves, and plan to exterminate them from the face of the earth, they rationalize evil as good; or, they just don't create a word for evil; or they create a syllogism, start it with a biased premise, and make whatever they want to believe about themselves logical; which is one of the reasons St. Francis said "Satan is Logic."[59] The Houyhnhnm's grand maxim is "to cultivate reason, and to be wholly governed by it." Bernard's answer to such a maxim, which Swift poses, would be the following:

> If the mind does not rely upon itself, but is strengthened by the Lord, it can gain command over itself that no unrighteousness will have power over it.[60]

In Gulliver's further praise of the Houyhnhnms, Swift has Gulliver's master, as symbolic of Aristotle, ironically attack one of his own disciples, in the Aristotelian theory of Abelard's "Sic and Non"; in Abelard's rationalistic approach to Church doctrine, especially the doctrine of the Trinity; and in Abelard's emphasis on dialectic argument and proof rather than faith; all of which is an allusion to Bernard, who had Abelard persecuted as a heretic. Gulliver says:

> Neither is reason among them a point problematical as with us, where men can argue with plausibility on both sides of a question; but strikes you with immediate conviction; as it must needs do where it is not mingled, obscured, or discoloured by passion and interest. I remember it was with extreme difficulty that I could bring my master to understand the meaning of the word "opinion," or how a point could be disputable; because reason taught us to affirm or deny only where we are certain; and beyond our knowledge we cannot do either. So that controversies, wranglings, disputes, and positiveness in false or dubious propositions are evils unknown among the Houyhnhnms [216].

For the most part, the preceding is an allusion to Bernard's *Consideration* (Intention on the true is called "*consideration*"), in which he distinguishes between opinion, faith, and understanding, and cautions against confusing them, as the Houyhnhnms seem to do. "Opinion," he says, "is to hold as true something you do not know to be false."

> It is based on "plausibility." It differs from faith and understanding in being fallible; it seeks, rather than grasps, truth. Each person is justified in holding his own opinion in matters which are not subject to faith or understanding. But such opinions should be held and asserted tentatively, not dogmatically; we must avoid the common error of confusing opinion with understanding, believing something concerning which we should remain in doubt.

The most important distinction is "faith," which Bernard says, and Swift agrees: "reveals truth undiscoverable empirically because of the fallibility of empirical knowledge or because the objects are not sensible things; and reveals truths undiscoverable rationally because of the limits of human understanding."[61]

Swift's sermon "On the Trinity" is a good example, especially for those who doubted and still doubt Swift's faith, even to the extent of Glendinning's asking in 1998, "Did Swift believe in God?"

Swift introduces the sermon quoting Scripture: "For there are three that bear record in Heaven, the Father, the Word, and the Holy Ghost; and these Three are One" (John 5:7). He goes on to repeat the doctrine of the Trinity, "as it is positively affirmed in Scripture":

> ... that God is there expressed in three different names, as Father, as Son, and as Holy Ghost; that each of these is God, and that there is but one God. But this union and distinction are a mystery utterly unknown to mankind.
> This is enough for any good Christian to believe on this great article, without ever inquiring any farther. And this can be contrary to no man's reason, although the knowledge of it is far from him.... It is impossible for us to determine, for what reason God thought fit to communicate some things to us in part, and leave some part a mystery: but so it is in fact.... It may be thought a strange thing, that God should require us to believe mysteries, while the reason or manner of what we are to believe is above our comprehension, and wholly concealed from us: neither doth it appear at first sight, that the believing or not believing them doth concern either the glory of God, or contribute to the goodness or wickedness of our lives. But this is a great and dangerous mistake. We see what a mighty weight is laid upon faith, both in the Old and New Testaments. In the former we read, how the faith of Abraham is praised.... Our Saviour is perpetually preaching faith to his disciples, and reproaching them with the want of it; and St. Paul produceth numerous examples of the wonders done by faith. And all this is highly reasonable; for, faith is an entire dependence upon the truth, the power, the justice, and the mercy of God; which dependence will certainly incline us to obey him in all things. So

that the great excellency of faith consists in the consequence it hath upon our actions: as, if we depend upon the truth and wisdom of a man, we shall certainly be more disposed to follow his advice. Therefore let no man think that he can lead as good a moral life without faith as with it; for this reason, because he who hath no faith, cannot by the strength of his own reason or endeavours so easily resist temptations, as the other, who depends upon God's assistence in the overcoming of his frailties ... faith is a virtue, by which any thing commanded us by God to believe, appears evident and certain to us, although we do not see, not can conceive it; because by faith we entirely depend upon the truth and power of God.... Without faith we can do no works acceptable to God; for, if they proceed from any other principle, they will not advance our salvation; and this faith, as I have explained it, we may acquire without giving up our senses, or contradicting our reason.

As we can see, Swift's faith in faith is very much like Bernard's. And his statement on reason seems an echo of Bernard's criticism of Abelard. For example:

It would be well, if people would not lay so much weight on their own reason in matters of religion, as to think every thing impossible and absurd which they cannot conceive. How often do we contradict the right rules of reason in the whole course of our lives? Reason itself is true and just, but the reason of every particular man is weak and wavering, perpetually swayed and turned by his interests, his passions, and his vices. Let any man but consider, when he hath a controversy with another, though his cause be ever so unjust, though the whole world be against him, how blinded he is by the love of himself, to believe that right is wrong, and wrong is right, when it makes for his own advantage. Where is then the right use of his reason, which he so much boasts of, and which he would blasphemously set up to control the commands of the Almighty?[62]

The African slave trade and white supremacy are good examples, except that almost the whole world believed that wrong was right because it made for the world's advantage. At the end of the *Travels* African slave ship captain, white supremacist Gulliver, is depicted as guilty of the final blasphemy.

When Gulliver says, in praise of the Houyhnhnms, that "controversies, wranglings, disputes, and positiveness in false or dubious propositions are evils unknown among the Houyhnhnms, we find that statement corrected in Swift's sermon "On the Wisdom of This World," proving that those whom the Houyhnhnms symbolize are the cause of those evils:

Christianity itself has very much suffered, by being blended up with Gentile philosophy. The Platonick system, first taken into religion, was thought to have given matter for some early heresies in the church. When disputes began to arise, the peripatetick forms were introduced by Scotus, as best fitted for controversy. And, however this may now have become necessary, it was surely the author of a litigious vein, which has since occasioned very pernicious consequences, stopped the progress of Christianity, and been a great promoter of vice, verifying that sentence given by St. James, and mentioned before,

"Where envying and strife is, there is confusion and every evil work." ... Diogenes said, Socrates was a madman; the disciples of Zeno and Epicurus, nay of Plato and Aristotle, were engaged in fierce disputes about the most insignificant trifles.[63]

Bernard's criticism of Abelard, who was a disciple of Aristotle, has a profound impact on the climax of *Gulliver's Travels*, as we shall see. For now, it serves as a telling summary, satirically, of Gulliver's praises of the Houyhnhnms and their grand maxim. In his criticism of Abelard, Bernard says the following:

> Being prepared to give a reason for everything, even those things which are above reason, he presumes both against reason and against faith. For what is more contrary to reason than to try to transcend reason by reason? And what is more contrary to faith, than to refuse to believe whatever he cannot attain by reason?[64]

Continuing on with his account of the manners and customs of the Houyhnhnms, which reflect the ideals of Plato's *Republic*, Gulliver mentions their discrimination customs. For example, "the race of inferior Houyhnhnms bred up to be servants ... are allowed to produce three of each sex, to be domestics in the noble families." Also:

> In their marriages they are exactly careful to choose such colours as will not make any disagreeable mixture in the breed.

Prejudice, discrimination, supremacy, notions of inferior/superior, Jim Crow, apartheid, and slavery, as these two examples demonstrate, can hardly be called "virtues," and thus contradict one of the Houyhnhnm creeds: "They will have it that nature teaches them to love the whole species, and it is reason only that maketh a distinction of persons, where there is a superior degree of virtue," which is corrected by allusion to Swift's sermon "On Mutual Subjection," in which is stated:

> No one human creature is more worthy than another in the sight of God, farther than according to the goodness or holiness of their lives.[65]

The allusion is also to one of Bernard's sermons, in which is stated:

> Although the virtues have their origin from the emotions, which are functions of the will, they have their operation in different faculties, prudence and temperance in the reason, fortitude and justice in the will.[66]

Swift is satirizing the origins and definition of virtue as practiced by the Houyhnhnms symbolic of Plato. (How anyone could write a book about virtues and name its hero Plato would to Swift constitute the height of absurdity.) To Swift, Bernard is *the* authority on virtue, in saying:

To strengthen your heart and to wait upon the Lord—that is virtue.... For it is Christ who must be relied upon for virtue.[67]

The Houyhnhnms do not know Christ, nor did Plato, nor does Gulliver.

To believe that Plato is the definitive authority on virtue, one would have to esteem prejudice, discrimination, bigotry, apartheid and genocide as virtue, which, of course, some do, all the way through the African slave trade and its attendant atrocities—lynchings, jailings—to the twentieth-century South African plan to exterminate black people from the face of the earth by scientific means. The following is an example of Plato's kind of "virtue," which the Houyhnhnms reflect in their grand debate. Gulliver's master "agreed entirely with the sentiments of Socrates, as Plato delivers them; which, says Gulliver, I mention as the highest honour I can do that prince of philosophers." In Plato's *Republic*, Socrates idealizes for the imitation of man, using horses as the model; and genocide:

> ... our rulers will find a considerable dose of falsehood and deceit necessary for the good of their subjects ... the use of these things regarded as medicines might be of advantage. And this lawful use of them seems likely to be often needed in the regulations of marriages and births ... the best of either sex should be united with the best as often, and the inferior with the inferior, as seldom as possible; and they should rear the offspring of the one sort of union, but not of the other, if the flock is to be maintained in first-rate condition. Now these goings-on must be a secret which the rulers only know, or there will be a further danger of our herd ... breaking out into rebellion.... The proper officers will take the offspring of the good parents to the pen or fold, and there they will deposit them with certain nurses who will dwell in a separate quarter; but the offspring of the inferior, or of the better when they chance to be deformed, will be put away in some mysterious, unknown place, as they should be. The proper officers will provide for the nurture of the better, and will bring the mothers to the fold when they are full of milk, taking the greatest possible care that no mother recognizes her own child.[68]

The Houyhnhnms reflect a similar, unnatural lack of feeling in the "regulation" of children:

> ... if a Houyhnhnm hath two males, he changeth one of them with another who hath two females: and when a child hath been lost by casualty, where the mother is past breeding, it is determined what family in the district shall breed another to supply the loss.

But the most violative of the laws of human nature is exposed by the connection Swift brings to light between the genocide alluded to in Plato's *Republic* by the genocide debated by the Houyhnhnms. Its relevance to Swift's protest of white racism, white supremacy, and the African slave trade and its legacy, as a mirror held up to white people, is unmistakable:

> The question to be debated was whether black people (the yahoos) should be exterminated from the face of the earth [218].

It's undeniable the debate is about black people because only white racist stereotypes are used to describe these yahoos as animals. To keep them from "infesting the whole nation" and "to get rid of this evil," the Houyhnhnms made a general hunting, "and at last enclosed the whole herd":

> and destroying the older, every Houyhnhnm kept two young ones in a kennel, and brought them to such a degree of tameness, as an animal so savage by nature can be capable of acquiring; using them for draught and carriage. That there seemed to be much truth in this tradition, and that those creatures could not be "ylnhniamsby" (or "aborigines" of the land) because of the violent hatred the Houyhnhnms, as well as all other animals bore them; which although their evil disposition sufficiently deserved, could never have arrived at so high a degree, if they had been aborigines, or else they would have long since been rooted out. That the inhabitants taking a fancy to use the service of the yahoos, had very imprudently neglected to cultivate the breed of asses, which were a comely animal, easily kept, more tame and orderly, without any offensive smell, strong enough for labour, although they yield to the other in agility of body; and if their braying be no agreeable sound, it is far preferable to the horrible howlings of the yahoos [219].

Ironically, as a symbol, Gulliver's master is quite right and quite responsible: no other race has been so consistently subjected to so violent a hatred as black people by white people, and for no reason other than the monstrous arrogance that has deformed the soul of white people. This is what Swift means in the end when he has Gulliver refer to white people as "lumps of deformity and diseases both in body and mind, smitten with pride." And Swift is, of course, perceptive as well as prophetic in his fiercely indignant exposing of white people's hatred and contempt of black people: they teach every other race to hate black people, and teach black people to hate themselves and each other. White people divide to conquer. The root cause of the tragedy in Rwanda is the former Belgian slave master colonialists, who set one black group or tribe against another, to divide and conquer. The criticism of black people as "savage by nature," according to Gulliver's master, pertains instead to white people, Swift is saying ironically. And in another comparison of Gulliver to these yahoos, we are again reminded that he is white and they are black, when Gulliver's master says that Gulliver is "an exact yahoo in every part, only of a whiter colour, less hairy."

As the preceding discussion has had to do with the "grand debate," the "only debate that ever happened in their country": whether black people should be exterminated from the face of the earth. Gulliver had offered the solution of "castration" to his master, who presented to the general assembly that:

> This invention might be practised upon the younger yahoos here, which, besides rendering them tractable and fitter for use, would in an age put an end to the whole species without destroying life [220].

There is in addition, a twenty-first century invention similarly reminiscent of Plato's solution to the problem of "undisirables," an invention suggested by former Secretary of Education, Bill Bennett, which might explain his choosing the name "Plato" for the hero of his book, *Virtues*. On a radio broadcast, Bennett said:

> I do know that it's true that if you wanted to reduce crime, you could — if that were your sole purpose — you could abort every black baby in this country, and your crime rate would go down (Bob Herbert, "Impossible, Ridiculous, Repugnant," *New York Times*, OP-ED., 6 Oct. 2005, Sec. A, p. 37, col. 1.).

Obviously, the former Secretary of Education has not done his homework. Not to mention white crimes via the African slave trade; the fact of "the many thousand gone" (Baldwin), black men, women, and children lynched by white people; the fact that white serial killers far outnumber black serial killers, and far outnumber them in number of people killed by one person; the fact of Timothy McVeigh; the fact of James Byrd and Matthew Sheppard; the fact of white junior high and high school student murderers at Columbine, Moses Lake, Washington; Pearl, Mississippi; West Paduka, Kentucky; Jonesborough, Arkansas; and Littleton, Colorado, would seem to challenge the accuracy of Bill Bennett's statement, and we haven't even considered white-collar crimes and "high crimes."

Castration, and lynching, suggested by the black men "tied by the neck with strong withes, fastened to a beam," are two forms of viciousness most infamously and universally associated with black victims. Matching Swift's depiction of the character of white people, a twentieth-century example, one of thousands, is vivid testimony to the prophetic genius of Swift, to the depths of his courageous social, moral, and religious conscience, and to the social, historical, and twenty-first century relevance of *Gulliver's Travels*. Not unmindful of James Byrd in the 1990s, this example is of the lynching of twenty-three-year-old Claude Neal in Marianna, Florida, on October 27, 1934, which Swift would not have considered a digression, or irrelevant, but to the point:

> After taking the nigger to the woods about four miles from Greenwood, they cut off his penis. He was made to eat it. Then they cut off his testicles and made to eat them and say he liked it…. Then they sliced his sides and stomach with knives and every now and then somebody would cut off a finger or a toe. Red hot irons were used on the nigger to burn him from top to bottom. From

time to time during the torture, a rope would be tied around Neal's neck and he was pulled up over a limb and held there until he almost choked to death when he would be let down and the torture began all over again.

The man who castrated Neal seemed ecstatic over his handiwork. Castration of animals was a common practice in farm communities at the time, and some members of the group had the required skill to commit this act.... Those unable to attack Neal alive or to witness his destruction wished to commit an act of aggression against his corpse and, after he was interred, against others of his race. The lynch mob delivered Neal's body shortly after 1 a.m. to the Cannidy house; and the crowd rushed up to see him and someone called, "There he is sure as the world." A reporter who was present described the scene: "In a few minutes several cars, one after another, rolled into the yard. From one of them a rope jerked spasmodically as the car struck bumps and gullies in the road. On the end of the rope was Neal dead. His body was covered with dust, scarred and torn by knives and horribly mutilated."

When the car dragging Neal's body arrived in front of the Cannidy house, the man riding the rear bumper cut the rope. The lynch mob having completed its task literally cut itself away from the incident at that point. Its members did not participate in later actions against blacks.... Several people drove knives into the corpse, reportedly "tearing the body almost to shreds." Sixty-year-old George Cannidy than took a .45 and pumped three bullets into the forehead of the corpse.... The crowd then had its way. Howard Lester's informants told him that many people subjected the body to other indignities. Several kicked it and others drove cars over it. Perhaps the most terrifying remark in Lester's summary of the Neal lynching was this one:

> It is reported from reliable sources that the little children, some of them mere tots, who lived in the Greenwood neighborhood, waited with sharp sticks for the return of Neal's body and that when it rolled in the dust on the road that awful night these little children drove their weapons deep into the flesh of the dead man.

> ... another mob was organized and it brought the body to the courthouse at 3 o'clock this morning where it hanged him on a tree on the east side of the courthouse lawn.... Those who were there before 6:30 a.m. got a chance to view Neal's skinned and mutilated body.... Photographers were on the scene early and took hundreds of pictures of Neal's remains. They had reckoned their business investments prudently because, once the corpse was removed, disappointed latecomers were willing to pay fifty cents a photograph. These photographs were hawked in a crowd which was still enraged over having been left out of the spectacle when so much had been promised; some took solace when persons in the crowd exhibited fingers and toes from Neal's body. To own them conferred genuine status. One store owner recalled the pride with which a man came into his store that morning and declared, "See what I have here." It was one of Neal's fingers.[69]

This is the kind of venomous hatred of black people by white people that moved famed attorney William Kunsler to say, when he marched with King, "I've never seen anything like it. It's Mother's milk."

5. Black Superiority

An immortalized example emphasizing Swift's purpose in exposing the horrors of white racist hatred of black people is the difference in treatment of the black civil rights worker, Cheney, compared to the treatment of his two white civil rights companions, Goodman and Schwerner. Goodman and Schwerner were each fatally shot one time. Chaney, on the other hand, was badly beaten, shot several times, his body mutilated.

The hatred infiltrates the language as well. Gulliver says, for example:

> I know not whether it may be worth observing, that the Houyhnhnms have no word in their language to express any thing that is evil, except what they borrow from the deformities or ill qualities of the [black people].

Such languaging is further proof of the currency of *Gulliver's Travels*. A book published in 1992 makes the point regarding the "insidious virus of superiority":

> ... there is no word in the language that packs the punch for whites that "nigger" does for blacks.... We've never created that, which is almost to immunize white people, to say we're not going to have a term like that no matter how degraded you are as a white person.[70]

Swift's condemnation of white people is revealed in his use of the irony of self-betrayal in depicting Gulliver's unwitting condemnation of white people to cover up his paramount reason for wanting to live out the rest of his life among the Houyhnhnms in that Antichrist cesspool of white supremacy, African slaves and genocide, Houyhnhnmland (suggestive of Hinnomland), white-everyman-Gulliver's utopia (*The Republic*). His paramount reason is the Houyhnhnm's condescending to distinguish him from black people. He covers this up with a *lengthy* litany that is more of a scathing indictment of white people than of black people, in exposing immoralities and crimes characteristic of white civilization, of which "animals" (as black people are perceived) are not capable. Gulliver says:

> I enjoyed perfect health of body and tranquillity of mind; I did not feel the treachery or inconstancy of a friend, nor the injuries of a secret or open enemy. I had no occasion of bribing, flattering or pimping to procure the favour of any great man or of his minion. I wanted no fence against fraud or oppression; here was neither physician to destroy my body, nor lawyer to ruin my fortune; no informer to watch my words and actions, or forge accusations against me for hire: here were no gibers, censurers, backbiters, pickpockets, highwaymen, housebreakers, attorneys, ... politicians ... murderers, robbers ... no leaders or followers of party and faction: no encouragers to vice, by seducement or examples: no dungeon, axes, gibbets, whipping-posts, or pillories: no cheating shopkeepers or mechanics; no pride, vanity, or affectation; no fops, bullies, drunkards, strolling whores, or poxes, etc., etc., etc.

Although he perceives black people as "animals," and animals are not capable of any of these things he lists above, he still sees white people as superior, and is grateful that the Houyhnhnms condescend to distinguish him from black people.

Gulliver goes from no regrets to high hopes, the latter in adoration of the Houyhnhnms. His adoration of the Houyhnhnms reflects white people's Humanistic adoration of the Greek and Roman philosophers who are the foundation of western civilization Swift is digging up. Gulliver, for example, speaks of the discourses of his master and friends, to which he was "graciously suffered" to attend, as if he'd been admitted to the discourses of Socrates, Glaucon, Polemarchos, Thrasymachos, Adeimantos, and Cephalos. In that Socrates held up horses for the imitation of human kind, Gulliver's statement, "they were all pleased to descant in a manner not very advantageous to human kind," is indicative. And Gulliver is depicted as reflecting the teaching of the Greek philosophers, and what that teaching cost him. "Whether out of ignorance, fraud, or logic," he says that,

> ... his Honour, to my great admiration, appeared to understand the nature of yahoos much better than myself. He went through all our vices and follies, and discovered many which I had never mentioned to him, by only supposing what qualities a yahoo of their country, with a small proportion of reason, might be capable of exerting; and concluded, with too much probability, how vile as well as miserable such a creature must be.

By "a yahoo of their country" is meant a black person, an African slave. Gulliver's hypocritical confession that follows seems an attempt to cover up the fact he cannot argue with the logic of his master's statement, which forces his self-consciousness as to being that "creature"; and becoming what he's been taught, as he says:

> I freely confess, that all the little knowledge I have of any value was acquired by the lectures I received from my master, and from hearing the discourses of him and his friends; to which I should be prouder to listen, than to dictate to the greatest and wisest assembly in Europe. I admired the strength, comeliness, and speed of the inhabitants; and such a constellation of virtues in such amiable persons produced in me the highest veneration. At first, indeed, I did not feel that natural awe [fear] which the yahoos [blacks] and all other animals bear towards them; but it grew upon me by degrees, much sooner than I imagined, and was mingled with a respectful love and gratitude, that they would condescend to distinguish me from the rest of my species [black people] [224].

As this adoration of the ancient Greek philosophers, combined with the Greek love of horses, is a prelude to the climax of *Gulliver's Travels*, and to its dominantly urgent theme of conversion, the opening paragraph of Swift's sermon "On the Wisdom of This World" is significantly enlightening in validating white-everyman-Gulliver's veneration:

> It is remarkable, that about the time of our Saviour's coming into the world, all kinds of learning flourished to a very great degree; insomuch that nothing is more frequent in the mouths of many men, even such who pretend to read and to know, than an extravagant praise and opinion of the wisdom and virtue of the Gentile sages of those days, and likewise of those ancient philosophers who went before them, whose doctrines are left upon record, either by themselves, or other writers. As far as this may be taken for granted, it may be said, that the Providence of God brought this about for several very wise ends and purposes: for it is certain, that these philosophers had been a long time before, searching out where to fix the true happiness of man; and not being able to agree upon any certainty about it, they could not possibly but conclude, if they judged impartially, that all their inquiries were, in the end, but vain and fruitless: the consequence of which must be, not only an acknowledgment of the weakness of all human wisdom, but likewise an open passage hereby made, for letting in those beams of light, which the glorious sunshine of the Gospel than brought into the world, by revealing those hidden truths, which they had so long before been laboring to discover, and fixing the general happiness of mankind, beyond all controversy and dispute ... that to be the true wisdom only, "which cometh from above,
> ... a great many of those encomiums given to ancient philosophers, are taken upon trust, and by a sort of men, who are not very likely to be at the pains of an inquiry, that would employ so much time and thinking. For, the usual ends why men affect this kind of discourse, appear generally to be either out of ostentation, that they may pass upon the world for persons of great knowledge and observation.[71]

This is like Gulliver, who "reads the best authors ancient and modern," with no scale of values.

The climax begins with "consideration" ("the intention of the mind when it is searching for the true"),[72] with Gulliver's self-examination. Speaking of white people, since he doesn't consider black people human, nevertheless comparing blacks and whites, he says:

> When I thought of my family, my friends, my countrymen, or human race in general, I considered them as they really were, yahoos in shape and disposition, only a little more civilized, and qualified with the gift of speech, but making no other use of reason than to improve and multiply those vices whereof their brethren in this country had only the share that nature alloted them [225].

In other words, white people make no other use of reason than to invent unnatural or monstrous vices, and more than alloted human nature, whereas black people have only the vices of human nature. White people violate the laws of human nature by a degenerate way of life, such as white supremacy, racism, and African slave trade, the animalization, dispossession, oppression, menticide, and genocide of black people. The irony of ironies in *Gulliver's Travels* is that black people are superior to white people, that white people are inferior to black people. Swift has Gulliver realize this as the truth for which his mind is intent upon searching, in keeping with the distinction Swift makes between superiority and inferiority: "No one human creature is more worthy than another in the sight of God, farther than according to the goodness or holiness of their lives."[73] One can hardly call the monstrous vices mentioned above either good or holy, it goes without saying. Gulliver's reaction to his anagnorisis, his realization, calls to mind ancient Greek tragedy as well as the prophet Ezekiel: "They shall loathe themselves for the evils which they have committed in all their abominations." Gulliver's reaction:

> When I happened to behold the reflection of my own form in a lake or fountain, I turned away my fact in horror and detestation of myself, and could better endure the sight of a common yahoo, than of my own person [225].

This scene is to be understood in terms of one of Bernard's sermons on conversion from "A Mirror That Flatters Not," which Swift alludes to ("...for perhaps it is necessary to Preach the Gospel even to the dead."):

> That God's Voice offers itself to all, and presents itself to the Soul that's unwilling to hear it.
> Nor need we much to labour to come to hear this Voice, the labour will be rather to stop thine ears that thou must not hear it. For the Voice itself offers itself, intrudes itself; nor does it cease continually to knock at everyone's door. In fine, "Forty years," says he, "I have been very neer to that generation, and have said they always err with their heart." He is still very neer unto us, he still speaks, and perhaps there is not who hears him. He still says, "these err with their heart": still Wisdom cries in the streets, "Transgressors, return to your heart." For this is the beginning of our Lord's speaking; and this Word seems to have gone before to all those who are converted to their heart, not only calling them back, but also bringing them back again, and setting them before their own face: for it is not only a Voice of power, but also a Ray of light, telling men of their sins, and enlightning the hidden things of darkness. Nor is there any difference betwixt the internal Voice and Light, the same Son of God being the Word of the Father, and the Splendor of his Glory; and the substance also of the Soul, in its kind spiritual, and uncompounded, without any distinction of senses is whole seeing, if we may call it a whole, and also in like manner whole hearing. Or what is done by that either Ray of Light or Word, but that only the Soul is made to know itself? For the Book of Conscience is opened, the miserable order of the Life is unfolded, a sad Story is repeated, Reason is enlighten'd, and the unfolded Memory is exhibited to certain eyes, as it were of the Soul. But both is not so much any thing of the Soul, as the Soul it self so that the same is both the beholder, and the beholded: the Soul set before her own face, and by sturdy apparitors, to wit, of thoughts sent into her, she is compelled, as a guilty Criminal, to appear before her own Tribunal. And who is able to undergo this judgment without being troubled? "My Soul is troubled at myself, says the Prophet of our Lord," Psal. 142. and doest thou

wonder that thou canst not be set before thy face without reprehension, without turbation, without confusion?⁷⁴

Gulliver's reprehension, perturbation, confusion, and self-loathing are not the climactic tragedy as much as the fact that he is doomed because he has no recourse for salvation, although he thinks he has, and resorts to that which in the first place, brought him to this juncture, to that which made him the monster he is: white supremacy, based on pride in reason. After "turning away his face" from its reflection "in horror and detestation of himself," he says, turning to pride in reason:

> By conversing with the Houyhnhnms, and looking upon them with delight, I fell to imitate their gait and gesture, which is now grown into a habit, and my friends often tell me in a blunt way that I 'trot like a horse'; which, however, I take for a great compliment: neither shall I disown, that in speaking I am apt to fall into the voice and manner of the Houyhnhnms, and hear myself ridiculed on that account without the least mortification.

There will be more than "the least mortification," meaning death, not humiliation, because philosophers do not leave hope at the bottom because "nothing is more contrary to reason than to try to transcend reason by reason."⁷⁵

> The conversion of the Souls is the work of God's Voice, and not of man's.... To this internal Voice therefore I exhort you to listen with the ears of your heart; and that you would make it your business rather to hear God speaking within you, than man speaking without you.⁷⁶

The latter, "man speaking without you," translated "philosophers speaking without you," is the crux of the problem, as Gulliver ironically betrays himself confessing pride in reason unwittingly as the cause of his downfall. This is the confession that leads directly into his anagnorisis:

> I freely confess, that all the little knowledge I have of any value was acquired by the lectures I received from my master [Socrates, Plato, Aristotle], and from hearing the discourses of him and his friends.

In other words, Gulliver's tragic flaw was in choosing Aristotle over Christ, which dictated his choice of white supremacy, the African slave trade, and constituted his forfeiture of the image and likeness of Christ for the image and likeness of a monster, which "trotting like a horse" demonstrates. But the tragedy is, it could not have been any other way; given his initial choice, the end is in the beginning. "Trotting like a horse" means his only recourse is the bound cycle of pride in reason.

Swift's allusion to Bernard affords the perfect conversionary context for Swift's meaning. Bernard's statement, "When a man thus takes stock of himself in the clear light of truth, he will discover that he lives in a region where likeness to God has been forfeited," is exactly the cause in the region called Houyhnhnmland, with its monsters called Centaurs, and their monstrous enslavement and planned genocide of black people. The key to Gulliver's tragedy is in the balance of Bernard's statement: "...and groaning from the depths of a misery to which he can no longer remain blind, will he not cry out to the Lord as the Prophet did: 'In your truth you have humbled me'?"[77] No, because Gulliver does not know God, and he is not humbled. Having started with Aristotle, he lost the knowledge of God within himself.

The climax is the turning point because self-knowledge is pivotal. At the climax, Gulliver is depicted as finding out the truth about himself and white people in general, which Swift wants white people in general to do, without "dissimulation," with "no attempt at self-deception, but a facing up to their real selves without flinching and turning aside." "When white people thus take stock of themselves in the clear light of truth, they will discover that they live in a region" of white supremacy, the African slave trade, and other atrocities against black people, "a region where likeness to God has been forfeited." As a consequence of this discovery, Swift wants white people "to groan from the depths of a misery to which they can no longer remain blind" ("the reason is blinded by pride"), the misery of self-hatred derived from self-knowledge and the remembrance of certain flagitious and facinorous acts against black people. Swift emphasizes the irony in Gulliver's discovery that, not only are white people *not* superior to black people, they are inferior to black people. In other words, the contrary is true, black people are superior to white people. The reason being: "No one human creature is more worthy in the sight of God than according to the goodness and holiness of their life;" and white people "make no other use of reason than to multiply and increase the vices of human nature," such as the African slave trade and the animalization of black people; but black people have *only* the vices of human nature. Swift is also emphasizing Gulliver's self-hatred and hatred of white people in general, as the proper reaction, expressing Swift's own feelings toward the horrors committed by white people against black people. Such justifiable hatred, is what Swift means by advocating misanthropy, in his letter to Alexander Pope, previously quoted. But Swift wants self-hatred to humble white people, and make them "cry out to the Lord as the Prophet did: "In your truth you have humbled me." He has Gulliver demonstrate from the climax to the end, the consequences of not crying out to the Lord as the Prophet did, and, more importantly, of not being able to. And he is not humbled. So that, his despairing hatred of himself and white people in general, culminates in the end in his self-betraying diatribe against white supremacy, and against white people as "lumps of deformity and diseases both in body and mind, smitten with pride."

But there is more to the climax that contributes to Gulliver's rage at the end. As integral to self-knowledge, came the realization of "how cruelly he tore out his own very bowels (heart), under the pretext of a miserable hunting" of African slaves. "Neither indeed could he then be sensible of it, when with "insatiable desire" catching human prey, "like the spider catches the vile prey of a few sorry flyes," he seemed to "make Nets of his own Bowels (heart)." At the climax, he realized this too late.

Gulliver does not repent because he cannot repent, having, in repeatedly resisting the promptings of the Holy Spirit, committed the final blasphemy, the unforgivable sin. Swift's message in Gulliver's damning, is in Bernard's words to Satan, that, God "neither can nor should suffer his goodness to be blasphemed with impunity;" that, God "so softens the sentence of punishment that," should Gulliver wish to recover himself, God "will not refuse forgiveness." But Gulliver's "hardness and impenitent heart" has continued for so long, that, he "canst not so wish," that is, he is no longer capable of wishing to recover himself, "and so [he] canst not escape from [his] punishment either."

Gulliver is "like unto a man beholding his natural face in a glass: For he beholdeth himself, and goeth his way, and straightway forgetteth what manner of man he was" (James 1:23–24), in that the first thing he tells the reader after "mortification" is:

> In the midst of all this happiness, when I looked upon myself to be fully settled for life, my master sent for me one morning a little earlier than his usual hour.

Gulliver may straightway have forgotten what manner of man he is, but the effect of what manner of man he is must be reckoned with. What makes the climax a turning point is the change in Gulliver wrought by his having committed the final blasphemy, the unforgivable sin: (His self-hatred upon self-knowledge constitutes the cumulative effects of a habitual unwillingness to hear the Voice of God presenting itself to the soul that's unwilling to hear it.):

> It is far worse than "grieving the Spirit." The sin against the Holy Ghost implies a state of final and hopeless impenitence, and is committed by those who have again and again wilfully resisted the influences and warnings of the Holy Ghost, and have made themselves incapable of repentance, and consequently of pardon.[78]

Such is Gulliver's state at the climax. Proof of his wilful resistance is afforded by the Scriptures alluded to for the dates of each of Gulliver's African slave trade voyages, Scripture which he wilfully resists or he wouldn't have made the voyages. By this time he has made himself incapable of repentance, and consequently of pardon, for although he hates himself he cannot repent.

Bernard's definition of the final blasphemy underscores Gulliver's change by being closer to the action from the climax on:

> There is a final impenitence, the greatest crime of all, an unforgivable blasphemy. In his agitation he is either swallowed up by excessive sadness and lost in a deep depression from which he will never have the consolation of emerging, in accord with Scripture's saying that the wicked man shows only contempt when caught in the midst of evils; or he will dissimulate, flatter himself with false reasonings and, as far as in him lies, surrender irrevocably to the world, to find his pleasure and delight in what advantages it offers. But just when he believes that he has peace and security, misfortunes of all kinds will overwhelm him and he will not escape. Thus despair, the greatest evil of all, follows on ignorance of God.[79]

"Just when he believes that he has peace and security" is when Gulliver states: "In the midst of all this happiness, when I looked upon myself to be fully settled for life," with his master's news, "misfortunes of all kinds will overwhelm him and he will not escape;" thus despair sets in, confirming his ignorance of God.

Gulliver's master's news is that Gulliver must be banished from Houyhnhnmland because the representatives at the general assembly "had taken offence at the master's keeping a yahoo (Gulliver) in his family more like a Houyhnhnm than a brute animal."

> That he was known frequently to converse with Gulliver, as if he could receive some advantage or pleasure in Gulliver's company: that such a practice was not agreeable to reason or nature, or a thing ever heard of before among them.

This sounds like the kind of racism whites practices against blacks, so Gulliver should be well acquainted with it, ironically. Gulliver adds:

> they alleged, that because I had some rudiments of reason, added to the natural pravity of those animals [the black yahoos], it was to be feared I might be able to seduce them into the woody and mountainous parts of the country, and bring them in troops by night to destroy the Houyhnhnm cattle, as being naturally of the ravenous kind, and averse from labour.

This is another way of saying white people are inferior and black people superior, in pitting the unnatural (as in monstrous) depravity of which the reason of white people is capable of devising against the natural depravity and ravenousness of the black yahoos. Swift more subtly again projects the inferiority of white people, in Gulliver's saying of his master that "for his own part he could have been content to keep me in his service as long as I lived, because he found I had cured myself of some bad habits and dispositions, by endeavouring, as far as my inferior nature was capable, to imitate the Houyhnhnms." But he is "daily pressed to have the assembly's exhortation executed." Gulliver doesn't hesitate to tell the reader that the Houyhnhnms "have no conception how a rational creature can be compelled, but only advised or exhorted, because no person can disobey reason, without giving up his claim to be a rational creature," which is exactly what Swift in promoting, the giving up of one's claim to being a rational creature, as in rationalism. But given the fundamental definition of rational, "having reason," the Houyhnhnms are confusing the reason with the will. In the sense of "having reason," one can disobey reason without giving up one's claim to be a rational creature:

> Reason is given to the will for instruction, not destruction. It would be to the destruction of the will, however, were it to impose any necessity on which would prevent it from moving freely in accordance with its judgment. Such necessity might push it (consenting to appetite or evil spirit) toward wrong, making an animal of it, not knowing, or even actively resisting the things which are of the Spirit of God; or (following grace) toward right, making it spiritual, able to judge all things, but itself judge by no one. If, I say, the will were incapable of reaching out to any of these because of some prohibition of the reason, it would no longer be will. For the presence of necessity means the absence of will.[80]

It is important to note, with regard to the African slaves and all that they are accused of doing and being, that Bernard asks and answers the question: "On what basis, in fact, can one impute anything to a man, whether good or bad, if he is not known to have the free disposal of himself? Necessity excuses from both. For necessity's presence means freedom's absence; and where there is no freedom, neither is there merit, nor consequently judgment...."[81]

Gulliver more and more begins to show signs of being guilty of the final blasphemy as defined by Bernard: "excessive sadness, deep depression, contemptuous, dissimulation, false reasonings, irrevocable surrender to the world, and despair."[82] His reaction to the Houyhnhnm's decree is indicative. He says:

> I was struck with the utmost grief and despair at my master's discourse, and being unable to support the agonies I was under, I fell into a swoon at his feet; when I came to myself he told me that he concluded I had been dead.... I answered, in a faint voice, that death would have been too great an happiness; that although I could not blame the assembly's exhortation, or the urgency of his friends, yet, in my weak and corrupt judgment, I thought it might consist with reason to have been less rigorous.

He goes on to say, with self-betraying irony: "I looked on myself as already devoted to destruction." He's been devoted to the destruction of black people for most of his life, and therefore has been devoted to his own destruction in terms of salvation. Ironically, he obtusely alludes to the way to prevent both kinds of destruction when he says:

> That the certain aspects of an unnatural death was the least of my evils: for, supposing I should escape with life by some strange adventure, how could I think with temper of passing my days among yahoos [white people], and relapsing into my old corruptions, for want of examples to lead and keep me within the paths of virtue?

The allusion is to "he leadeth me in the paths of righteousness for his name's sake. Yea, though I walk through the valley of the shadow of death, I will fear no evil, for thou art with me" (Ps. 23).

After presenting his master with humble thanks for the offer of his servants' assistance in making a vessel, and "desireing a reasonable time for so difficult a work," Gulliver says to the reader:

> I told him I would endeavour to preserve a wretched being; and, if ever I returned to England, was not without hopes of being useful to my own species, by celebrating the praises of the renowned Houyhnhnms, and proposing their virtues to the imitation of mankind.

The latter is not only an allusion to a statement by Socrates in Plato's *Republic* but, in "celebrating the praises of the renowned Houyhnhnms," reflects the very adoration Swift describes in the first paragraph of his sermon "On the Wisdom of This World."

Gulliver is given two months to construct a boat. He goes to that part of the coast where the rebellious crew of his African slave ship had set him on shore. Getting upon a height, he sees in the distance a small island about five leagues off, and resolves "it should, if possible, be the first place of my banishment, leaving the consequence to fortune [not to God]."

In depicting Gulliver's "mechanics," Swift intends the same purpose in his use of irony, as in "A Modest Proposal." Gulliver says:

> I finished a sort of Indian canoe, but much larger, covering it with the skins of [black people] well stitched together, with hempen threads of my own making. My sail was likewise composed of the skins of the same animal; but I made use of the youngest I could get, the older being too tough and thick, and I likewise provided myself with four paddles.... I tried my canoe in a large pond near my master's house, and then corrected in it what was amiss; stopping all the chinks with [black people's] tallow, till I found it staunch.... And when it was as complete as I could possible make it, I had it drawn on a carriage very gently by [black people] to the seaside.

Swift thus calls attention to the savage abuse of black people by white people by having Gulliver use their skins to cover his canoe, as he would call attention to the abuse by the English of the Irish children by proposing that they be eaten.

When it came time for his departure, Gulliver takes leave of his master, "his eyes flowing with tears, and his heart quite sunk with grief." He says:

> I was forced to wait above an hour for the tide.... I took a second leave of my master: but as I was going to prostrate myself to kiss his hoof, he did me the honour to raise it gently to my mouth [228].

Swift's depiction of Gulliver kissing the hoof of the Antichrist is an allusion to Bernard's explanation of the meaning of "the kiss," to emphasize Gulliver's incapacity for conversion, his rejection of Christ, and his blasphemy against the Holy Ghost, the unforgivable sin ("The blasphemy against the Holy Ghost shall not be forgiven unto men" (Matt. 12:31).

Bernard describes "three stages of the soul's progress under the figure of three kisses": "the kiss of the Lord's feet, hands and mouth." The first stage is:

> Prostrate yourself on the ground, take hold of Christ's feet, sooth them with kisses, sprinkle them with your tears and so wash not them but yourself.[83]

This first stage Swift alludes to when he has Gulliver say, "...as I was going to prostrate myself to kiss his hoof...." "The first stage is the sign of a genuine conversion of life,"[84] of which Gulliver is incapable. The second stage is the kiss of the Lord's hand: "The Lord's hand gives the power to persevere and raises up."[85] Swift alludes to the second stage by having Gulliver say, "...he did me the honour to raise it gently [as if a hand] to my mouth." There is further instruction. Bernard says, "...you must kiss his hand, that is, you must give glory to his name, not to yourself."[86] We're not sure Gulliver isn't giving glory to himself on the sly when he says, "Detractors are pleased to think it improbable, that so illustrious a person should descend to give so great a mark of distinction to a creature as inferior as I."

Finally, Bernard speaks of the Holy Spirit as the kiss of the mouth:

> It is by giving the Spirit, through whom God reveals, that he shows us himself.... This revelation which is made through the Holy Spirit not only conveys the light of knowledge but also lights the fire of love, as St. Paul testifies: "The love of God has been poured into our hearts by the Holy Spirit which has been given us."[87]

Swift alludes to the kiss of the mouth when Gulliver's wife kisses him with the kiss of her mouth upon his return home, when he is incapable of love. These "stages of the soul's growth in love," figured by the three kisses, serve as a foil for Gulliver's desperate spiritual condition. He is not able to prostrate himself at the feet of Christ, weeping and deploring the evil he has done, and "then reach out for the hand that will lift him up." He is like Satan, whom Bernard addresses, saying that God would not be so hard on him, should he repent and ask forgiveness, that God "will not refuse forgiveness" should Satan so wish it:

> but after thy hardness and impenitent heart thou canst not so wish, and so thou canst not escape from they punishment either.[88]

The same hardness and impenitent heart is owned by Gulliver after so many years in the African slave trade.

He begins his "desperate voyage" on "February 15, 1714–15." He says:

> My design was, if possible, to discover some small island uninhabited ... so horrible was the idea I conceived of returning to live in the society and under the government of yahoos [white people]. For in such a solitude as I desired, I could at least enjoy my own thoughts, and reflect with delight on the virtues of those inimitable Houyhnhnms, without any opportunity of degenerating into the vices and corruptions of my own species.

Not only are "his own thoughts" and "reflections on the virtues" of "those inimitable Houyhnhnms [Greek philosophers] contrary to "that contemplative gift by which ... the Lord shows himself to the soul,"[89] the "virtues" of the "inimitable" Greek philosophers [Houyhnhnms], provide white-everyman-Gulliver with numerous "opportunities of degenerating into the vices and corruptions," of which he took abundant advantage, as we've seen. And in continuing to do so, he further proves there is nothing more contrary to reason than to try to transcend reason by reason. He has descended to the Twelfth Step of Pride, Habitual Sinning, where "the fool saith in his heart, 'There is no God.'" He does not consent to be saved. ("To consent is to be saved.")[90]

So his "desperate voyage" is more desperate than he thinks, "desperate" being synonymous with hopeless despair, as the OED defines it for the period, which means it is characteristic of the final blasphemy. So is "contempt," which Gulliver expresses when he says: "so horrible was the idea ... of living in the society and under the government of white people." In representing the bulk of white people, in hating himself he is hating them.

The African slave trade is a created context for Gulliver's desperate voyage. He mentions the Cape of Good Hope, Madagascar, and New Holland twice. Immediately afterward he postures as an Amerigo Vespucci, using map and chart placements as a smoke screen to cover up his African slave trade activities. The African slave trade makes Gulliver's voyage all the more desperate, bench marked as it is by the Scriptures for the date he began this desperate voyage, "February 15, 1714–5, at 9 o'clock in the morning." The first Scripture for that morning was chosen to identify Gulliver with the Jews who provoked the Lord. It's an ominous warning coinciding with "desperate":

> ... the ground clave asunder that was under them And the earth opened her mouth, and swallowed them up, and their houses, and all that appertained to them went down alive into the pit, and the earth closed upon them: and they perished [Num. 16].

In the second Scripture for the morning of February 15, white people, because of the African slave trade, are condemned for the mocking and crucifying of Jesus Christ, by Christ's own decree: "As ye do unto the least of these [African slaves] my brethren, ye do it unto me" (Mark 15).

Gulliver's "desperate voyage" takes him first to an small island that seems uninhabited. On his fourth day there, he sees twenty or thirty naked natives, men, women, and children. One of the "savages" spies Gulliver, and "discharged an arrow, which wounded [him] deeply on the inside of [his] left knee." He says, "I shall carry the mark to my grave. I apprehended the arrow might be poisoned, and paddling out of reach of their darts ... I made a shift to suck the wound, and dress it as well as I could." This incident identifies Gulliver with Chiron, the best known of the Centaurs, who, like Gulliver, has a knowledge of medicine; and whom Dante places in hell's Circle of the Violent, where the African slave trade would place Gulliver. Chiron was also wounded in the knee, but fatally, by Hercules. Gulliver's wound in the knee is not fatal, but he will "carry the mark to his grave." As Chiron hastens toward death, he gives up his immortality to Prometheus, who created man out of clay. Just as Chiron gives up his immortality to a false god, Gulliver gives up his immortality to a false god, Greek philosophy, symbolized by the Houyhnhnms, and thereby makes himself a candidate for the kind of immortality defined by St. Augustine, which is also exemplified by the "struldbruggs":

> ... those who are excluded from eternity because they are separated from God are still immortal; this immortality means their punishment and damnation. They are excluded from God; this means they are excluded from love — love is the ground of being — and they deserve no pity. There is no unity of love between them and the others.[91]

Gulliver is separated from God; and his contempt for black people and white people, including himself, his wife, and his children, as we shall see, obviously means "there is no unity of love between him and others." When he sees a sail "to the north-northeast" (Satan's seat), he says:

> I was in some doubt, whether I should wait for them or no; but at last my detestation of the [white race] prevailed, and turning my canoe, I sailed and paddled together to the south, and got into the same creek from whence I set out in the morning, choosing rather to trust myself among these barbarians,

than live with European yahoos.

His contempt is, again, indicative of the final blasphemy, which separates him from God, for "love of others in the path which leads from knowledge of yourself to knowledge of God."⁹²

With the approach of a Portuguese African slave ship, Swift brings *Gulliver's Travels*, a protest of white supremacy and the African slave trade in defense of "real" Christianity, full circle, condemning the launching of the African slave trade by the Portuguese. We are given another allusion to the African slave trade in Gulliver's hiding place — "behind a stone by the little brook, which, as I have already said, was excellent water." We are reminded of a traditional African slave ship stop for water:

> The ship came within a half a league of this creek, and sent out her long-boat with vessels to take in fresh water (for the place it seems was very well known) [230].

The Portuguese seamen find Gulliver flat on his face behind the stone. They conclude he's not "a native of the place, who all go naked." They see by his "complexion" Gulliver must be a European, "but were at a loss to know what I meant by yahoos and Houyhnhnms, and at the same time fell a laughing at my strange tone in speaking, which resembled the neighing of a horse" (230).

Further instances of "the great power of habit and prejudice" (121) are brought to mind when Gulliver says of the seamen: "When they began to talk, I thought I never heard or saw any thing so unnatural; for it appeared to me as monstrous as if a dog or a cow should speak in England, or a yahoo in Houyhnhnmland, but especially when Gulliver speaks of the seamen in traditional white supremacist terms, notwithstanding their being African slave trade monsters. He speaks of them as "The honest Portuguese," and as having "great humanity," and their captain as "a very courteous and generous person." Worst of all, however, he still animalizes black people, comparing them with "a dog or a cow." The words Gulliver uses, "unnatural" and "monstrous," are ironically more appropriate for himself and the seamen, than for the use he puts them to.

As to Gulliver's state of mind, we get another clue, this from the Portuguese seamen, who "all conjectured that my misfortunes had impaired my reason." Gulliver's symptoms are described in "A Tritical Essay Upon the Faculties of the Mind": That the opinions of philosophers lead men from one errour to another.... For such opinions cannot cohere; but like the iron and clay in the toes of Nebuchadnezzar's image, must separate and break in pieces." Man is clay; the opinions are iron, which cause a separation and breaking in pieces in the mind of the adherent of clay, such as Gulliver. Therefore, at the same time that he is showing signs of the final blasphemy, he is showing signs of schizophrenia, at least according to the *Merriam Webster* dictionary definition, although I have as well the permission of a neurologist to call Gulliver's condition schizophrenia:

> Schizophrenia—A psychotic disorder characterized by disturbance in thinking involving a distortion of the usual logical relations between ideas, a separation between the intellect and the emotions so that the patient's feelings or their manifestations seem inappropriate to his life situation, and a reduced tolerance for the stress of interpersonal relations so that he retreats from social intercourse into his own fantasy life and commonly into delusions and hallucinations — may go on to marked deterioration or regression in behavior though often unaccompanied by further intellectual loss.

The definition's mention of "a separation between the intellect and the emotions" reminds us of something Bernard teaches: "that the will [emotions] are the reason [intellect] always act together. Willing implies choosing that which is willed; and choosing implies willing that which is chosen. The joint action of will and reason is consent."[93]

If they don't act together, a separation is indicated, presumably. And Gulliver obviously demonstrates "a reduced tolerance for the stress of interpersonal relations," as we have seen; and it gets worse. He exemplifies the definition.

For example, although he says the African slave ship captain, Pedro de Mendez, "was a very courteous and generous person," and "desired to know what I would eat or drink ... and spoke many obliging things," Gulliver remained silent and sullen, and says: "I was ready to faint at the very smell of him and his men." Gulliver goes on to say:

> ... he ordered me a chicken and some excellent wine, and then directed that I should be put to bed in a very clean cabin. I would not undress myself, but lay in the bed-clothes, and in half an hour stole out, when I thought the crew was at dinner, and getting to the side of the ship was going to leap into the sea, and swim for my life [like some of the African slaves], rather than continue among yahoos [white people]. But one of the seamen prevented me, and having informed the captain, I was chained to my cabin.

He continues: "After dinner Don Pedro came to me, and desired to know my reason for so desperate an attempt."

Bernard has the reason in one of his conversionary sermons from "A Mirror That Flatters Not." Its relevance starts at the climax, when Gulliver "happened to behold the reflection of his own form in a lake or fountain," and says, "I turned away my face in horror and detestation of myself":

> He who loves Wickedness, hates both his own Soul and Body.... Does he not

hate his own body, for which he daily merits more and more fire in Hell; for which, according to his hard and impenitent heart, he "treasures up wrath against the day of wrath?" Notwithstanding this hatred as well of the Body as of the Soul, is rather in effect than affection. So the phrenetick man hates his own flesh, when he endeavours to mischief himself; the deliberation of reason being asleep in him. But can there be a worse phrensie than impenitency of heart, and an obstinate resolution to go on in sin? For such a one lays violent hands upon himself; nor does he tear and gnaw his flesh, but his mind. If thou hast seen a man fret, and scratch his hands till they bleed again, thou hast in such an one a clear and lively pourtraicture of a Soul when it sins. For the pleasure gives place to grief, and pain succeeds the itching delight. Nor was he ignorant of it, that so it would be; but dissembled it when he scratched himself. So we tear and wound our unhappy Souls with our own hands; but with this difference, that we wound them so much the more grievously, by how much a spiritual Creature is more excellent, and more hardly cured. Nor do we this out of hatred or ill-will, but out of a stupid internal insensibility. For the Soul being poured out abroad, it has no sense of its internal dammages; because it is not within itself, but in the belly perhaps, or under the belly. In fine, some men's Souls are in their Platters, and others in their Coffers; "where thy treasure is," says our Lord, "there also is thy heart." And what wonder, if the Soul feel not its own wounds, when forgetful of it self, and wholly absent from it self, it was gone into a far Country? But the time will come, when returning home to it self, it shall understand how cruelly it tore out its own very bowels, under the pretext of a miserable hunting. Neither indeed could it then be sensible of it, when with insatiable desire catching at the vile prey of a few sorry flyes, like the spider, it seemed to make Nests of its own Bowels.

It is not difficult to see Gulliver in Bernard's sermon. His "violent thirst" and "insatiable desire" for the African slave trade tell us he loves wickedness, the African slave trade epitomizing wickedness by the violation of the laws of nature. White people have to *love* wickedness to "make no other use of reason than to improve and multiply the vices allotted by nature," the vices of human nature, which Gulliver realizes at the climax. The fact that he tries to cover up his slave trade activities means he knows he's wrong but continues in the trade notwithstanding. That's what you call *love* of wickedness. No wonder, when he sees himself as he really is, he hates himself, "turns away his face in horror and detestation of himself." We know it's an intensely fierce hatred because he can "better endure the sight of a common [black person] than of his own person," and we've had unforgettable descriptions of his hatred of black people.

Gulliver's worsening desperate state answers Bernard's question: "But can there be a worse phrensie than impenitency of heart, and an obstinate resolution to go on in sin?" Gulliver, having made himself incapable of repentance, demonstrates this in "trotting like a horse," which proves he has lost the wisdom which is able to grasp intuitively the ultimate principles, the knowledge of God, within himself, because he started with the external world, as Aristotle taught. His worsening condition indicates, in effect, that he is "laying violent hands upon himself." He "tears and wounds his unhappy Soul with his own hands." Bernard says we do this out of "a stupid internal insensibility," which is one of the main points Swift makes with having Gulliver start out with Curiosity, feeding the eyes and ears, Aristotle's system of knowledge, which is "the Soul being poured out abroad," and as a result, having "no sense of its internal damages; because it is not within it self," but, as in Gulliver's case, is in his "Coffers," indicative of the "far Country" (Africa) Gulliver's Soul has gone into both literally and figuratively on prosperous voyages to fill his coffers. Gulliver's own words, "insatiable desire," expose him as the personification of Bernard's prophetic conclusion: Let's just say the time came at the climax, "when returning home to itself" Gulliver's Soul came to understand "how cruelly it tore out its own very bowels [heart] under the pretext of a miserable hunting [for African slaves]. Neither indeed could it then be sensible of it, when with "insatiable desire" catching as prey thousands of African slaves; Gulliver, like the spider catching flies, made Nests of his own Bowels [heart]."

Examples continue to mount. The captain makes him promise not to attempt anything against his life, or else he will continue a prisoner until they arrive in Lisbon. Gulliver promises, saying he would suffer the greatest hardships rather than return to live among yahoos [white people]. He says: "I strove to conceal my antipathy to human kind, although if often broke out.... But the greatest part of the day, I confined myself to my cabin, to avoid seeing the crew."

> The captain had often entreated me to strip myself of my savage dress, and offered to lend me the best suit of clothes he had. This I would not be prevailed on to accept, abhorring to cover myself with anything that had been on the back of a yahoo [white person]. I only desired he would lend me two clean shirts, which having been washed since he wore them, I believed would not so much defile me. These I changed every second day, and washed them myself.

Ironically, of course, Gulliver's hatred and contempt of white people is a reflection of his hatred and contempt for himself.

His condition worsens with paranoia. The Portuguese African slave ship, Captain Pedro de Mendez commanding, arrived at Lisbon, the first major African slave market, on November 5, 1715. Gulliver is conveyed to the captain's own house, and requests to be led up to the highest room backward. He tells the reader, speaking of the captain:

> I conjured him to conceal from all persons what I told him of the Houyhnhnms, because the least hint of such a story would not only draw numbers

of people to see me, but probably put me in danger of being imprisoned, or burnt by the Inquisition.... He gained so far upon me, that I ventured to look out of the back window. By degrees I was brought into another room, from whence I peeped into the street, but drew my head back in a fright. In a week's time he seduced me down to the door. I found my terror gradually lessened, but my hatred and contempt seemed to increase. I was bold enough to walk the street in his company, but kept my nose well stopped with rue, or sometimes with tobacco.

As in the beginning, Swift alludes to his sermon "On the Testimony of Conscience," in the captain's putting it upon Gulliver as "a point of honour and conscience" that he ought to return to his native country, live at home with his wife and children. He tells Gulliver of an English ship in the port just ready to sail.

Gulliver leaves Lisbon the 24th day of November, in an English merchantman (African slave ship), "but who was the master I never inquired," he says, and adds (with double entendre on "commerce"): "During this last voyage I had no commerce with the master or any of his men, but pretending I was sick kept close in my cabin," which means he did not traffick in African slaves on this his last African slave trade voyage, but not for the reasons exquisitely stated in the Scripture alluded to by the date of this last voyage: The Epistle of Paul to Philemon.

To allude to The Epistle of Philemon on the date of an African slave trade voyage in a book that protests the African slave trade in defense of "real" Christianity is to allude to Scripture that protests slavery in defense of "real" Christianity while defining "real" Christianity in the context of legalized slavery. To the extent that "real" Christianity is Christ, and the Spirit of the Lord anointed Christ to "proclaim release to the captives," to free the slaves, in other words, both Paul and Swift have the best authority for their defense.

Paul, in his beseeching, relies on Philemon's love and faith in Jesus Christ to make the communication of that love and faith effectual by acknowledging every good thing which is in him in Christ Jesus by freeing his slave, Onesimus (6). Paul says he has "great joy and consolation in Philemon's love, because the hearts of the saints are refreshed by Philemon," whom he calls "brother." Because of his rank and authority, Paul could order Philemon to free Onesimus, but he wants Philemon to be persuaded by love to free him, by the love Paul has already made much of in praise, and to which Paul has gone from calling Philemon "our dearly beloved, and fellow-labourer" to calling him "brother." Paul is shrewdly persuading Philemon to do the right thing for the right reason, which is right desire. After projecting the "real" Christian aspect of their relationship by calling

Philemon "brother," Paul makes it even more difficult for Philemon to not desire to free Onesimus for love's sake, by emphasizing the "real" Christian aspect of the "new" relationship of Onesimus to them both. Paul says:

> I beseech thee for my son Onesimus, whom I have begotten in my bonds: Which in time past was to thee unprofitable, but now profitable to thee and to me:

Since Paul has fathered the rebirth of Onesimus in Christ, Paul feels justified in speaking of Onesimus as his son. And by comparing the financial master/slave relationship to the Christic father/son relationship, Paul can say, without fear of contradiction, that the former was unprofitable, and that now Onesimus is profitable to them both as a "fellow-labourer" in Christ; for, "What shall it profit a man, if he shall gain the whole world, and lose his own soul?" (Mark 8:36). The answer, it goes without saying, is "nothing," as any "real" Christian knows. Moreover, by calling Onesimus his son, Paul is making it harder for Philemon not to free Onesimus. It would be refusing to free Paul's son. In sending Onesimus back as Paul's "own heart," Paul makes it even harder for Philemon but his own case more justifiable:

> Whom [Onesimus] I have sent again: thou therefore receive him, that is, mine own bowels [heart]: Whom I would have retained with me, that in thy stead he might have ministered unto me in the bonds of the gospel: But without thy mind would I do nothing; that thy benefit should not be as it were of necessity, but willingly.

He's saying he could have kept Onesimus with him to minister unto him in the bonds of the gospel in place of Philemon, but that he does not want to force Philemon's hand. Also, if Onesimus can work in Philemon's "stead," it subtly suggests equality between master and slave — an extra nudge. But Paul returns slave to master so that master can free slave willingly, for love of Christ's sake. That would not only free Onesumus from the bondage of slavery, but Philemon as well. And Paul wants Philemon to experience the greater salvational benefit accruing from master freeing slave because he wants to, not because he has to, and not just to please Paul, a much greater benefit than keeping Onesimus, whose name means "benefit." In other words, Paul is offering Philemon an opportunity for a blessing Philemon could not have foreseen:

> For perhaps he therefore departed for a season, that thou shouldst receive him for ever; Not now as a slave, but above a slave, a brother beloved, specially to me, but how much more unto thee, both in the flesh, and in the Lord?

Paul is pulling out all the stops. Forcing Philemon to put his love and faith toward Jesus Christ on the line, as well as his relationship with Paul, his superior. Paul is determined to make his offer one that can't be refused. He presents Onesimus first as his own son, then as his own heart, and finally as Paul himself:

> If thou count me therefore a partner, receive him as myself.

In other words, in the words of "real" Christianity, "As ye do unto the least of these my brethren, ye do it unto me."

Paul seems to be taking nothing for granted. Ironically, but in keeping with tradition, he takes full responsibility for Onesimus, with a twist:

> If he hath wronged thee, or oweth thee ought, put that on mine account; I Paul have written it with mine own hand, I will repay it: albeit I do not say to thee how thou owest unto me even thine own self besides.

"It was customary, when the possession of a slave was passed to another, or when a slave was freed, for any debts or penalties outstanding to be assumed by the slave himself or by the new owner." But in Paul's reminding the slave owner of the greater debt he owes, the implication is that Philemon "ought not to request payment of debts Onesimus may owe, or even accept it."[94]

Presumably Philemon owes Paul his life in Christ. But Paul softens his tone from that reminder to words evocative of Christ, which in a way are also a reminder as well as a call for Philemon's obedience to his love and faith in Christ. Paul ends assuming Philemon will not disappoint him in that regard:

> Yea, brother, let me have joy of thee in the Lord: refresh my heart in the Lord. Having confidence in thy obedience I wrote unto thee, knowing that thou wilt also do more than I say.

What Paul means by the latter statement is that he expects Philemon to not only free Onesimus but to return Onesimus to him, and Paul is perhaps providing a convenient way the latter can be accomplished, in saying:

> But withal prepare me also a lodging: for I trust that through your prayers I shall be given unto you.

As commentary on Gulliver's last African slave trade voyage, Paul's Epistle to Philemon is a fitting, spiritual, moral, religious, and human rights justification for a protest of the African slave trade and white supremacy; and given Gulliver's condition, a mental and emotional health justification as well. One African slave ship captain from the pages of history, said, looking back on his Guinea voyages, that the trade

> renders most of those who are engaged in it too indifferent to the sufferings of

their fellow creatures, and the necessity of treating the Negroes like cattle gradually brings a numbness upon the heart.[95]

A historian agrees:

> That to me was the distinguishing feature of the trade: not its dangers, not the loss of life it involved, not even the cruelties it inflicted on millions, but rather the numbness of the traders and their loss of human sympathies.[96]

Gulliver's African slave ship from Lisbon casts anchor in the Downs on the fifth of December, 1715, at about nine in the morning. He says, "...at three in the afternoon I got safe to my house at Redriff." But he is not "safe" at home, as we shall see. Two of the Scriptures Swift alludes to for the fifth of December bring *Gulliver's Travels* full circle. Gulliver's first voyages were "into the Levant." The Scripture alluded to for his last voyage describes the destruction of Tyre and Sidon, slave markets of the Levant, symbolic of African slave trade markets such as Lisbon, London, Amsterdam, Liverpool, New York, Newport, Charleston, etc., which Swift is condemning. The second Scripture is a catalogue of the faith of many, including the giant of faith, Samson, with whom, in Lilliput, the giant of no faith, Gulliver, is compared as the ironic opposite.

About his arrival home, Gulliver states:

> My wife and family received me with great surprise and joy, because they concluded me certainly dead;

He *is* certainly dead. The novel up to this point has demonstrated the death of Gulliver's Will, Memory, and Reason, the faculties of the soul of white people. He is also dead according to the following, as previously shown:

> A soul which lacks knowledge of truth [Christ] cannot be said to be alive, but is so far dead in itself; likewise one which does not yet possess love is without sensitivity.[97]

To the contrary as to love and sensitivity, Gulliver tells us:

> I must freely confess the sight of them [his wife and family] filled me only with hatred, disgust, and contempt, and the more by reflecting on the near alliance I had to them.... And when I began to consider, that by copulating with one of the yahoo species I had become a parent of more, it struck me with the utmost shame, confusion, and horror.

He goes on to say:

> As soon as I entered the house, my wife took me in her arms, and kissed me, at which, having not been used to the touch of that odious animal for so many years, I fell in a swoon for almost an hour.

With the kiss of Gulliver's wife, Swift alludes to "the kiss of the mouth," "the third stage of the soul's growth in love ... that contemplative gift by which a kind and beneficent Lord shows himself to the soul with as much clarity as bodily frailty can endure":

> The kiss is the gift of the Holy Spirit. The bride has no doubt that if the Son will reveal himself to anybody, it will be to her. Therefore, she dares to ask for this kiss, actually for that Spirit in whom both the Father and the Son will reveal themselves to her.... The Holy Spirit indeed is nothing else but the love and the benign goodness of them both. When the bride asks for the kiss therefore, she asks to be filled with the grace of this threefold knowledge, filled to the utmost capacity of mortal flesh. But it is the Son whom she approaches, since it is by him it is to be revealed.... It is by giving the Spirit, through whom he reveals, that he shows us himself; he reveals in the gift, his gift is in the revealing. Furthermore, this revelation which is made through the Holy Spirit, not only conveys the light of knowledge but also lights the fire of love, as St. Paul again testifies: "The love of God has been poured into our hearts by the Holy Spirit which has been given us."[98]

Unlike the bride, Gulliver does not ask for this kiss. Swift depicts "that contemplative gift by which the Lord shows himself to the soul,"[99] the Holy Spirit, to expose Gulliver's blasphemy against the Holy Spirit, his ignorance of Christ, his lack of love and sensitivity, his "certainly dead" soul. Swift's ingenious use of the irony of self-betrayal makes this depiction more powerfully effective, in that he has Gulliver utter charged words evocative of Christ, the Holy Spirit, "the kiss of the mouth," obtusely and unwittingly. This demonstrates Gulliver's having lost the wisdom which is able to grasp intuitively the knowledge of God within himself, as a result of having pursued the Aristotelian–Thomist method of starting with the external world. For example, Gulliver says:

> At the time I am writing it is five years since my last return to England: during the first year I could not *endure* my wife or *children* in my *presence*, the very *smell* if them was intolerable, much less could I *suffer* them to *eat* in the same *room*.

These words are evocative of signs of the second coming of Christ, and of the end of the world, as revealed by Jesus to his disciples:

> And because iniquity shall abound, the love of many shall wax cold. But he that shall endure unto the end, shall be saved [Matt. 24:12–13].

One of his disciples asks Jesus: "Are there few that be saved?" Jesus said unto them:

> Strive to enter in at the strait gate: for many, I say unto you, will seek to enter in, and shall not be able. When once the master of the house is risen up, and hath shut the door, and ye begin to stand without, and to knock at the

door, saying, Lord, Lord, open unto us; and he shall answer and say unto you, I know you not whence ye are: Then shall ye begin to say, We have eaten and drunk in thy *presence*, and thou hast taught in our streets. But he shall say, I tell you, I know you not whence ye are; depart from me, all ye workers of iniquity. There shall be weeping and gnashing of teeth [Luke 13:23–28].

"Presence" is also relevant to Swift's condemnation of Gulliver as a white supremacist, in Christ's teaching of humility:

When thou art bidden, go and sit down in the lowest room; that when he that bade thee cometh, he may say unto thee, Friend, go up higher: then shalt thou have worship in the presence of them that sit at meat with thee. For whosoever exalteth himself shall be abased; and he that humbleth himself shall be exalted [Luke 14:10–11].

In addition, "presence" is relevant in the mention of "Who shall be punished with everlasting destruction from the *presence* of the Lord, and from the glory of his power" (Gulliver, for example):

... them that know not God, and that obey not the gospel of our Lord Jesus Christ [II Thess. 8–9].

The "day of the Lord" is also alluded to in Swift's use of "smell": "It shall come to pass, that instead of sweet smell there shall be stink" (Is. 3:24).

"*Suffer*" relates to "*children*": "Suffer little children, and forbid them not to come unto me: for of such is the kingdom of heaven." "To *eat* in the same *room*," is an allusion to Christ's last supper in the "upper room." Christ sends two of his disciples to say to a certain man: "The Master saith, 'Where is the guest chamber, where I shall *eat* the passover with my disciples?" (Emphasis added).

And he will shew you a large *upper room* furnished and prepared: there make ready for us (Emphasis added). [Mark 14:14–15].

Swift has Gulliver go on to say, speaking of his wife and children, and then of his horses:

To this *hour* they dare not presume to touch my *bread*, or *drink* out of the same *cup*, neither was I ever able to let one of them take me by the *hand*. The first money I laid out was to buy two young stone-horses, which I keep in a good stable, and next to them the groom is my greatest favourite; for I feel my spirits revived by the smell he contracts in the stable (Emphasis added).

The first sentence is an allusion to the last supper:

And when the hour was come, he sat down, and the twelve apostles with him.... And he took bread, and gave thanks, and brake it, and gave unto them, saying, This is my body which is given for you: this do in remembrance of me.

> Likewise also the cup after supper, saying, This cup is the new testament in my blood, which is shed for you. But, behold, the hand of him that betrayeth me is with me on the table.

Although Gulliver's wife and children "dare not presume to touch [his] bread, or drink out of the same cup," Christ's disciples did presume to touch his bread, "he brake it [a loaf] and give it unto them," and did presume to drink out of the same cup: "Christ took the cup, and give thanks, and said, 'Take this, and divide it among yourselves.'" "Touch" may also be an allusion to the risen Christ, when Christ says to Mary Magdalen, "Touch me not, for I am not yet ascended to my Father" (John 20:17). This is made even more probable by the transition Swift makes from the betrayal of Christ in the first sentence to the betrayal of Christ in the second sentence, which proceeds to the crucifixion, death, burial and ascendency of Christ.

"Hand" at the end of the first sentence and "money" (thirty pieces of silver) in the second sentence both refer to the betrayal of Christ by Judas. "Laid out" refers to the crucifixion and death of Christ: Joseph of Arimathea took the body of Christ down from the cross, "and wrapped it in linen, and *laid* it in a sepulchre that was hewn in *stone*, wherein never man before was *laid*" (Emphasis added). White-everyman-Gulliver's betrayal and crucifying of Christ is projected by his "buying two stone-horses," signifying his worship of Greek and Roman philosophers and pride in reason, which the stone-horses (Houyhnhnms) symbolize, instead of worshipping Christ. This is also signified by his keeping his stone-horses in the place signifying where Christ was born, "in a good stable."

In Gulliver's statement that, next to his horses, "the groom is my greatest favourite; for I feel my spirits revived by the smell he contracts in the stable," Swift uses Bernard's depiction of "the soul's relations with God in terms of the love which unites a bride to her bridegroom" as the third coming of Christ, "a hidden one in which one sees Christ within one's self and is saved" (Christ revealing himself through the Holy Spirit, "the kiss of the mouth"). The "groom" Gulliver mentions, a caretaker of horses, is an ironic allusion to Christ the bridegroom. "Contracts" refers to the marriage contract. "Spirits revived" refers to the resurrection. What this means is, the rejection of Christ for philosophy and pride in reason, which the horses symbolize. For example, Gulliver says:

> My horses understand me tolerably well; I converse with them at least four hours every day. They are strangers to bridle or saddle; they live in great amity with me, and friendship to each other.

The heresy in this is implied in the Scriptures alluded to, for God says:

"I" will instruct thee and teach thee in the way which thou shalt go: I will guide thee with mine eye. Be ye not as the horse, or as the mule, which have no understanding, whose mouth must be held in with bit and bridle....

An horse is a vain thing for safety: neither shall he deliver any by his great strength.

In other words, Gulliver is way off base, ominously. All signs point to his doom, to his being lost beyond recall. All of his obtuse allusions to Christ prove his soul is dead. "The death of the soul is separation from God, which is effected by sin."[100] Swift's ingenious method of proving Gulliver does not know God proves Gulliver's soul is separated from God, and there is no hope of resurrection because "the resurrection of the soul is effected by Christ's humble and secret coming,"[101] which Gulliver has been depicted as dead to.

By all indications his body is dead as well. "The death of the body is separation of the soul from the body, effected by the penalty of sin."[102] Gulliver's soul is separated from his body because his body "trots like a horse," but "the invisible soul is created in the image of God; wherefore the scripture says, "God made man in his image and likeness." "Upright indeed."[103] Gulliver's *not* Upright body is separated from his Upright soul, man in the image of God. Inasmuch as Swift identifies the Centaurs (Houyhnhnms) with sin, and has Gulliver "trot like a horse," it's fair to say that in Gulliver, "sin and flesh are much alike." And it fits Bernard's description of what happens after "the laying aside of [Gulliver's] body, as Swift depicts it from one of the conversionary sermons in "A Mirror That Flatters Not," which tells of "The punishment as well of Soul as Body, and fruitless Repentance after death."[104]

As Swift has just demonstrated, all of the doors of Gulliver's body, the five senses, are dead, that his soul's returning home to itself, "when it shall understand how cruelly it tore out its own very bowels, under the pretext of a miserable hunting" of African slaves with "insatiable desire," is projected as after death. The punishment is depicted in the last chapter, as Gulliver takes leave of the reader for the last time. The basis of the punishment is explained in the following, to be understood in terms of Gulliver's soul:

> This return into it self, shall without doubt be at least after death, when all the doors of the Body shall be shut up ... so that it necessarily remains in itself, all egress out of itself being now impossible unto it. But it will be a sad and most pernicious return, and everlasting misery, when it shall be able to have repentance, but not be able to do any penitential work; for when the Body shall be wanting, there can be no action.... But whosoever shall not return unto himself before the laying aside of his body, must necessarily remain in himself for ever. But in what a self? In such a self, as he shall have made himself in this life; unless perhaps he shall sometimes be worse, for better shall he never be who is bad; for this very Body which now he put off, he must one day receive

again; not to do penance, but to be punished in it, when after a certain sort the condition of the flesh and of sin shall be much alike: for as sin shall be able always to be punished, but never be expiated or satisfied for; so neither in the Body shall the torments possibly be ended, nor yet the Body be consumed with the torments. Deservedly indeed shall everlasting vengeance and rage be against the sinner, because his fault can never be blotted out; and neither shall the substance of his flesh fail, lest together with it the affliction of his flesh should be forced to fail also.[105]

The "vengeance and rage" Bernard speaks of is reflected in Gulliver's diatribe against white supremacy in the very end. Gulliver never repented nor did penitential works. He remains in himself, in the self that we have seen, only worse. He's worse because his lies are more outrageous and his hypocrisy more blatant. Whereas because he never mentioned the African slave trade nor colonialism, in the final chapter he talks about little else, but still without exposing himself as an African slave trader, an African slave ship surgeon and captain; but more and more the "worm of conscience" gives him away, although he maintains his white supremacist character.

Setting the tone, he begins his good-by with an outrageous lie:

> Thus, gentle reader, I have given thee a faithful history of my travels for sixteen years, and above seven months [234].

First of all, his "Thus, gentle reader" smacks of connivance, a wink or secret understanding between him and the white reader, that what has gone on before, to which the "Thus" pertains, has *not* been a "faithful history." This means that Swift indicts white people in general, but he does anyway by making Gulliver white-everyman. This tells us that Swift could assume that readers of his day would know by Gulliver's itinerary that Gulliver's travels were only to African slave trade ports of call. Thus, Gulliver's wink reflects the conspiracy of silence on the outside regarding the African slave trade, as well as inside the book, the one reflecting the other.

As is obvious, Gulliver has not presented "a faithful history of his travels for sixteen years, and above seven months"; far from it, because he never once mentions the African slave trade, the sole purpose of his travels. Also, his African slave trade travels cover twenty-five years, not sixteen or seventeen. He goes on to say the opposite of the truth when he says that in giving his history he "has not been so studious of ornament as of truth," giving African slave trade ports of call ornamental names such as Lilliput, Brobdingnag, Laputa, and Houyhnhnmland, to cover up his slave trading. He continues with his lies:

> I could perhaps like others have astonished thee with strange improbable tales; but I rather chose to relate plain matter of fact in the simplest manner and style, because my principal design was to inform, and not to amuse thee.

5. Black Superiority 219

On the contrary, he rather chose to astonish us with strange improbable tales of six inch people, giants, flying islands, talking horses, etc., to cover up, not to inform, about the African slave trade and his involvement in it.

His most audacious lies have to do with covering up his African slave trade involvement. These lies are of the nature of guilt protesting too much, and they blow his cover. For example, at the height of the African slave trade, when over three million slaves a year are being shipped from Africa to the New World, he says: "It is easy for us who travel into remote countries, which are seldom visited by Englishmen or other Europeans, to form descriptions...." And then he claims to "relate only plain facts that happen in such distant countries where we have not the least interest with respect either to trade or negotiations." Was there any other interest?

He goes on to attack critics in much the same tone as Swift does in "A Tritical Essay," reflecting Boccaccio's attack in "Defense of Poetry":

> So that I hope I may with justice pronounce myself an author perfectly blameless, against whom the tribe of answerers, considerers, observers, reflecters, detecters, remarkers, will never be able to find matter for exercising their talents.

In "A Tritical Essay," Swift calls critics "capering Momuses,"[106] which is what Boccaccio calls them. In addition, Boccaccio attacks critics for:[107]

> BOCCACCIO: the foolishness of condemning what one does not readily understand.... Why then keep up this bray? They suffer from a morbid envy that will not endure what it cannot explain.
> (SWIFT: They must pardon me, if I venture to give them this advice, not to rail at what they cannot understand: it does but discover that self-tormenting passion of envy, than which the greatest tyrant never invented a more cruel torment.)
> BOCCACCIO: Why do such incompetents usurp the bench to judge that of which they know nothing? O base impiety, vile offense, hateful presumption — that a child born blind should openly attempt to distinguish colors.
> (SWIFT: I must be so bold to tell my critics and witlings, that they can no more judge of this, than a man that is born blind, can have any true idea of colours.)
> BOCCACCIO: Why do they keep up this ignorant yelping?
> (SWIFT: I have always observed, that your empty vessels sound loudest ... a writer need no more regard them than the moon does the barking of a little senseless cur.)

He adds the preposterous lie: "I write without passion, prejudice, or ill-will against any man or number of men whatsoever," (only black men, but he doesn't consider them human). That lie, not coincidentally but guilty by association, brings him back to the subject of the African slave trade:

> I confess, it was whispered to me that I was bound in duty, as a subject of

England, to have given in a memorial to a secretary of state, at my first coming over; because, whatever lands are discovered by a subject belong to the crown. But I doubt whether our conquests in the countries I treat of would be as easy as those of Ferdinando Cortez over the naked Americans [236].

The lands Gulliver travels to had already been just "taken" by the English or other European countries for the African slave trade. And the conquest of Mexico by Cortez was anything but easy; it was deplorable. And Cortez brought African slaves with him. Gulliver's is a hypocritical confession whose hypocrisy reveals the intensity of Swift's protest of white supremacy, the African slave trade, and colonialism. Swift is also ripping to shreds white people's hypocritical reverence for the ideals of Plato and Aristotle the Houyhnhnms hypocritically represent — the very ideals that fostered white supremacy, the African slave trade, and colonialism. For example, Swift has Gulliver desire of the Houyhnhnms what's already been done:

> I rather wish they were in a capacity of disposition to send a sufficient number of their inhabitants for civilizing Europe, by teaching us the first principles of honour, justice, truth, temperance, public spirit, fortitude, chastity, friendship, benevolence, and fidelity.

And he adds pointedly, "The *names* of all which virtues are still retained among us in most languages, and are to be met with in modern as well as ancient authors; which I am able to assert from my own small reading" (Emphasis added). Well, now we have it on the best authority on hypocrisy and the nominal. He did, however, give us a slightly different impression earlier, when he said: "My hours of leisure I spent in reading the best authors ancient and modern, being always provided with a good number of books." His lack of a scale of values in what he reads goes along with nominal virtues and hypocrisy.

Attempting, through hypocrisy, fraud, and lying — a cover-up — Gulliver instead does just the opposite by unwittingly exposing England's entrance into the African slave trade:

> But I had another reason which made me less forward to enlarge his Majesty's dominions by my discoveries. To say the truth, I had conceived a few scruples with relation to the distributive justice of princes upon those occasions. For instance, a crew of pirates are driven by a storm they know not whither, at length a boy discovers land from the topmast, they go on shore to rob and plunder, they see an harmless people, are entertained with kindness, they give the country a new name, they take formal possession of it for the king, they set up a rotten plank or a stone for a memorial, they murder two or three dozen of the natives, bring away a couple more by force for a sample, return home, and get their pardon. Here commences a new dominion acquired with a title by "divine right." Ships are sent with the first opportunity, the natives

driven out or destroyed, their princes tortured to discover their gold, a free license given to all acts of inhumanity and lust, the earth reeking with the blood of its inhabitants: and this execrable crew of butchers employed in so pious an expedition, is a modern colony sent to convert and civilize an idolatrous and barbarous people [237].

How could anyone not know what Swift is protesting here through Gulliver's characteristic obtuseness, his being "wholly unmoved at all the scenes of blood and desolation" (109), lacking human feeling, which allows such "pious expeditions" to thrive? Swift thus exposes white people's inhumanity using a description of a common occurrence to convey it, while signifying England's entry into the African slave trade.

In another hypocritical confession, it's hard to tell whether Gulliver leans too far over backward or falls flat on his face, especially considering England's reputation for "probably inflicting more suffering on the Negroes than any other nation." Referring to the above description of a colony, Gulliver says:

> But this description, I confess, doth by no means affect the British nation, who may be an example to the whole world for their wisdom, care, and justice in planting colonies; their liberal endowments for the advancement of religion and learning; their choice of devout and able pastors to propagate Christianity; their caution in stocking their provinces with people of sober lives and conversations from this the mother kingdom; their strict regard to the distribution of justice, in supplying the civil administration through all their colonies with officers of the greatest abilities, utter strangers to corruption; and to crown all, by sending the most vigilant and virtuous governors, who have no other views than the happiness of the people over whom they preside, and the honour of the king their master [237].

First of all, there is not such thing as "wisdom, care, and justice in planting colonies" since planting colonies is an act of arrogance and malignant aggression performed by an "execrable crew of butchers" against a backdrop of "all acts of inhumanity and lust, the earth reeking with the blood of its inhabitants." Moreover, what Gulliver goes on to say applies to the *real* African slave trade ports he travels to:

> But as those countries which I have described do not appear to have any desire of being conquered, and enslaved, murdered or driven out by colonies...

although the rest is a lie:

> nor abound either in gold, silver, sugar or tobacco; I did humbly conceive they were by no means proper objects of our zeal, our valour, or our interest.

On the contrary, Swift chooses for Gulliver's travels those countries known to be objects of English and European zeal, interest, and "insatiable desire" *because* they abound in gold silver, sugar, and tobacco, although they are not "proper" objects of zeal, interest, or "insatiable desire."

Now, after all the atrocities against black people, and the lies, the conniving, the cover-up, the deceit, the hypocrisy, the arrogance, and the fraud, with which many objections can be raised, Gulliver has the presumptuous white supremacist with insensitive audacity to say: "Having thus answered the "only" objection that can ever be raised against me as a traveller," by which he means "as to the formality of taking possession in my sovereign's name,"

> I here take a final leave of my courteous readers, and return to enjoy my own speculation in my little garden at Redriff, to apply those excellent lessons of virtue which I learned among the Houyhnhnms, to instruct the yahoos of my own family as far as I shall find them docible animals, to behold my figure often in a glass, and thus if possible habituate myself by time to tolerate the sight of a human creature [238].

By this we know he remains in his Humanist self forever, only worse, he's now not only a supremacist racist, but a supremacist sexist as well, holding forth in the style of the humanist Thomas More, and as advised by Captain Pedro de Mendez, who told Gulliver he "might command in his own house, and pass his time in a manner as recluse as he pleased." In other words, he could just ignore his wife. With the same lack of passion, Gulliver married for money, and in the twenty-two years of his marriage he had seen his wife only a total of five years, two months, and ten days, up until his return from his last African slave trade voyage when she takes him in her arms and he faints, "having not been uses to the touch of that odious animal for so many years." And after being home for five years, he says:

> I began last week to permit my wife to sit at dinner with me, at the farthest end of a long table, and to answer (but with the utmost brevity) the few questions I ask her. Yet the smell of a yahoo continuing very offensive, I always keep my nose well stopped with rue, lavender, or tobacco leaves [238].

Thomas More, although not misanthropic, is as passionless, holding forth in the style of Plato's *Republic*. In his letter to Peter Gilles, apologizing for the many commitments that prevented his completion of *Utopia*, he says (including his wife among his many commitments):

> You see, when I come home, I've got to talk to my wife, have a chat with my children, and discuss things with my servants. I count this as one of my commitments, because it's absolutely necessary, if I'm not to be a stranger in my own home. Besides, one should always try to be nice to the people one lives with, whether one had chosen their company deliberately, or merely been thrown into it by chance or family-relationship — that is, as nice as one can without spoiling them, or turning servants into masters.[108]

Humanism, it seems, makes one less human, lacking in passion, "one of the four natural emotions," which "is not subject to reason."[109] Swift places Thomas More in Glubbdubdrib, the lower world. More puts his wife and children on a level with his servants. Similarly, Gulliver puts his wife and children on a level with African slaves ("to instruct the yahoos of my own family as far as I shall find them docible animals"). More refers to *Utopia* as "a feast of reason." Such a feast seems to have poisoned Gulliver.

Holding forth as his Houyhnhnm master (Socrates/Plato/Aristotle), it's only logical that Gulliver should become contemptuous (indicative also of the final blasphemy) of human kind, horses being superior, "the perfection of nature." Sin and flesh have become much alike, so the irony is that by "holding his figure often in a glass," he will not possibly "habituate [himself] in time to tolerate the sight of a human creature," because he is a monster, like the Houyhnhnms. This is underscored by his "return to enjoy his own speculations in his little garden at Redriff," and "to apply the virtues he learned from the Houyhnhnms," not for purposes of "speculative consideration." "Speculative consideration" is that which collects itself in itself and, so far as divinely assisted, withdraws itself from human affairs in order to contemplate God."[110] In other words, Gulliver has *not* "returned home": "This will be a returning home: to have left the land of the body for the region of the spirit, the most sublime dwelling of the blessed spirits."[111] But Gulliver lives in a land where likeness to God has been forfeit. He is bound to the cycle of reason.

His end is prefigured in "A Tritical Essay," in the punishment of Ixion, the father of the Centaurs (Houyhnhnms). Ixion was bound on a wheel that turned forever in hell as punishment for his gross ingratitude to Zeus, from whom Ixion had obtained purification after committing murder. Ixion showed gross ingratitude by trying to win the love of Hera, the wife of Zeus:

> Thereupon Zeus formed a cloud, Nephele, to resemble Hera, and by her Ixion became the father of the Centaurs.[112]

Gulliver's embrace of reason and Greek philosophy, "Nephele," instead of Christ, from whom he had received purification, is the gross ingratitude for which he is punished by being bound to the cycle of reason in hell, the remembrance of past sins such as the murder of African slaves. "The memory of past sins is what constitutes the torment of hell, which is everlasting because the sins cannot be eradicated from the memory."[113]

Gulliver's pain from the biting of his worm of conscience becomes more intense as the cause of his pain is revealed in the fierceness of his diatribe against white supremacy, which he nails down as patently unnatural, a degenerate way of life that violates the laws of nature. He runs the gamut of the natural vices, the vices of human nature, those that black people possess, as established by the climax. He then establishes the difference been natural and unnatural by making an all-out assault against white people as the worst people for having the worst vice: white supremacy. He says:

> My reconcilement to the yahoo-kind [white people] in general might not be so difficult if they would be content with those vices and follies only which nature hath entitled them to. I am not in the least provoked at the sight of a lawyer, a pickpocket, a colonel, a fool, a lord, a gamester, a politician, a whoremonger, a physician, an evidence, a suborner, a traitor, or the like; this is all according to the due course of things: but when I behold a lump of deformity and diseases both in body and mind, smitten with pride, it immediately breaks all the measures of my patience; neither shall I be ever able to comprehend how such an animal and such a vice could tally together. The wise and virtuous Houyhnhnms, who abound in all excellencies that can adorn a rational creature, have no name for this vice [pride] in their language, which hath no terms to express any thing that is evil, except whereby they describe the detestable qualities of their yahoos, [black people] among which they were not able to distinguish this of pride, for want of thoroughly understanding human nature, as it showeth itself in other countries, where that animal presides. But I who had more experience, could plainly observe some rudiments of it among the wild yahoos. I dwell the longer upon this subject from the desire I have to make the society of an English yahoo by any means not insupportable, and therefore I here entreat those who have any tincture of this absurd vice, that they will not presume to appear in my sight [239].

This is, of course, further proof that Gulliver's white supremacist pride is not quenched. Here again he is extolling its source, the Humanist practice of condemning black people as "evil" and "detestable" while simultaneously giving them human nature *and* animal nature and confusing the two in schizophrenic fashion by attributing "pride," of which animals are not capable, to "wild yahoos," again perceiving black people as wild animals.

The rage of the proud blasphemer Gulliver is identifiable with the rage of the proud blasphemer Capaneus in Dante's Bernardian *Inferno*, the intensity of whose torment compels Dante the pilgrim to exclaim: "O vengeance of God, how much should you be feared by all who read what was revealed to my eyes!" The same could be exclaimed in Gulliver's case. Dante asks Virgil:

> ... who is that great one who seems not to heed the fire, and lies disdainful and scowling, so that the rain seems not to ripen him? And that same one, who had perceived that I was asking my leader about him, cried out, "What I was living, that am I dead...."

(Gulliver can say the same.)

> Then my leader spoke with such force as I had not heard him use before, "O

Capaneus! in that your pride remains unquenched you are punished the more: no torment save your own raging would be pain to match you fury."[114]

Gulliver's pride remains unquenched. He is tormented by the remembrance of white supremacy, which manifested as the African slave trade, and which torments him by being unquenched. But he is not "bitten so much with the remembrance of Pride and Envy, as with the remembrance of certain flagitious and facinorous acts" against African slaves.[115] And in Gulliver's hell, there is a conversionary message for white people, too late for Gulliver, which makes it all the more urgent: "That the worm of Conscience ought here to be felt, and by little and little extinguished; and not to be cherished and nourished to immortality." Bernard speaks of "the punishment as fruitless Repentance after death," when one "must necessarily remain in himself for ever":

> But in what a self? In such a self, as he shall have made himself in this life; unless perhaps he shall sometimes be worse, for better shall he never be who is bad; for this very Body which now he puts off, he must one day receive again; not to do penance, but to be punished in it, when after a certain sort the condition of the flesh and of sin shall be much a-like [Dorian Gray]: for as sin shall be able always to punished, but never be expiated or satisfied for; so neither in the Body shall the torments possibly be ended, not yet the Body be consumed with the torments.

So that is how Gulliver ends. He is bitten by the worm of conscience, not only with the remembrance of pride (white supremacy), but also with "the remembrance of certain flagitious and facinorous acts" (the African slave trade). He suffers the everlasting misery of remaining in himself forever.

> Deservedly indeed shall everlasting vengeance and rage be against the sinner, because his fault can never be blotted out; and neither shall the substance of his flesh fail, lest together with the affliction of his flesh should be forced to fail also.

This is what Swift is saying in advocating misanthropy (hatred by white people of themselves), that they *deserve* "everlasting vengeance and rage" for their flagitious and facinorous acts against black people. He has Gulliver demonstrate the proper attitude or misanthropy in calling white people "lumps of deformity and diseases both in body and mind, smitten with pride," and in reflecting how they should view themselves: "When I happened to behold the reflection of my own form in a lake or fountain, I turned away my face in horror and detestation of myself...."

> To the nine black men whose bodies they found,
> When looking for Cheney they went down.
> Cheney, Goodman, and Schwerner, now renowned.
> How many more black men lynched then drowned?

Chapter Notes

Introduction

1. Jonathan Swift, Epitaph in "Dr. Swift's Will," in *Dean Swift's Works in Nineteen Volumes*, Arranged by Thomas Sheridan, A.M., vol. 1 (London: J. Johnson, J. Nichols, et al., 1801), 530. For those who question Swift's belief in God, the following, which has always been accessible, should settle the issue: "Dr. Swift's Will": "In the name of GOD, Amen. I Jonathan Swift, doctor in divinity, dean of the cathedral church of St. Patrick, Dublin, being at this present of sound mind, although weak in body, so here make my last will and testament, hereby revoking all my former wills.
'Imprimis.' I bequeath my soul to God, (in humble hopes of his mercy through Jesus Christ) and my body to the earth," etc.

2. Giovanni Boccaccio, "The Defense of Poetry," in *Genealogies of the Pagan Gods*, p. 26.
3. Ibid., 24–25.
4. Ibid., 39.
5. Ibid., 40.
6. Ibid., 40.
7. Ibid., 79.
8. Charles Rowen Beye, *Ancient Greek Literature and Society* (Garden City, New York: Anchor Press/Doubleday, 1975), 5.
9. Swift, "The Abolishing of Christianity," vol. 2, *Works*, 383.
10. Ibid., 397.
11. Ibid., 398.
12. Henry Fielding, *Introduction to Jonathan Swift, "Gulliver's Travels" and Other Writings*, ed. Louis A. Landa (Boston: Houghton Mifflin, 1960).
13. Louis A. Landa, ed., *Introduction to Jonathan Swift, "Gulliver's Travels" and Other Writings*, (Boston: Houghton Mifflin, 1960).
14. Robert Grosseteste, in David L. Jeffrey, *The Early English Lyric & Franciscan Spirituality* (Lincoln: University of Nebraska Press, 1975), 93.
15. Bernard of Clairvaux, *The Steps of Humility*, trans. George Bosworth Burch (Cambridge: Harvard University Press, 1950), 30.
16. Ibid., 39.
17. Grosseteste, 93.
18. L.J. Morrissey, *Gulliver's Progress* (Hamden, CT: Archon Books, 1978), 32.
19. Swift, "A Sermon on Mutual Subjection," vol. 10, *Works*, 39–40.
20. Swift, "A Sermon on Brotherly Love," vol. 10, *Works*, 56.
21. Stephen G. Nichols, Jr., *Romanesque Signs: Early Medieval Narrative and Iconography* (New Haven, CT: Yale University Press, 1983), 2.
22. Ibid.
23. Ibid.
24. Paul Tillich, *A History of Christian Thought: From Its Judaic and Hellenistic Origins to Existentialism*, ed. Carl E. Braaten (New York: Simon and Schuster, 1968), 197.
25. Bernard of Clairvaux, *On the Song of Songs*, Sermon 35 (Kalamazoo: Cistercian Publications, 1980), 170.
26. Ibid., Sermon 35, 171.
27. Tillich, 184.
28. Bernard in Burch, 40.
29. Tillich, 186.
30. Bernard in Burch, 225.
31. Tillich, 186.
32. Ibid., 184.
33. Ibid., 112.
34. Bernard in Burch, 6.
35. Ibid., 133.
36. Bernard, Sermon 31, 126.
37. Ibid.
38. Bernard in Burch, 133–159.
39. Bernard in Burch, 133–159.
40. *The Interpreter's Bible: A Commentary in Twelve Volumes* (Nashville: Abingdon Press, 1978).
41. Bernard in Burch, 133–159.
42. Ibid.
43. Bernard in Burch, 38.

44. Swift, "Sermon on the Wisdom of This World," vol. 10, *Works*, 146–147.
45. Ibid.
46. Ibid., 137.
47. Swift, "A Tritical Essay Upon the Faculties of the Mind," vol. 5, *Works*, 5.
48. Ibid., 2.
49. Tom Wolfe, "Sorry But Your Soul Just Died," *Forbes ASAP*, December 2, 1996, 211.
50. Irenaeus, *Against Heresies, The Ante-Nicene Fathers: The Writings of the Fathers Down to A.D. 325*, eds. The Rev. Alexander Roberts, DD, and James Donaldson, LLD, vol. 1, *The Apostolic Fathers*: Justin Martyr — Irenaeus (Buffalo: The Christian Literature Publishing Company, 1885), I: 315.
51. Swift, "Sermon on the Wisdom of This World," vol. 10, *Works*, 138.
52. Irenaeus, 315.
53. Swift, "Sermon on the Wisdom of This World," 136.
54. Irenaeus, 315
55. Ibid., 316.
56. Ibid., 315.
57. *Hamlet*, ed. G.B. Harrison (New York: Harcourt Brace, 1948).
58. Daniel P. Mannix in collaboration with Malcolm Cowley, *Black Cargoes: A History of the Atlantic Slave Trade, 1518–1865* (New York: Viking Press, 1962), 59.
59. Ibid., 60.
60. Ibid.
61. Nichols, 2.
62. Bernard, "A Mirror That Flatters Not," trans. Anonymous, (London, 1677), Translator's Preface.
63. Bernard in Burch, 10.
64. Bernard, "Mirror," 2.
65. Irenaeus, 316.
66. Bernard, "Mirror," 2–3.
67. Bernard in Burch, 181.
68. *Everyman*, in David Bevington, *Medieval Drama* (Boston: Houghton Mifflin, 1975), 963.
69. Ibid., 953.
70. Ibid., 956.
71. Ibid., 958.
72. Ibid, 963.
73. Philip Schaff, ed. *A Dictionary of the Bible* (Philadelphia: American Sunday-School Union, 1885).
74. Tillich, 186.
75. James Baldwin
76. Swift, "A Sermon on Mutual Subjection," vol. 10, *Works*, 36.
77. Bernard in Burch, 39.
78. Swift, "The Difficulty of Knowing One's Self," vol. 10, *Works*, 17.
79. Ibid.
80. Wole Soyinka, Nobel Peace Lecture 1986, in Publication of the Modern Language Association, vol. 102, 5, (October 1987): 764.
81. Swift, "A Tritical Essay," vol. 5, *Works*, 8.
82. *Othello*, ed. G.B. Harrison (New York: Harcourt, Brace, 1948) 5, 2, 163. References are to act, scene, and line.
83. Swift, "Dr. Swift to Mr. Pope," vol. 14, *Works*, 37.
84. Swift, "A Tale of a Tub," vol. 2, *Works*, 1.
85. Malcolm X, an expression he used to signal he was ready to be introduced to an audience and didn't want a big fanfare.

Chapter 1

1. Augustine, in Hugh Thomas, *The Slave Trade: The Story of the Atlantic Slave Trade, 1440–1870* (New York: Simon and Schuster, 1999), 30.
2. Mannix, *Black Cargoes*, 32.
3. Thomas, 115.
4. Mannix, Cowley, 32.
5. Ibid., 32–33.
6. Ibid., 28.
7. Ibid., 33.
8. Landa, Introduction to *Gulliver's Travels*.
9. Mannix, Cowley, 33.
10. Ibid., 32.
11. Deborah Wyrick, "Gulliver's Travels and the Early English Novel," in *Critical Approaches to Teaching Swift*, Peter J. Schakel, ed. (New York: AMS, 1992), 132–48.
12. Ibid.
13. Ibid.
14. Ibid.
15. Winston S. Churchill, *A History of the English Speaking Peoples*, vol. 3, *The Age of Revolution* (New York: Dodd, Mead, 1957), 86.
16. Wyrick.
17. *Encyclopedia Britannica*.
18. Wyrick.
19. Ibid.
20. Ibid.
21. Ibid.
22. Ibid.
23. Ibid.
24. Mannix, Cowley, *Black Cargoes*, 121.
25. Ibid., 105.
26. Johannes Menne Postma, *The Dutch in the Atlantic Slave Trade, 1600–1815* (Cambridge, MA: Cambridge University Press, 1990), 11.
27. Ibid.
28. Landa, Introduction.
29. Mannix, Cowley, 71.
30. Ibid., 60.
31. Ibid.
32. Donald Greene, Introduction, *The Age of Exuberance: Background to Eighteenth Century English Literature*. (New York: Random House, 1970).

Notes—Chapter 1

33. Ibid.
34. Bernard, Sermon 30, 121.
35. Bernard in Burch, 225.
36. Greene, Introduction.
37. Aristotle, *Politics*, trans. Trevor J. Saunders, (Penguin Classics, 1981).
38. Ibid., 64–69.
39. Ibid., 75.
40. Ibid., 71–72.
41. Ibid., 79.
42. Mannix, *Black Cargoes*, 47.
43. Ibid., 72.
44. Ibid., 73.
45. Ibid., 50.
46. Ibid., 50–51.
47. Ibid., 52.
48. Ibid.
49. Swift, "A Tale of a Tub," vol. 2, *Works*.
50. Mannix, Cowley, 53.
51. Greene, Introduction.
52. Mannix, Cowley, 3.
53. Postma, 15.
54. Mannix, Cowley.
55. Ibid., 69.
56. *Gulliver's Travels*, 16.
57. Mannix, Cowley, 112.
58. Ibid., 105.
59. Ibid., 106.
60. Ibid., 107.
61. Ibid., 106.
62. Ibid., 115.
63. Hugh Thomas, *The Slave Trade* (New York: Simon and Schuster, 1997), 428.
64. Postma, 164.
65. Mannix, Cowley, 74.
66. Ibid., xiii.
67. Ibid., 145.
68. Fage, J.D., *A History of West Africa* (London: Cambridge University Press, 1969), 226.
69.
70. Thomas, 82.
71. Fage, 227.
72. Ibid., 225.
73. Ibid., 244–245.
74. Ibid., 245.
75. Ibid., 244.
76. *Encyclopedia Britannica*.
77. Mannix, Cowley, 47.
78. Ibid., 48.
79. Thomas, 406.
80. Ibid.
81. Postma, .
82. Ibid., 17.
83. Mannix, Cowley, 3–4.
84. Ibid., 5.
85. Postma, 13.
86. Ibid., 18.
87. Ibid.
88. Mannix, Cowley, 4.
89. Mannix, Cowley, .
90. Ibid., 66.
91. Postma, 78–79.
92. Thomas, 430.
93. Postma, 111.
94. Ibid., 15.
95. Irvin Ehrenpreis, *Swift, the Man, His Works, and the Age*, vol. 2, *Dr. Swift* (Cambridge: Harvard University Press, 1967), 542.
96. "Gulliver's Passage on the Dutch Amboyna," *English Language Notes*, June 1964.
97. Victoria Glendinning, *Jonathan Swift, a Portrait* (New York: Henry Holt, 1998), 45.
98. Ibid., 43.
99. Ibid.
100. Postma, 111.
101. Ibid., 9.
102. *Encyclopedia Britannica*.
103. Thomas, 76.
104. Ibid., 77.
105. Mannix, Cowley, 111.
106. Churchill, vol. 3, 86.
107. Glendinning, 106.
108. Ehrenpreis.
109. Ehrenpreis.
110. William Rose Benet, *The Reader's Encyclopedia*, 2nd edition (New York: Thomas Y. Crowell Company, 1965).
111. Thomas, 236.
112. *The Reader's Encyclopedia*.
113. Thomas, 241.
114. Thomas, 203.
115. Thomas, 240.
116. Mannix, Cowley, 60.
117. Ibid., 5.
118. Bernard, Sermon 30:10.
119. Archbishop Desmond Tutu, interview by Bill Moyers, [Name of TV program], PBS, [Date].
120. Samuel Holt Monk in a Norton Critical Edition of *The Writings of Jonathan Swift*, eds. Robert A. Greenberg and William Piper (New York: W.W. Norton), 645.
121. Ibid., 644.
122. Allan Bloom, in Norton, 658.
123. Norman O. Brown, in Norton, 611.
124. Monk, 646.
125. Laura Brown, "Reading Race and Gender," Critical Essay on Jonathan Swift, ed. Frank Palmeri (New York: Macmillan, 1993), 121–140. (First pub. in *Eighteenth-Century Studies* 23:4 (1990), 425–43.
126. Ibid.
127. Ibid.
128. Ibid.
129. Ibid.
130. Ibid.
131. Ibid.
132. Ibid.
133. Ibid.
134. Ibid.

135. Ibid.
136. Ibid.
137. Edward Albee, personal interview with Charlie Rose on PBS.
138. Brown.
139. Ibid.
140. Ibid.
141. Ibid.
142. Swift, "Thoughts on Various Subjects," vol. 5, *Works*, 463.
143. Toni Morrison, *Beloved* (New York: Alfred A. Knopf, 1987).
144. Morrison, 151.
145. Mannix, Cowley, 32.
146. Ibid., xiii.
147. Bernard in Burch, 12.
148. Swift, in a letter to Alexander Pope.

Chapter 2

1. Geoffrey Chaucer, *The Tales of Canterbury*, ed. Robert A. Pratt (Boston: Houghton Mifflin Company, 1974), 10.
2. Swift, "The Epistle Dedicatory, to His Royal Highness Prince Posterity" (The citation out of Irenaeus), in "A Tale of a Tub," vol. 2, *Works*, 49.
3. Swift, "Sermon on the Testimony of Conscience," vol. 10, *Works*, 43.
4. Ibid., 44.
5. Ibid., 45–46.
6. Ibid., 46.
7. Ibid., 46–47.
8. Ibid.
9. *Reader's Encyclopedia*, 485.
10. Swift, "Sermon on the Testimony of Conscience," 47.
11. Ibid.
12. Ibid., 47–48.
13. Ibid., 48.
14. Ibid., 49–50.
15. Ibid., 51.
16. Ibid., 52–54.
17. Mannix, Cowley, 33.
18. Bernard, Sermon 36.
19. Bernard in Burch, 12.
20. Ibid.
21. Ibid.
22. Ibid.
23. Ibid.
24. Ibid., 34.
25. Dante, *Inferno*, trans. Charles S. Singleton (Princeton, NJ: Princeton University Press, 1977), II, 61.
26. Bernard, "The First Step of Pride, Curiosity," in Burch, 181.
27. *The Los Angeles Times*.
28. Augustine, *The City of God* (London: Everyman, 1945), XV, xxiii, 310.
29. Bernard, Sermon 31.
30. Grossteste, 93.
31. Tillich, 184.
32. Bonaventure, *De Reductione Artium Ad Theologiam*, trans. Emma Therese Healy (New York: Saint Bonaventure College, 1939), 39–41.
33. Ibid., 41.
34. Ibid.
35. Mannix, Cowley, xiii.
36. Ibid., 32.
37. Ibid., 121.
38. Ibid., 120.
39. Ibid., 116.
40. Bernard in Burch, 12.
41. Swift, "Thoughts on Various Subjects," vol. 5, *Works*, 463.
42. Bernard, "The Second Step of Pride, Frivolity," in Burch, 199.
43. Swift, "Thoughts on Religion," vol. 10, *Works*.
44. Swift, "Sermon on Mutual Subjection," vol. 10, *Works*.
45. Bernard, "The Second Step of Truth," in Burch, 153.
46. Bernard, "The Fifth Step of Pride, Singularity," in Burch, 209.
47. Plato, *The Republic*, in *Great Dialogues of Plato*, trans. W.H.D. Rouse, eds. Eric H. Warmington and Philip G. Rouse, (New York: NAL Penguin, 1984). 122.
48. Bernard, "The First Step of Pride, Curiosity," in Burch, 181.
49. Ibid., 189.
50. Ibid., 189–191.
51. Schaff, *A Bible Dictionary*.
52. Mannix, Cowley, x.

Chapter 3

1. Bernard, *On Grace and Free Choice*, in *Bernard of Clairvaux Treatises III*, trans. Daniel O'Donovan osco, intro. Bernard Mcginn (Kalamazoo: Cistercian Publications, 1977), 65.
2. Ibid., 55.
3. Ibid., 56.
4. Ibid., 79.
5. Read, 207.
6. Peter Claver, in *Oxford Dictionary of Saints*, ed. David Farmer (New York: Oxford University Press, 1997).
7. Ibid.
8. Bernard, "The First Step of Pride" in Burch, 193.
9. Ibid.
10. Bernard, *On Grace*, 74.
11. Bernard, "The First Step of Pride," 191.
12. *Oxford Companion to Classical Literature*, ed. Sir Paul Harvey (Oxford: Clarendon Press, 1955).
13. Dante Alighieri, *Inferno*, in *The Divine*

Comedy, trans. and with a commentary by Charles S. Singleton (Bollingen Series LXXX Princeton, NJ: Princeton University Press, 1977), XXXIV, 28–29.
14. Augustine.
15. Bonaventure, "The Second Light."
16. Bernard, "The First Step of Pride, Curiosity."
17. *Inferno*, I, 3.
18. Ibid., XXXI, 20.
19. Ibid., XXXI, 22–33.
20. Ibid., XXXI, 34–39.
21. Ibid., XXXI, 12–18.
22. Singleton, *Inferno* Commentary, 565.
23. Ibid., 566.
24. *La Chanson de Roland*, 1920–1922.
25. *Inferno*, XXXI, 77–81.
26. Swift, "Thoughts."
27. Milton, *Paradise Lost*, in *John Milton, Complete Poems and Major Prose*, ed. Merritt Y. Hughes (New York: The Odyssey Press, 1957), 11–37, 64–71.
28. *Inferno*, XXXI, 85–88, 91–96, 106–111.
29. Ibid., XXXI, 139–145.
30. Mannix, Cowley, 47.
31. Singleton, *Inferno* Commentary, 575.
32. *Inferno*, XXXI, 49–57.
33. Swift, "Sermon on the Testimony of Conscience."
34. Bernard, "The First Step of Pride, Curiosity," in Burch.
35. Bernard in Burch, 30.
36. Ibid., 39.
37. Grosseteste.
38. Bernard, Sermon 31.
39. Ibid.
40. Bernard in Burch, 39.
41. *The Republic*.
42. Swift, "Sermon on Brotherly Love."
43. Augustine.
44. Bernard in Burch, 39.
45. Bonaventure, "The Soul's Journey Into God," in *The Classics of Western Spirituality*, trans. Ewert Cousins (New York: Paulist Press, 1978), 71–72.
46. Bernard, Sermon 37.
47. Bernard in Burch, 7.
48. *Paradise Lost*.
49. Bernard, Sermon 28.
50. Mannix, Cowley, 116.
51. *Paradise Lost*, II, 930–938.
52. Ibid., II, 951–967.
53. Ibid., II, 1002–1003.
54. Ibid., I, 777–781.
55. Ibid., II, 1009.
56. Ibid., II, 621–628.
57. Ibid., II, 629–643.
58. Bernard in Burch, 30.
59. Bernard, "On Grace," 74.
60. *Paradise Lost*, IV, 66–75.
61. Ibid., V, 520–543.
62. Bernard, "On Grace," 57.
63. Swift, "A Tritical Essay," 8.

Chapter 4

1. Swift, "Sermon On Mutual Subjection," vol. 10, *Works*.
2. Swift, "Sermon On Brotherly Love," vol. 10, *Works*.
3. Bernard, Sermon 28.
4. Bernard, Sermon 31.
5. Ibid., 126.
6. *Inferno*, I, 1–41.
7. Bernard, 31.
8. *Inferno*, I, 37–41.
9. Swift, "A Tritical Essay," 5.
10. *Paradise Lost*, III, 496.
11. Ibid., 518–519.
12. Ibid., 510–511.
13. Swift, "A Tritical Essay," 8.
14. Dante, *The Inferno* trans. John Ciardi, A New Translation, (New York: Penguin, 1982), 49.
15. Bernard, "The First Step of Pride, Curiosity," 191.
16. *Paradise Lost*, III, 444–459.
17. Ibid., 524–526, 541–544.
18. Swift, "Sermon On the Wisdom of This World."
19. *Inferno*.
20. Bernard, Sermon 35.
21. Bernard, "Mirror."
22. Bernard in Burch, 12.
23. Bonaventure, the third light, the "inner" light, or the light of philosophical knowledge, in *Retracing the Acts of Theology*.
24. *The Republic*.
25. *The Oxford Companion to Classical Literature*, Compiled and edited by Sir Paul Harvey (Oxford: Clarendon Press, 1955).
26. Bernard in Burch, 33.
27. Swift, "A Tritical Essay."
28. Bernard in Burch, 12.
29. *The Republic*.
30. Swift, *A Tale of a Tub*.
31. Landa, Intro. to *Gulliver's Travels*.
32. Bernard, "The First Step of Pride, Curiosity."
33. Bernard in Burch, 39.
34. Bernard, Sermon 31.
35. Swift, "A Tritical Essay."
36. Landa, Intro. to *Gulliver's Travels*.
37. *Inferno*, IV, 106, 118–120.
38. *Hamlet*, I, .
39. *Hamlet*, I, 15–20.
40. Ibid., 1, 4, 39–44.
41. Bernard in Burch.
42. *Hamlet*, 1, 5, 24–25.
43. Singleton, *Inferno* Commentary, 62.
44. *De Casibus*, Intro.

45. Swift, "Tatler," No. 81.
46. Augustine.
47. *Inferno*, XII, 47–48, 102–107.
48. Orosius, *Historiarum adversum paganos libri VII*, (III, 7, 18, 23), in Singleton, *Inferno* Commentary, 196–197.
49. Lucan (Phars. X, 30–36), in Singleton, *Inferno* Commentary, 197.
50. Charles Roland Beye, *Ancient Greek Literature and Society* (New York: Anchor Press/Doubleday, 1975), 5.
51. Tom Wolfe.
52. Boccaccio, *De Casibus*.
53. Ibid.
54. Mannix, Cowley, 32.
55. Ibid., 33.
56. Swift, "The Sentiments of A Church of England Man," vol. 2, *Works*, 369.
57. Swift, "Thoughts on Religion," vol. 10, *Works*, 169.
58. *Inferno*, III, 45–50, 103–108.
59. Bernard in Burch, 12.
60. Bernard, "Mirror."
61. Bernard, quoting Christ in Sermon 35.
62. John A. Dussinger, "'Christian' vs. 'Hollander': Swift's Satire on the Dutch East India Traders," *Notes and Queries* 211 (1966), 209–212.

Chapter 5

1. Philip Schaff, ed., *A Dictionary of the Bible* (Philadelphia: American Sunday School Union, 1885).
2. Bernard in Burch, 34.
3. Ibid.
4. Bonaventure, "The Fourth Light," in *De Reductione*.
5. Ibid.
6. Bernard in Burch, 225.
7. Ibid., 225.
8. Ibid., 227.
9. Ibid.
10. *Lear*, 4, 2, 43–49.
11. Mannix, Cowley, 50–51.
12. Ibid., 52.
13. Ibid.
14. Landa, notes to *Gulliver's Travels and other Writings By Jonathan Swift*.
15. Ibid.
16. *Hamlet*, 3, 2, 38–39.
17. Bernard in Burch.
18. Grossteste.
19. Bernard in Burch.
20. Landa, in Intro.
21. Glendinning.
22. Ibid.
23. Swift, "Sermon on the Testimony of Conscience," vol. 10, *Works*.
24. Mannix, Cowley, 33.
25. Glendinning, 187.
26. Ibid., 188.
27. Swift, "Sermon on Brotherly Love," vol. 10, *Works*.
28. Mannix, Cowley, 74.
29. Amerigo Vespucci, *Letters From A New World: Amerigo Vespucci's Discovery of America*, ed. Luciano Formisano, forward by Garry Willis, trans. David Jacobson (New York: Marsilio, 1992), 31–35.
30. Landa, Intro. to *Gulliver's Travels*.
31. Bernard, "Mirror."
32. Bernard, "On Grace," 59.
33. *King Lear*, 4, 2, 30–36.
34. Ibid., 37.
35. Ibid., 46–49.
36. Ibid., 4, 4, 126–127.
37. Landa, Intro. to *Gulliver's Travels*.
38. Glendinning, 185.
39. Bernard in Burch, 39.
40. Ibid., 39.
41. *The Oxford Companion to Classical Literature*.
42. Ibid.
43. Ibid.
44. Bernard, Sermon 35.
45. Aristotle, *Politics*.
46. Bernard, Sermon 35.
47. Francis Bacon, in Henry Adams, *Mont-Saint-Michel and Chartres* (New York: The Heritage Press, 1957), 306.
48. Swift.
49. Bernard in Burch, 109.
50. Ibid., 217.
51. Ibid., 27.
52. Bernard, *Consideration*, 142–143.
53. Bernard in Burch, 109.
54. Grossteste.
55. Mannix, Cowley, 108.
56. Swift, "Thoughts on Religion."
57. Tillich, 197.
58. Bernard, "On Grace," 55.
59. St. Francis, in *Mont-Saint-Michel*, 306.
60. Bernard in Burch, 31–32.
61. Ibid.
62. Swift, "Sermon on the Trinity," vol. 10, *Works*.
63. Swift, "Sermon on the Wisdom of This World," vol. 10, *Works*.
64. Bernard in Burch, Appendix B, "Bernard's Criticism of Peter Abelard's Theology," 268–274.
65. Swift, "Sermon on Mutual Subjection."
66. Bernard, "Misc. Sermon 72, 2 (XB 947)," in Burch, 25.
67. Bernard.
68. *The Republic*.
69. James R. McGovern, *Anatomy of a Lynching* (Baton Rouge: LSU Press, 1982), 80–85.
70. Lynne Duke, "The White Stuff: A Theory of Race, Author Andrew Hacker on 'The Insidius

Virus of Superiority,'" *The Washington Post*, Tues. April 1992, B1.

71. Swift, "Sermon On the Wisdom of This World."
72. Bernard in Burch, 28.
73. Swift, "Sermon On Mutual Subjection."
74. Bernard, "Mirror."
75. Bernard on Abelard in Burch, 270.
76. Bernard, "Mirror."
77. Bernard, Sermon 36.
78. *A Dictionary of the Bible.*
79. Bernard, Sermon 38.
80. Bernard, *On Grace*, 58.
81. Ibid., 59.
82. Bernard, Sermon 38.
83. Bernard, Sermon 3.
84. Bernard, Sermon 4.
85. Ibid.
86. Ibid.
87. Bernard, Sermon 8.
88. Bernard in Burch, "The First Step of Pride, Curiosity."
89. Bernard, Sermon 8.
90. Bernard, *On Grace*, 55.
91. Augustine.
92. Bernard in Burch, 39.
93. Bernard, *On Grace*.
94. *Interpreter's Bible.*
95. Captain John Newton, in *Black Cargoes*, x.
96. Malcolm Cowley, Intro. to *Black Cargoes*, xiv.
97. Bernard in Burch, 7.
98. Bernard, Sermons 4 (22) and 8 (46–52).
99. Ibid., 22.
100. Bernard in Burch, 8.
101. Ibid.
102. Ibid.
103. Ibid.
104. Bernard, "Mirror."
105. Ibid.
106. Swift, "A Tritical Essay."
107. Boccaccio, "Defense of Poetry."
108. Thomas More, "More's Letter to Peter Gilles," in *Utopia*, trans. Paul Turner (London: Penguin Books, 1965), 29–30.
109. Bernard in Burch, 60.
110. Ibid., 33.
111. Bernard of Clairvaux, *Five Books On Consideration: Advice to a Pope*, trans. John D. Anderson and Elizabeth T. Kennan (Kalamazoo: Cistercian Publications, 1976), 141.
112. *Oxford Companion to Classical Literature.*
113. Bernard in Burch, 12.
114. *Inferno*, XIV, 46–48, 49–51, 61–66.
115. Bernard, "Mirror."
116. Ibid.

Bibliography

Adams, Henry. *Mont-Saint-Michel and Chartres*. New York: The Heritage Press, 1957.
Albee, Edward. Interview by Charlie Rose, *The Charlie Rose Show*, June 6, 2005.
Aristotle. *The Politics*. London: Penguin, 1981.
Augustine. *The City of God*. London: Everyman edition, 1945.
Bernard of Clairvaux. *On the Song of Songs*. Sermons 1–86. Kalamazoo, Michigan: Cistercian Publications, 1980.
_____. *On Grace and Free Choice*. Kalamazoo, Michigan: Cistercian Publications, 1977.
_____. *A Mirror That Flatters Not*. London, 1677.
_____. *Five Books on Consideration: Advice to a Pope*. Kalamazoo, Michigan: Cistercian Publications, 1976.
Bevington, David. *Medieval Drama*. Boston: Houghton Mifflin, 1975.
Beye, Charles Rowan. *Ancient Greek Literature and Society*. New York: Anchor Press/Doubleday, 1975.
Blake, William. *The Marriage of Heaven and Hell*. In *The Complete Poetry and Prose of William Blake*. Edited by David E. Erdman. Berkeley: University of California Press, 1982.
Bloom, Allan. "An Outline of *Gulliver's Travels*." In *The Writings of Jonathan Swift*. A Norton Critical Edition. Edited by Robert A. Greenberg and William Piper. New York: W.W. Norton, 1973.
Boccaccio, Giovanni. "Defense of Poetry." In *Genealogies of the Pagan Gods*. Princeton: Princeton University Press, 1930.
_____. *The Fates of Illustrious Men*. Originally published as *Illustrium*. New York: F. Unger, 1965.
Bonaventure. *Retracing the Arts to Theology*. New York: Saint Bonaventure College, 1939.
_____. *The Soul's Journey Into God*. In *The Classics of Western Spirituality*. New York: Paulist Press, 1978.
Braaten, Carl E. *A History of Christian Thought: From Its Judaic and Hellenistic Origins to Existentialism*. New York: Simon and Schuster, 1968.
Brown, Laura. "Reading Race and Gender." *Eighteenth-Century Studies* 23.4, 1990.
Brown, Norman O. "The Excremental Vision." In *The Writings of Jonathan Swift*. A Norton Critical Edition. Edited by Robert A. Greenberg and William Piper. New York: W.W. Norton, 1973.
Burch, George Boswell, ed. *The Steps of Humility by Bernard, Abbot of Clairvaux*. Cambridge: Harvard University Press, 1950.

Chaucer, Geoffrey. *The Tales of Canterbury.* "Prologue." Edited by Robert A. Pratt. Boston: Houghton Mifflin, 1974.
Churchill, Winston S. *A History of the English-Speaking Peoples.* Vol. III, *The Age of Revolution.* New York: Dodd, Mead, 1957.
Cowley, Malcolm. Introduction. *Black Cargoes* by Daniel P. Mannix, in collaboration with Malcolm Cowley. New York: The Viking Press, 1968.
Dante. *Inferno.* Translated by John Ciardi. New York: Penguin, 1982.
_____. *The Inferno.* Translated by Charles S. Singleton. Bollingen Series LXXX. Princeton, NJ: Princeton University Press, 1977.
Duke, Lynne. "'The White Stuff: A Theory of Race,' Author Andrew Hacker on 'The Insidious Virus of Superiority.'" *The Washington Post,* April 14, 1992.
Dussinger, John A. "'Christian' vs. 'Hollander': Swift's Satire on the Dutch East India Traders." *Notes and Queries* 211 (1966).
Ehrenpreis, Irvin. *Swift: The Man, His Works, the Age.* Vol. II, *Dr. Swift.* Cambridge, Massachusetts: Harvard University Press, 1967.
Erdman, David E., ed. *The Complete Poetry and Prose of William Blake.* Berkeley: University of California Press, 1982.
Fage, J.D. *A History of Africa.* New York: Alfred A. Knopf, 1978.
Farmer, David, ed. *Oxford Dictionary of Saints.* New York: Oxford University Press, 1997.
Fielding, Henry. Introduction to *"Gulliver's Travels" and Other Writings By Jonathan Swift.* Edited by Louis Landa. Riverside ed. Boston: Houghton Mifflin Company, 1960.
Glendinning, Victoria. *Jonathan Swift, A Portrait.* New York: Henry Holt, 1999.
Greenberg, Robert A., and William Piper. *The Writings of Jonathan Swift.* A Norton Critical Edition. New York: W.W. Norton, 1973.
Greene, Donald. *The Age of Exuberance: Background to Eighteenth Century English Literature.* New York: Random House, 1970.
Harvey, Sir Paul. *The Oxford Companion to Classical Literature.* Oxford: Oxford University Press, 1955.
Hughes, Merritt Y., ed. *John Milton: Complete Poems and Major Prose.* New York: The Odyssey Press, 1957.
The Interpreter's Bible, A Commentary in Twelve Volumes. The Holy Scriptures. The King James and Revised Standard Versions with General Articles and Introduction, Exegesis, Exposition for Each Book of the Bible. Nashville: Abingdon Press, 1978.
Irenaeus. *Against Heresies.* In *The Ante-Nicene Fathers: The Writings of the Fathers down to A.D. 325.* Buffalo: The Christian Literature Publishing Company, 1885.
Jeffrey, David L. *The Early English Lyric & Franciscan Spirituality.* Lincoln: University of Nebraska Press, 1975.
La Chanson de Roland. In *The Norton Anthology of World Masterpieces.* 4th ed. New York: W.W. Norton, 1979.
Landa, Lewis, ed. *"Gulliver's Travels" and Other Writings by Jonathan Swift.* Riverside ed. Boston: Houghton Mifflin, 1960.
Lucan (Marcus Annaeus Lucanus). *Inferno* Commentary. Edited by Charles S. Singleton. Bollingen Series LXXX. Princeton, NJ: Princeton University Press, 1977.
Mannix, Daniel P. *Black Cargoes: A History of the Atlantic Slave Trade, 1518–1865.* New York: Viking Press, 1968.

McGovern, James. *Anatomy of a Lynching.* Baton Rouge: Louisiana State University Press, 1982.
Milton, John. *Paradise Lost.* In *John Milton: Complete Poems and Major Prose.* Edited by Merritt Y. Hughes. New York: The Odyssey Press, 1957.
Monk, Samuel Holt. "The Pride of lemuel Gulliver." In *The Writings of Jonathan Swift.* Edited by Robert A. Greenberg and William Piper. New York: W.W. Norton, 1973.
More, Thomas. "More's Letter to Peter Gilles." In *Utopia.* Translated by Paul Turner. London: Penguin Books, 1965.
Morrison, Toni. *Beloved.* New York: Alfred A. Knopf, 1987.
Morrissey, L.J. *Gulliver's Progress.* Hamden, Connecticut: Archon Books, 1978.
Nichols, Stephen G., Jr. *Romanesque Signs: Early Medieval Narrative and Iconography.* New Haven, Connecticut: Yale University Press, 1983.
Orosius. *Historiarum adversum paganos libri VII.* Quoted in Charles S. Singleton, *Inferno* Commentary. Bollingen Series LXXX. Princeton, NJ: Princeton University Press, 1977.
Plato. *The Republic.* Translated by Desmond Lee. London: Penguin Books, 1987.
Postma, Johannes Menne. *The Dutch in the Atlantic Slave Trade, 1600–1815.* Cambridge, Massachusetts: Cambridge University Press, 1990.
Schakel, Peter J. *Critical Approaches to Teaching Swift.* New York: AMS, 1992.
Schaff, Philip, ed. *A Dictionary of the Bible.* Philadelphia: American Sunday School Union, 1885.
Shakespeare, William. *Shakespeare: Major Plays and the Sonnets.* Edited by G.B. Harrison. New York: Harcourt, Brace, 1948.
_____. *Hamlet.* In *Shakespeare: Major Plays and the Sonnets.* Edited by G.B. Harrison. New York: Harcourt, Brace, 1948.
_____. *Othello.* In *Shakespeare: Major Plays and the Sonnets.* Edited by G.B. Harrison. New York: Harcourt, Brace, 1948.
_____. *King Lear.* In *Shakespeare: Major Plays and the Sonnets.* Edited by G.B. Harrison. New York: Harcourt, Brace, 1948.
Singleton, Charles S., ed. *Inferno* Commentary. Bollingen Series LXXX. Princeton, NJ: Princeton University Press, 1977.
Soyinka, Wole. Nobel Lecture 1986. In Publication of the Modern Language Association. Vol. 102, no. 5. October 1987: 764.
Swift, Jonathan. *Dean Swift's Works in Nineteen Volumes.* Edited by Thomas Sheridan. London: Nichols and Son, 1801; "The Abolishing of Christianity"; "A Sermon on Mutual Subjection"; "A Sermon on Brotherly Love"; "Sermon on the Wisdom of This World"; "A Tritical Essay Upon the Faculties of the Mind"; "The Difficulty of Knowing One's Self"; "A Tale of a Tub"; "Sermon on the Testimony of Conscience"; "Thoughts on Various Subjects"; "Thoughts on Religion"; "Tatler," No. 81; "The Sentiments of a Church of England Man"; "Sermon on the Trinity."
_____. *Gulliver's Travels.* In *"Gulliver's Travels" and Other Writings by Jonathan Swift.* Edited by Louis A. Landa. Riverside ed. Boston: Houghton Mifflin, 1801.
Thomas, Hugh. *The Slave Trade: The Story of the Atlantic Slave Trade, 1440–1870.* New York: Simon and Schuster, 1997.
Thrall, William Flint, and Addison Hibbard, rev. by C. Hugh Holman. *A Handbook to Literature.* New York: Odyssey Books, 1962.
Tillich, Paul. *A History of Christian Thought: From Its Judaic and Hellenistic Origins to Existentialism.* Edited by Carl E. Braaten. New York: Simon and Schuster, 1968.

Vespucci, Amerigo. *Letters from a New World: Amerigo Vespucci's Discovery of America*. Edited by Luciano Formisano. Translated by David Jacobson. New York: Marsilio, 1992.
Wilford, John Noble. "Science Times." *New York Times*, February 1, 2006.
Wolfe, Tom. "Sorry, But Your Soul Just Died." *Forbes ASAP,* December 2, 1996.
Wyrick, Deborah. "*Gulliver's Travels* and the Early English Novel." In *Critical Approaches to Teaching Swift*. Edited by Peter J. Schakel. New York: AMS, 1992.

Index

Abelard 185, 188
Aceldama 90
The Adventure 26, 39, 42, 52, 91, 98, 156
Against Heresies (Irenaeus) 15, 16
Albee, Edward 61
Alexander the Great 143
The Amboyna 51, 152
Amsterdam 51, 52, 133, 152, 153
Anakims 96
Ancient Greek Literature and Scoeity (Beye) 3
Antaeus 103
The Antelope 39, 74
Aquinas, Saint Thomas 8, 9, 10, 23, 184
Archimedes 131, 132, 135
"An Argument Against Abolishing Christianity" (Swift) 4, 5, 161
Aristotelian/Thomas method 10, 20, 67, 73, 214
Aristotle 4, 8, 10, 34, 56, 57, 68, 70, 144, 164, 173, 183, 185; system of knowledge 24, 34, 73, 77
Asiento 54
attack on critics (Swift and Boccaccio) 219
Augustine, Saint 10, 25, 98, 110, 184, 205
Augustinean/Bernardian method 10, 67, 184

Baal 76
Bacon, Francis 15, 175
Baldwin, James 21
Barbados 37, 53, 133, 158
Beloved (Toni Morrison) 62
Bennett, Bill 190–191
Berkeley, Bishop George 17, 32, 161
Bernard of Clairvaux, Saint 6, 9, 10, 73, 113, 117, 123, 128, 164, 185, 186, 188, 201, 213
Bernard's Satan 97, 98, 104, 121, 130
bill of lading 31–32
Blefuscu 41, 86
Boccaccio, Giovanni 2
Bonaventure, Saint 7, 10, 111
Brazil 39, 48
Bristol 39, 52, 74, 133
Brobdingnag 23, 43, 96

Brown, Laura 59
Buffon, George Louis Leclerc 60

calentures 53, 158
Calvinism 31, 67
Campechy 52, 157
Canary Islands 52, 53
Capaneus (*Inferno* char.) 224
Cape of Good Hope 43, 45, 47, 51, 122, 152, 204
Cape Town 45
centaurs 8, 15, 35, 164, 168, 223
Chaney, Goodman, and Schwerner 192, 225
Chanson de Roland 100
Chaos 126
Chiron 168, 205
Christian apologetics for the African slave trade 17, 32, 56
Claver, Saint Peter 93–94
Cocytus, *Inferno* (Dante) 98
The Company of Royal Adventurers of England Trading to Africa 26, 39
Consideration (Bernard) 180, 185, 195
Cooke, George Frederick 42
Curiosity (Bernard) 10, 19, 20, 34, 74, 81, 92, 99, 106, 137, 142

Dagon 76
Dante 7, 66, 165, 205
De Casibus Virorum Illustrium (*The Fate of Illustrious Men*) (Boccaccio) 3, 142, 245
De Reductione Artium Ad Theologium (*Retracing the Arts to Theology*) (Bonaventure) 7
Defense of Poetry (Boccaccio) 2–3, 218–219
Defoe, Daniel 28, 54
Deism 108
Dias, Bartolomeu 43
Dives 151
Druids 76
dungeon 47, 120, 126–128
Dutch 28, 39, 40, 44, 47, 51
Dutch East India Company 5, 42, 44, 45, 47, 51, 152
Dutch West India Company 49, 52

Eagles 47
East Indies 26, 28, 37, 39, 48, 152
Ebedmelech the Ethiopian 126–127
Ehrenpreis, Irving 51, 53
Elmina, West Africa 38, 48, 126
Emanuel 67
Emmanuel College, Cambridge 67
the English 41, 64, 153
"The Epistle of Paul to Philemon" 7, 210–212
epitaph (Swift's self-written) 1
Everyman (Anon.) 7, 19, 20

faculties and functions of the Soul (Bernard) 18, 73, 74, 92, 132, 133, 134, 135, 180, 207, 213
final blasphemy 199–200
First Ignorance (Bernard) 9, 128, 170
fixed melancholy 80
Flying Island 130
Fort St. George 38, 48, 49, 126, 146
Four Horses of the Apocalypse 182
four lights to human knowledge (Bonaventure) 7, 43, 74, 77–83, 93, 99, 105, 132, 134, 154, 155
Francis of Assisi, Saint 175, 185
frozen sea 98

Gama, Vasco da 43
Glendinning, Victoria 51, 160, 161, 166
Glubdubdrib 67, 140, 142, 147, 222
Goneril (*King Lear* char.) 157, 165–166
Grand Academy of Lagado 136, 137
Grand Debate (extermination of black people) 189–190
Great Tartary 98
Green, Donald 33
Grossteste, Robert 6, 159
Guinea trade 28, 37, 51, 152, 212

Hamlet (Shakespeare) 140–141
Hazael, King 94–95, 96
Henry the Navigator 43
Hinnom 90, 154
History of Jamaica (Long) 60
Homer 4, 144
Hope-well 47, 50
horse latitudes 39–40
Houyhnhnmland 10, 55, 154
Houyhnhnms 8, 17, 20, 21, 23, 56, 57, 167, 168, 181, 182

India 43
Indians 56
Inferno (Dante) 19, 66, 98–104, 129, 140, 224
intention on the expedient, the good, or the true (Bernard) 180
Irenaeus (*Against Heresies*) 15
Ixion 15, 168, 223

Jeremiah 19, 126
Jerome, Saint 8
Judas 90

King Lear (Shakespeare) 157, 165–166

Landa, Louis 5, 158, 160, 166
languaging 192–193
Laputa 23, 132
Lazarus 150
Leeward Islands 37, 53, 133, 158
the Levant 31
Lilliput 41
Lilliputians 23, 72, 75–88
Limbo, *Inferno* (Dante) 130, 132
"Limbo of Vanity," *Paradise Lost* (Milton) 130
Lindow Man, 76
Lisbon 133, 209
Liverpool 37, 42, 133
logos 8, 17
London 30, 32, 39, 133
Long, Edward (*History of Jamaica*) 60
Luggnagg 140, 147
Lynching 191–192

macrocosm/microcosm 77
Madagascar 43, 54, 55, 204
Medici, Lorenzo di Pierfrancesco de' 45
mercantile capitalism 27
Metamorphoses (Ovid) 168, 169
Middle Passage 37, 40
Milton's Satan 115, 119, 122, 124, 131
"A Mirror That Flatters Not" (Bernard) 11, 18, 19, 163, 196, 197, 207–208, 217, 227
misanthropy 21, 22, 65, 66, 198
A Modest Proposal (Swift) 202
Molucca Islands 43, 45
Monk, Samuel 62
morality vs. religion 70–72
More, Thomas 221, 222
Mori (Ghana) 48
Morrison, Toni 62, 63

Nagasaki 39, 51, 152
Nathan 95–96
Natural History (Buffon) 60
Neal, Claude 191
New Holland 46, 47, 48, 204
Nimrod 100–101
nominal Christianity 4, 15, 50, 128, 157, 161
north (Satan's seat [Bernard]) 121

Onesimus 210–212
Othello (Shakespeare) 22, 56

Paradise Lost (Milton) 101, 102, 115, 116, 119, 120, 121, 122, 124, 130–131
Paradise of Fools (Milton) 130
Paul, the Apostle 12
Philemon 210–212
Philistines 75–76
pirates 50, 52, 54
Plato 8, 34, 56, 57, 70, 132, 139
Politics (Aristotle) 23, 34, 35, 36, 73, 174, 183

Pope, Alexander 22
portrait of Gulliver (Donald Greene) 33
Portsmouth 52
Portuguese 39, 44, 45, 48, 64, 205–209
pride in reason 8, 9, 154
projectors/projects 137

Queen Anne Book of Common Prayer 6, 74, 88

real Christianity 4, 7, 18, 23, 91, 152
Redriff 42, 221, 222
The Republic (Plato) 136
The Royal African Company 39
The Royal Society 136

Samson 74–77
satire 5
schizophrenia 206
Second Ignorance (Bernard) 9, 132, 133, 150, 170, 175
Sephardim 31
"A Slave-ship Consignment" 49
Sloane, Sir Hans 37
Socrates 56, 135, 165
South Africa 40, 89
South America 28, 45
South Sea 28, 39, 53, 74
The South Sea Company 28, 53–55
southern monsoon 443
Soyinka, Wole 21
"speculative consideration" (Bernard) 222
Spice Islands 43, 51
Steps of Pride (Bernard) 7, 10, 13, 44, 63, 73, 83, 84, 86, 87, 92, 106, 124, 141, 154, 155, 156, 163, 178, 204
Steps of Truth (Bernard) 7, 11, 12, 13, 21, 62, 67, 94, 108, 127
Struldbruggs 149–150

Surat 42
Swallow 26
Swift, Jonathan, sermons: "On Brotherly Love" 8, 11, 161; "On Mutual Subjection" 8, 21, 147, 188; "On the Difficulty of Knowing Oneself" 11, 21; "On the Testimony of Conscience" 68–72, 209; "On the Trinity" 186, 187; "On the Wisdom of This World" 14, 15, 16, 131, 132, 187, 194–915

Table Bay (Cape Town) 45
The Tale of a Tub (Swift) 23, 67, 69, 136
The Tatler (Swift) 142, 145
Tenare and Tidore (*Paradise Lost*) 122
Tenariff 52, 53
three-cornered/triangular trade 40, 53, 158
"The Three Kisses" (Bernard) 202–203, 213–216
Timon (*Timon of Athens* char.) 22, 66
Tonquin 47, 49
Tory Party 28, 53
"A Tritical Essay Upon the Faculties of the Mind" (Swift) 3, 14, 22, 125, 168, 206, 219, 223

Universe of Death (*Paradise Lost*) 121–122, 128
Utopia (More) 221, 222

Van Dieman's Land (Tasmania) 28, 39, 41
Vespucci, Amerigo 45, 161–163
Virgil (*Inferno* char.) 99, 100

West Indies 26, 37, 53, 158
Whore of Babylon 132, 133
Wyrick, Deborah 27, 58

yahoos 5, 6, 35, 159, 160, 167–169, 172, 175, 178, 181, 183, 194, 195, 200, 209, 221, 222, 223

www.ingramcontent.com/pod-product-compliance
Lightning Source LLC
Chambersburg PA
CBHW051218300426
44116CB00006B/627